*Social History of Africa*

# RUNNING AFTER PILLS

# RUNNING AFTER PILLS

## POLITICS, GENDER, AND CONTRACEPTION IN COLONIAL ZIMBABWE

Amy Kaler

Social History of Africa
*Allen Isaacman and Jean Allman, Series Editors*

HEINEMANN
Portsmouth, NH • London

Heinemann
A division of Reed Elsevier Inc.
361 Hanover Street
Portsmouth, NH 03801-3912

Offices and agents throughout the world

ISBN 0–325–07044–X (Heinemann cloth)
ISBN 0–325–07043–1 (Heinemann paper)
ISSN 1099–8098

British Library Cataloguing in Publication Data

**Library of Congress Cataloging-in-Publication Data**

Kaler, Amy.
Running after pills: politics, gender, and contraception in colonial Zimbabwe / Amy
Kaler.
    p. cm.—(Social history of Africa, ISSN 1099–8098)
  Includes bibliographical references (p. ) and index.
  ISBN 0–325–07044-X (alk. paper)—ISBN 0–325–07043–1 (pbk. : alk. paper)
  1. Family planning—Zimbabwe—History. 2. Family planning—Political aspects—
Zimbabwe. 3. Contraception—Political aspects—Zimbabwe. 4. Contraception—Govern-
ment policy—Zimbabwe. 5. Sex role—Zimbabwe. 6. Human reproduction—Social
aspects—Zimbabwe. 7. Family policy—Zimbabwe. I. Title. II. Series.
HQ766.5.Z55K35   2003
363.9′6′096891—dc21        2002191302

Printed in the United States of America on acid-free paper

01   00   99   98   97   DA   1   2   3   4   5   6   7   8   9

# CONTENTS

# ILLUSTRATIONS

# ACKNOWLEDGMENTS

I would like to thank the Population Council, the MacArthur Foundation, the Social Science Research Council, the American Council of Learned Societies, the Woodrow Wilson Foundation, the Graduate School of the University of Minnesota and the Anna Welsch Bright Fund of the Department of Sociology at the University of Minnesota for supporting various components of this work.

My fascination with Zimbabwe began when I spent three years in the rural Shamva district as a teacher under the auspices of World University Service of Canada. Some of the roots of this project lie in the experiences of students at Chindunduma Government High School and their families, especially the Form Four graduates of 1993. I would like to thank Mr. Reginald Tambaoga Manyati and his family for their patience with my curiosity during those years.

I would also like to thank the people in Zimbabwe who helped me in their professional capacities: the staff of the Zimbabwe National Family Planning Council, especially the executive director Dr. Alex Zinanga and the provincial directors; the Minister of Health and Child Welfare Dr. Timothy Stamps and the archives staff in his Ministry; the archives staff of the Zimbabwe National Family Planning Council; the archivist of the *Zimbabwe Herald;* the staff of the National Deposit Library in Bulawayo; and the Women's Action Group for allowing me to attend their annual conference. Thanks also go to the Department of Sociology at the University of Zimbabwe for providing me with an institutional "home." The family of the late Paddy Spilhaus very kindly gave me a copy of the scrapbook on family planning, which she kept for years.

I owe a huge debt to my Wedza-based research assistant Mrs. Nyaradzo Shayanewako, not only for her help with translation and her introduction to the community in Wedza, but also for her enthusiasm for this project and the hospitality shown by her family. The Shayanewakos helped me to understand much more about Zimbabwean life than I would ever have learned without them, and MaiSimba enabled me to see resistance and subversive consciousness in everyday life.

I am also grateful for the help of Mrs. Ruth Kandawasvika, who assisted with some Harare-based interviews with non-family planning workers and who helped with transcription of Shona interviews. I would also like to acknowledge the Shona language teaching staff of Ranche House College, especially Mr. Kennedy Mujombi, Mrs. Beatrice Ngwenya, and Mr. Lazarus Chidaushe.

In North America, I am grateful for the support and stimulation provided by my all-star committee at the University of Minnesota: my advisor Ron Aminzade, Allen Isaacman, MJ Maynes, Barbara Laslett, Jennifer Pierce, and the late Susan Geiger. Susan Cotts Watkins of the University of Pennsylvania also gave me crucial feedback on many of the themes in this project.

I'd also like to acknowledge the people I never would have met were it not for the research and writing of this project, and who made this whole process much better than it had to be. In Zimbabwe they include Erica Bornstein, James Burns, Marc Epprecht and Allison Goebel, Tony King, and Tanya Lyons. In Minneapolis they include Pam Aronson, Bo Dong, Sara Dorow, Martha Easton, Heidi Gengenbach, Louise Guenther, Jinzhou Huang, Switbert Kamazima, David Lunsford and Perry Seymour, Derek and Becky Peterson, Sharon Preves, Sylvia Tamale, and Samuel Zalanga.

I'd like to thank my parents, John and Hilary Kaler, for the twin gifts of curiosity and a healthy skepticism about the workings of the world. Both have stood me in good stead.

And most of all, I want to record my appreciation for the presence of Guy Thompson before, during, and after this project. He's a model of critical engagement and intellectual joie de vivre, among many other things.

# 1

# INTRODUCTION

The contraceptive pill and injection are unique among technologies for their ability to stir up trouble: trouble between men and women, trouble between the old and the young, trouble between social conservatives and radicals, trouble of all sorts. The very existence of devices that reshape sex and child-bearing invokes any number of ideas and anxieties about men, women, their bodies, and their responsibilities to the others who populate their social world.

Implicit in these contraceptive devices are questions about rights, freedoms, duties, and power. Do women have absolute rights to their bodies? Should a wife be able to use contraceptives without her husband's consent? Are wombs and women public property to be regulated by the state, or should the having or not having of children be a private decision? Is childbearing a duty one owes to a nation, a state, a lineage, or a deity? Do contraceptives change the link between sex and babies, producing new cohorts of unrestrained or immoral women? As such questions show, studying contraceptives and listening to what people say about them let us see the ways that fertility and sexuality underpin—and undermine—ideas about our bodies, gender, our families, and our nations. Contraception, I argue, is about much more than whether a particular baby will be born at a particular time; it is about the struggle over who will direct the material and symbolic resources represented by a fertile young woman's womb. At base, contraceptives are about power.

The contraceptive pill and injection are conduits for power, the power to have or not have a baby. When new contraceptives arrive, they precipitate radical and hotly contested shifts in the allocation of power over fertility. As we shall see, the advent of the pill and Depo-Provera in colonial Zimbabwe allocated this power to some—individual women and the nurses and distributors who supplied them—and took it away from others—husbands, female in-laws, and the traditional healers who had previously been the gatekeepers for indigenous means of regulating fertility. Most troublingly, the new contraceptives represented a reallocation of power over African childbearing, away from African families and communities, and toward the white colonial state.

bent on "cutting down the nation" by any means necessary. These multiple shifts in power and the anxieties and hopes that they generated are the subject of this book.

To examine these shifts in power, I trace the social history of contraception in colonial Zimbabwe by interviews with 58 former family planning workers from across the country and 67 ordinary Zimbabweans aged 40 and older, from a resettlement area near the town of Wedza, and through archival research. My observations form the six chapters that follow.

This particular historic moment was a roiling and volatile time for Rhodesians, black and white, as the country struggled out of decades of white domination to become the new nation of Zimbabwe in 1980. Contraceptives were strongly associated with the white regime, and were named as symbols of white efforts to wipe out or degrade blacks. The use of the pill and Depo became a political issue, and as we shall see, the nationalist struggle moved into family planning clinics and marital bedrooms, as well as the guerrillas' bush camps and the diplomats' chambers.

At the same time, the politicization of the pill and Depo coexisted with eternal domestic tensions—young people were chafing at the restrictions of their elders, and women were negotiating their relationships to their husbands and the dues they owed their husbands' families. The pill and the injection added fuel to these long-simmering fires and produced gendered and generational disputes as to who, exactly, would be able to control a young wife's womb.

## SEX, REPRODUCTION, AND POWER IN SOCIAL HISTORY AND DEMOGRAPHY

Women's fertility in Africa has always been linked to the psychopolitical and spiritual well-being of communities. Fears of infertility act as metaphors for political instability and economic hard times, and dropping birthrates are symbolically linked to declining temporal power (see, e.g., Feldman-Savelsberg 1994:471 and Vaughan 1989:135). Morality is also indexed by reproduction, as women's failures to conceive or give birth are ascribed to their or their neighbors' sexual misdeeds (Johnson 1995; Callahan 1997). Conversely, reproductive sins, such as aborting or having sex during pregnancy, are thought to bring sickness and catastrophe to entire communities (see, e.g., Bledsoe [1990] on *amakombela* or Obbo [1993] on *amakiro*). Colonial regimes in Africa, as well as their successors, struggled to control reproductive practices, which they deemed not just undesirable, but actually dangerous to the health of the body politic (Cooper and Stoler 1989). Throughout African history, sex and reproduction have been invested with power and symbolism above and beyond the mere biological mechanics of the acts.

Curiously, the association among sex, contraception, and power has until recently received scant attention from those scholars most concerned with fer-

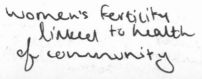

tility—demographers. Since demography's birth in the 1940s and 1950s, demographers have looked to the notion of modernization to explain why people use contraception and have fewer babies (Szreter 1993). They argue that the cost-benefit ratio for having children changes as economic modernization occurs, and that couples behave like rational consumers in maximizing the efficient use of their time and resources by reducing their production of children. Control of fertility as a means of asserting power and contraceptive-based strategies for resisting power have not figured into demographers' descriptions of fertility and reproduction until quite recently.

This book is part of a new and different configuration of demography, in which cultural meanings and struggles on multiple levels are foregrounded.[1] These new studies disrupt the "orderly theories" (Watkins, Rutenberg, and Green 1995) favored by their predecessors, with their attention to "disorderly" behavior and ideas. Of such writers, three have been particularly influential in helping me frame this project.

The new cultural demography has been strongly influenced by Geoffrey McNicoll, whose germinal 1980 article was an early argument for complexifying, rather than attempting to simplify, the determinants of fertility. Through application of his institutional analysis, he demonstrated that social and political institutions existing at all levels from the family to the nation have a place in decision making, as does the eruption of historic discontinuities. Although McNicoll avoids the issues of power, resistance, and coercion, he laid the groundwork for later theorists who had specifically feminist concerns about power and agency.

His materialist approach to fertility behavior was refined by Faye Ginsburg and Rayna Rapp's concern with the symbolic meanings and discursive uses of fertility, in their 1991 manifesto for a politics of reproduction. They called attention to "the ways in which [processes of fertility and birth] figure into understandings of social and cultural renewal" (311), opening the way for the methods that I use in this book—personal narrative and document analysis. Ginsburg and Rapp focus mainly on the state, but in this book I extend their insight that "throughout history . . . power has depended directly and indirectly on defining normative families and controlling populations" (314) to other forms of social control, such as patriarchy or different forms of colonialism.

Caroline Bledsoe brought these concerns with power, history, and meaning to the very tangible and concrete materials of modern contraception—the pills and injections themselves. In her work on The Gambia, Sierra Leone, and the print media of southern Africa (Bledsoe 1990, 1994; Bledsoe and Hill 1993), Bledsoe treats contraceptive methods as examples of "traveling technology," which take root in places other than where they originated and acquire meaning other than what their originators intended. Contraceptives, in other words, become icons of various sorts, signifying modernity, decadence, rebellion, or freedom, depending on who was looking at them. In this book, I focus on the iconicity of the pill and, later, the Depo-Provera injection, broadening and deepening Bledsoe's notions of contraceptives as cultural objects.

## HISTORIC CONTEXT: THE LIBERATION WAR

This book covers events between 1957 and 1980, and reaches even further into the past through the memories of those who are quoted in its pages. However, the defining historic event of this book is Zimbabwe's liberation war, fought in the 1970s by African guerrillas against the white settler government. The reasons for this war are manifest in the contrast between the lives of the black majority and of the white minority, who ruled what was then Rhodesia in the racist fashion of apartheid South Africa.

In 1977, the population of Rhodesia was approximately 6.8 million, of whom 95% were Africans, 4% whites, and 1% classed as Asian or "coloured." Nineteen percent lived in urban areas, mainly Salisbury and Bulawayo, while the majority lived in the countryside. The rural areas were divided into areas designated as European commercial farming and areas designated for Africans, which encompassed both the densely populated Tribal Trust Lands (TTLs), in which grazing rights and other usufructuary rights were held communally, and the much smaller African Purchase Areas, where farmers could hold individual title to land. The average income for families in the TTL was estimated at "less than $Rhodesian 15 per month," and had declined 40% in real terms between 1948 and 1977 (Gilmurray, Riddell, and Sanders 1979:18). Pneumonia and homicide were the leading causes of death among Africans in the TTLs; and bilharzia and malaria were endemic (26, 28). In addition to these absolute deprivations, Africans also suffered great relative deprivation compared with the white population. See Table 1 for a summary of African-white differentials in income, health, and education as of 1977.

During the 1970s, warfare in the rural areas added chaos and insecurity to poverty. Most military action took the form of hit-and-run guerrilla attacks by the liberation forces, which exacted harsh reprisals from the armies of the white government. Civilians in the rural areas bore the brunt of these attacks and counterattacks, and risked severe punishment from the state for helping or cooperating with the independence fighters, known to the peasants as the *vakomana* (the boys) and to the government as terrorists. The best estimate of total deaths in the war is about 30,000, which were overwhelmingly African civilians. At least 375,000 were internally displaced by being forced into so-called protected villages, encampments designed by the government to prevent civilians from aiding the guerrillas.

The toll of deaths and chaos intensified toward the end of the war, so that 45% of all black civilians killed during the war were killed in 1978. The number of guerrillas in Rhodesia was estimated at 3,200 in 1977; within two years

**Table 1.1**
**African-White Discrepancies in Rhodesia, 1977**

| Parameter | African Population | White Population |
|---|---|---|
| Average monthly wage (for those employed) | $49 | $513 |
| Infant mortality per thousand | 120-220 | 17 |
| Population densities in rural areas per square mile | 46 | 1 |
| Percentage completing secondary education | .04% | 33% |
| Government educational expenditure per enrolled pupil | $46 | $531 |

*Sources:* Average monthly wage: Gilmurray et al. 1979:17; Infant mortality: Gilmurray et al. 1979:22; Population densities: Kriger 1992:54 (figures for 1969); Secondary education completion rates: Kriger 1992:61; Educational expenditures: Kriger 1992:61.

this had increased to 28,000 combatants (Sibanda 1989). The logistics of moving this many guerrilla fighters into the field meant decreasing the amount of discipline and training they received and, as a consequence, the last years of the war are marked both in the history books and in people's memories by indiscipline and misbehavior on the part of the guerrillas (see Nhongo-Simbanegavi 1998).

The guerrilla forces were divided into two organizations: the Zimbabwe African National Union (ZANU) and the Zimbabwe African Patriotic Union (ZAPU). Both were Marxist in ideological orientation and received substantial help from neighboring socialist countries, as well as from the Soviet Union and China. The military toll of the war, combined with international condemnation of the Rhodesian regime, forced the regime to sit down with ZANU and ZAPU and accept national elections brokered by the United Kingdom in 1980. Despite the hardships of the war years, most Zimbabweans saw their hopes for a peaceful, democratic future embodied in ZANU and its leader, Robert Mugabe, and Mugabe's party won a landslide electoral victory. Mugabe became the first democratically elected prime minister of Zimbabwe, to enormous popular acclaim.

This book is about the dark days of the war and the years leading up to it, however, not about the victories that ended the war. During the war years, all families, including all those whose stories are in this book, were touched in some way. Even if they were not directly involved as combatants on either side, the restrictions and privations of the war were visited on all Africans. Mr. E.G. Watungwa, an African Member of Parliament (MP), told the Parliament:

> I believe I cannot associate myself with the name "terrorist" because I find on every road I travel, every African is [treated as] a terrorist. I say this because when I come from my house to town every Saturday morning the police are on the road checking. Every white man passes through with his car but every African is stopped and searched. I cannot see who I can call a terrorist and who is not a terrorist. I do not know who is a law-abiding African and who is not a law-abiding African. As far as I am concerned in the present stage every African, whether in a suit or in rags, is treated as a terrorist. (Parliamentary Debates vol.83 no.15, March 29, 1973, col.1140, cited in Catholic Commission for Justice and Peace [CCJP] 1976:2)

An old man, whose village had been destroyed by a Rhodesian barrage from the air and who had been forced at gunpoint by Rhodesian soldiers to destroy his own crops, in order to prevent him from feeding the guerrillas, said

> If we report the terrorists, they come and kill us. If we do not report them, the soldiers come to torture us and destroy our homes and fields. But even if we report the terrorists, the soldiers torture us all the same because they think we are trying to set them up. We do not know what to do. (CCJP 1976:40)

In addition to being caught in the battlefield of the hit-and-run war, the African population was subject to the increasingly punitive laws that the Rhodesian government brought in to try to reduce African support for the guerrillas and prevent the establishment of liberated zones. These laws indemnified the Rhodesian security forces for any offenses they might commit while in pursuit of terrorists and established a separate system of on-the-spot courts for dealing with offenses related to terrorism, without habeas corpus or accountability to higher authorities. The security forces and local government authorities were also empowered, as of 1973, to exact collective fines from villages suspected of supporting the guerrillas and, as of 1972, to enact dusk-to-dawn curfews, which blanketed most of the country by the middle of the war (CCJP 1976). Health and welfare conditions deteriorated further. Malnutrition accounted for a growing proportion of African deaths. By 1978, the International Red Cross and Christian Care were supplying emergency food and seed rations to more than 2 million people, yet their efforts only reached part of the people in need as so much of the country had become "no go" areas (Gilmurray et al. 1979:31).

What exactly did the people make of the guerrillas who precipitated this crackdown, some of whom were their own sons and daughters? Scholars of the liberation war period are divided as to the nature of the relationship between the guerrillas and the people. Kriger (1988, 1992) believes that coercion and threats played a major role in obtaining peasant support for the guerrillas and "reject[s] the concept of sustained support or voluntary cooperation between guerrillas and peasants or local elites" (1988:306). Frederikse (1984) argues that the guerrillas' normative appeals to cultural tradition and pride were successful and that violent coercion was rarely necessary. Ranger (1985) cites peasant receptiveness to the cultural nationalist arguments of the guerrillas, as well as peasants' economic grievances and objections to the colonial government's agricultural policies. Lan (1985) believes that the guerrillas' appeal to religious beliefs and practices won them considerable peasant support, more so than their anticolonial, revolutionary messages. These debates among scholars suggest a very complex and locally-inflected relationship between the liberation forces and the peasants.

Since Kriger's work in the mid-1990s, many social scientists, especially non-Zimbabweans, have produced revisionist histories of the liberation war that emphasize the use of coercion and violence by the comrades. Such histories are intended as a corrective to the hagiographies and party histories of the early 1980s, which stressed perfect harmony in guerrilla-peasant alliances. However, my own experience living and doing research in rural Zimbabwe has convinced me that the coercion paradigm is no more tenable than the paradigm of solidarity and cooperation. I have come to believe that most Zimbabweans, especially in rural areas, strongly supported the agenda of the liberation movements, especially the return of the ancestral land, and were proud of the *vakomana* (the boys) in the liberation armies. During the 1970s, thousands of Zimbabwean civilians went out of their way to listen to, cook for, and assist the guerrillas, out of their conviction that the comrades offered the best hope of redeeming Zimbabwe from its oppressors. At the same time, the day-to-day experience of living with the comrades produced stresses. This was particularly true when resources were scarce and both comrades and civilians needed to eat. A goat, a chicken, or a vegetable garden could become an object of struggle between local families and guerrillas, and the guerrillas usually won.[2] Nonetheless, most of the Zimbabweans I knew as colleagues or as interviews subjects looked back with pride on what they had done to help the boys, despite the incidents of misunderstanding or indiscipline that arose.

The war's greatest legacy, apart from its political gains, was the disruption it wrought on established hierarchies and the opportunities it provided for disaffected people, particularly women and youth, to assert themselves against local structures of power. Kriger refers to these as "struggles within the struggle" (1988, 1992) that shaped many people's experiences of the war as strongly as did the nationalism of the liberation movements.

*[Handwritten margin notes: "relationship between Guerrillas and civilians"; "but they couldn't just be wanting support since they were retrospectively"]*

The ambiguity of the ways that women were imagined within the liberation movement: side-by-side with gun-toting male comrade, yet dressed in traditional wrap-
around cloth and headscarf, while the man wears a military uniform. Source: *The
Zimbabwe Review*, January 1978, p. 10.

The very presence of the liberation forces brought new resources into age-old
gender and generational struggles. Alliances with the guerrillas provided women
and youth with new ways to assert their freedom, making the 1960s and 1970s a
time of unprecedented social ferment (20). For example, in zones controlled by
the guerrillas, they provided a new authority to which women could appeal to
protest their husbands' abuses of power, and by incorporating male and female
adolescents as assistants and messengers, they provided an escape from paternal
control (Gaidzanwa 1992:111–13; Kriger 1991; Stott 1989:22–23).

However, at the same time as the guerrillas' presence provided opportunities to shift balances of power in gendered and generational struggles, the
guerrillas themselves were concerned to assert themselves as the agents of
authentic African culture calling for a return to tradition and rejection of the

debasements of colonialism. Kriger calls this position "cultural nationalism," which she defines as appeals to the norms of an idealized Zimbabwean culture, in order to "build a spiritual and cultural base for African nationalism and denounce European culture" (96).

In the realm of marriage and family, cultural nationalism took the form of insisting that both genders conform to gender-specific norms of ideal patriarchal behavior.[3] For men, this meant providing adequately for wives and children rather than spending money on drinking and prostitutes. For women, this meant the expansion of the definition of maternal duties to include feeding and caring for their fictive children among the liberation forces (Kaler 1997; Staunton 1991). In this respect, the liberation movement did not attempt to change gender hierarchies and actually provided reinforcement to certain patriarchal values.

Of particular salience to this book, cultural nationalism meant strong opposition to such non-African things as the pill and the Depo-Provera shot, which were regarded as tools of the colonial regime. The pill and the shot were destroying Zimbabwean society both literally (by reducing the number of new people being born) and culturally (by encouraging women toward promiscuity and taking away men's control of the children born into their families), argued the ideologues of the nationalist forces. The specter of control over African women being wrested away from African men by Europeans armed with pills and injections was a potent one, invoked to rouse the support of men already made anxious by the rapid social changes that were depriving male elders of control over women (Kaler 1998). Thus, the liberation forces active in the rural areas remained staunchly pronatal and anticontraception on the level of rhetoric, if not always in their actions.

## HISTORIC CONTEXT: COLONIAL DEVELOPMENT AND THE "IMPROVEMENT" OF AFRICANS

The dominant historic context for this book is the liberation war. However, the history of contraception is also situated within a different context—that of the colonial projects designed to reshape African sexual and reproductive practices. Although the Rhodesian state provided very little in the way of health services for Africans, Rhodesia in the 1970s was heir to a wide range of programs, both governmental and nongovernmental, aimed at "socializ[ing] African women as biological reproducers" (Hunt 1988:430). These domesticity projects were the focus of persuasive, rather than coercive, attempts to civilize Africans (Hansen 1992, Kaler 1998, Kirkwood 1984, Ranchod-Nilssen 1992, Weinrich 1982). Such programs included marriage counseling, homecraft clubs for women, and classes in child care, home economics, and nutrition. These classes were aimed not only at changing superficial behavior, but also at getting Africans to adopt a moral, social, and economic order, one which was founded on European nuclear family models and the values they supposedly embodied (Comaroff and Comaroff 1992, see also Hunt 1990). Family planning fit right into this trajectory of molding proper families, although it ventured more deeply into the sexual heart of marriage than did any of its predecessors.

These domestication projects were not always adopted wholecloth by African women. Many women used the projects to further their own personal agendas, very different from what the white government might have had in mind. This process of subversion reached its apotheosis with family planning, but had its precedents in the ways that African beneficiaries appropriated their own domestication in previous decades.

For example, Weinrich describes how the new forms of marriage brought by Christian missionaries were selectively adapted by Africans. Church marriage, rather than marking the beginning of the marital relationship, was gradually transformed into the end stage of a series of nuptial rituals, which could include multiple wedding ceremonies. Often, the church wedding was only held after several children had already been born, and was used as a celebration of fertility as well as a nuptial rite (Weinrich 1982:82). This adaptation of a European ritual was not to the liking of many religious authorities, and marriage legislation and practice became a highly contentious arena of governance (see also Jeater 1993).

Kaler (1997) and Ranchod-Nilsson (1992) studied homecraft clubs for rural women sponsored by the National Federation of Women's Institutes of Rhodesia. These clubs were set up explicitly to teach home management skills to rural women, but women soon discovered that the laudable domestic purpose of the clubs gave women a sanctioned way to escape from their husband's watchful eyes and socialize, and share strategies among women about how to maximize their control of the household's financial resources. Ranchod-Nilsson argues that the homecraft clubs led to the unintended consequence of "the development of a gender consciousness that rural women eventually expressed during the liberation war" (197). While the women's clubs were used as a vehicle by white colonial rulers to convert African women to particular political positions, these ideologies were largely ignored by the women, who made use of the clubs to suit their own domestic strategies and agendas, most particularly securing their own income independent from their husband's.

In even earlier days, young women and teenage girls used the missions and the mission schools—where "good wives" were trained—as havens from undesired marriages or control by their parents, which they found too restrictive (Jeater 1993, Schmidt 1992). The threat of running away was used by girls to bargain for less onerous conditions at home. Angry fathers and prospective husbands arrived at the missions, demanding to get their women back, while the girls themselves appealed to the norms of the missionaries to justify their choice of a life, which they perceived as offering more autonomy. These confrontations between white men and African men over the activities

*[handwritten margin note: conflict between white men + African men over African women]*

of African women form one of the dominant motifs in the history of contraception, some four decades later.

## SHONA CULTURE AND REPRODUCTION

As is clear from these examples, African women had a long history of taking what the state offered them and using it for their own ends, foreshadowing their adoption of contraceptives. This appropriation, however, was not simply a means of adopting new objects and ideas wholecloth, but of integrating them with and juxtaposing them to longstanding practices concerning fertility and gender. Here, I summarize briefly some of these longstanding practices, bearing in mind the large gap that exists between ideals and actual experiences. (This section pertains to the Shona, who make up roughly 85% of the population.[4])

Shona society can be characterized as pronatal, but this pronatalism was *[handwritten: pronatal]* much more complex than the simple desire to have as many children as possible. Ideas about the moral goodness and rightness of being fertile and having children permeated the cluster of beliefs and practices that my interviewees described as "our Shona culture." The idea of "our Shona culture" as an explanation for all kinds of behavior was invoked so often in interviews that in transcription and coding I began to abbreviate it simply as OSC. *[handwritten: OSC = explanation for behavior]*

"Our Shona culture" and "our Shona tradition" were described as powerful forces, which dictated norms of conduct and belief and which provided explanations for behavior and events. However, asserting that something is "traditional" or part of "our culture" is not an unproblematic description of the past or a guide to contemporary practices (Hobsbawm and Ranger 1983, see also Kaler 2001). The power to define certain things as traditional and thereby to hallow them with cultural authenticity is a valuable asset in cultural disputes. Those who claim cultural authority for their position through associating it with tradition can legitimate themselves and delegitimate their opponents.[5] *[handwritten: meaning of "tradition"]*

Tradition was frequently invoked to explain reproductive customs and practices; however, it was not a unified and internally coherent monolith. Male infertility is a case in point—some people told me that in OSC no one could ever suggest that a couple's infertility was attributable to the male partner, and all traditional ways of dealing with childlessness, be they religious or medical, focused on the woman. However, others told me about specific traditional rituals for detecting and curing infertility in adolescent boys, which *[handwritten: contradictions in interviews]* presumes that it is possible for a man to be infertile. I also heard enough about deviant and counternormative behavior, such as abortion or non-procreative sex, to make it clear that tradition did not dictate actual lived experience.

So if OSC does not exist as a unified body of ideas, and it is not a force that determines people's lives, what is it? In this book, OSC appears in two forms: (1) as a collection of practical knowledge, such as how to find the particular

*[handwritten at bottom: OSC 1. collection of knowledge 2. Authority]*

herbs that would suppress ovulation; and (2) as a reservoir of authority, something to be drawn on to legitimate one's desires for power.

According to OSC, childbearing was the central, defining act of a person's
life—central not only to individual identity but to the purpose of life on earth.
"*Upenyu hwemunhu vana*"—a person's life is children—is a Shona proverb
that came up again and again (Mutambirwa 1979:97). A person's offspring
were his or her contribution to the world, binding him or her to the future and
the past, and carrying the obligation to assume moral responsibilities. Offspring were necessary for the creation of the good community. In Shona culture, therefore,

> the single most important condition necessary for maintaining justice and
> peace is "*kuva tsanga,*" to have or leave a seed through which human pro-
> creation can be maintained . . . as giver or contributor to the pool of life, it
> is believed that [a parent] becomes bound to protecting justice. (98)

For women, childbearing shaped and defined their marriage, which in turn
defined their life chances. Children were born into the male ancestral lineage,
and therefore the husband had the spiritual responsibility of producing more
progeny for his ancestors. However, a wife's biological responsibility for the
quantity and quality of children meant that her fertility was absolutely central
to her life, as well as to the relationship between husband and wife. Husbands
acquired rights to direct their wives' fertility for the benefit of the lineage as a
whole, a presumption that had major ramifications for the spread of contraceptives (Batezat and Mwalo 1989:49, Chinemana 1988, Stott 1989:6, Weinrich 1979:47–48).

Women's reproductive successes or failures were of interest for many people besides herself and her husband. The "patriarchal, patrilocal, and potentially polygynous" nature of Shona cultural life meant that fertility and
reproductive rectitude were a community concern (Stott 1989:6, see also
Batezat and Mwalo 1989, Courville 1993). For example, a woman's paternal
aunts often played a key role in organizing her reproductive life. Their authority derived from the fact that it was the bride-price that had been paid for
them, which enabled their brother—the woman's father—to get married and
found a family, and so they had an interest in seeing that family be perpetu-
ated. For the same reasons, a woman's brothers also had an interest in regulating how and when she got pregnant, as it was their sister's *lobola*, which
could be used for their payments to their own fiancées' families, and that
*lobola* was contingent on her childbearing success. The family into which a
woman married had even more concern with the quality and number of her
pregnancies, as these pregnancies enhanced the patrilineage. Many Shona
women remember older female in-laws commenting on the size, weight, and
frequency of a woman's children, including comments on lack of sexual self-

control or irresponsibility if the children were spaced unhealthily close together (see also Mutambirwa 1979).

Shona societies had many ways of regulating fertility, not only to ensure that children were born, but also to control the tempo and total number of births, in order to ensure quality of children as well as quantity (known as *kurera vana*, the spacing of children in order to raise them well). *Kurera vana* was primarily the responsibility of the husband, secondarily the responsibility of the wife, and tertiarily the responsibility of the grandparents and the community. If one link in this chain failed in their responsibility to space children, the next link was expected to take it on (Mutambirwa 1979:99). While it was the husband's duty to find contraceptives for his wife, she was expected to be counseled about the importance of child-spacing by her female relatives, especially her paternal aunts and grandmother, ideally following the birth of the first child.[6]

However, the ideals of marriage and childbearing described above were just that—norms and ideal types, rather than patterns of practice. Actual practices of union-formation and childbearing changed in response to changing social and economic conditions, as well as in response to individual interests. In an early-1980s survey of primaparas, Meekers (1993) found an increasing number of women expressing a preference for unions not anchored by the payment of bride-price to their families, for informal sexual unions, and, most significantly, for having children outside the framework of parental control of female reproductive capacities before marriage (40–51). The causes of this increasing irregularity were varied, including urbanization, waged employment for young men, and rising demands for bride-price (itself due to various different forms of impoverishment), but the net result was that "the erosion of the social control of the lineage . . . leads to an increasing prevalence of irregular forms of unions" (52). This erosion meant an increasing number of babies were being born outside the traditional framework of marriage and fertility regulation.

All of this evidence points to tensions over control of women's and girls' reproductive resources, with tradition and OSC invoked by some and struggled against by others. The stage was thus set for turbulence and conflict attending the arrival of pills and injections that could prevent a woman from getting pregnant—indeed, one might say that the debates and struggles within families and communities were overdetermined by colonial history and Shona cultural norms.

## HOW I DID THIS RESEARCH

My story is a bit long, a bit short, very complicated, and very interesting.
—interview with Mrs. Shamiso Kudakwashe

During 1996 and 1997, I collected three types of data: archival materials; interviews with African men and women who had been employed as family planning workers in the 1960s and 1970s; and interviews with middle-aged and elderly men and women.

I used the National Archives of Zimbabwe (NAZ), where the Family Planning Association of Rhodesia (FPAR) deposited its papers sporadically during the 1960s and 1970s, as well as the archives of the Ministry of Health, the *Zimbabwe Herald,* and the Zimbabwe National Family Planning Council (ZNFPC). Because of the limitations of archival materials—almost everything was written either by whites or for a white audience, and the FPAR was not very meticulous in its record keeping until the mid-1970s—these documents only hint at the complexities and debates that surrounded family planning in African communities.

The resulting book is based mainly on the memories of family planning workers (FPWs), supplemented with memories of non-FPWs. FPWs' knowledge about the conflicts attending the introduction of these new methods of birth control stems from two sources—their own lifelong immersion in Zimbabwean culture and their professional duty to negotiate both that culture and the political currents sweeping through the nation to promote new means of fertility regulation. Their work lives, at the juncture of the Rhodesian state's project of modernization and containment of a perceived demographic threat, and the daily lives of local communities gave them a unique perspective on the conflicts and shifts of power precipitated by the pills and injections. Who then were the FPWs? Were they drastically different from the people among whom they worked? Were they subaltern beneficiaries of the largesse of colonialism or members of the small African elite?

According to a 1974 survey of 74 FPWs, the only such research ever carried out, the average age of female FPWs was 34, ranging from 25 to 54. All had had some exposure to formal education. Eighty percent had completed primary education only, and 20% had some form of secondary education, mostly nurse or nurse-aid training. Almost all had some prior experience of working outside the home, 40% as primary school teachers. They had an average of three-and-a-half children, ranging from one to seven.

Among male FPWs, the average age was also 34, with a range from 26 to 50. They were more highly educated than their female counterparts, as 76% had some form of secondary education, including correspondence course, while 53% had the equivalent of 10 years formal education and 12% the equivalent of 12 years. Sixty percent had worked as teachers and 37% had clerical or sales experience. They averaged three children, ranging from one to seven (Geraty 1974: passim). To situate these people in the context of their peers, a 1975 survey of 10,890 Rhodesian African adults found that 27.7% of women had no formal education whatsoever and only 3.6% had been educated beyond primary school. Only 9% of African women did paid work outside the home, mostly as seasonal agricultural laborers. Among men, 19.5%

had no formal education at all, and 9.3% had some kind of secondary education. (Weinrich 1979:35, 39).

Wages for FPWs started relatively low, but climbed rapidly relative to the wages of other employed Africans. Mr. Richard Chipango, who began his work as an FPW in 1968, recalls that his starting salary was $Rhodesian 30 per month, with frequent increments, so that within a couple of years "I was happy because I was getting more than what nurses were getting." Other FPWs recalled being envied by local nurses, because they earned more despite not having the same amount of education. By the end of the 1970s, the average salary of an educator was approximately $Rhodesian 173 per month. In 1974, 80.6% of African families in the rural areas earned less than $Rhodesian 25 per month, while in the urban areas 42.5% earned less than $Rhodesian 25 per month, and only 2.5% earned more than $Rhodesian 125 per month (Weinrich 1979:50).[7] The FPWs were somewhat more educated and economically well-off than most of their cohort.

Despite their comparative wealth, FPWs were strongly rooted in the communities where they worked. In 1972, 71% of educators were employed in the community in which they resided, in many cases for their entire lives. Many of the educators, particularly women, had been active members of local women's clubs or church groups, and this affiliation was often the basis for their recruitment (interview with Mr. Peter Dodds). Nurses and clinic-based personnel tended to be more mobile, often changing their work location two or three times in their career. This profile suggests that the FPWs were likely to belong to locally prominent families, of successful farmers, low-level civil servants such as police constables, or small entrepreneurs. This is particularly true for those who started working in the very early days. As the FPW corps expanded and recruitment drives were launched, more men and women from lower socioeconomic strata were recruited so that the FPWs came to resemble the people among whom they worked.[8]

FPWs held common world views, as well as social characteristics. All the interviewees shared an attachment to a view of the world common in the social sciences and social policy, according to which people are utility-maximizing consumers whose consumption patterns are shaped by rational decisions based on available knowledge. Resistance to family planning was conceptualized as a problem of inaccurate or incomplete knowledge, leading to wrong ideas about the true nature of family planning. The cure for these misconceptions was more and better information, so that potential users could make better rational calculations. I attribute this emphasis on economic rationality and information saturation to the FPWs' perceptions of themselves as rational, modern[9] people, shored up by the prominence of rationality and utility calculations in the thinking of most pillars of the family planning establishment, in Rhodesia and abroad, during the 1960s and 1970s.

Over the course of my research, I traveled throughout rural, urban, and peri-urban Zimbabwe, doing interviews in every province. I also interviewed several of the white founders of the Family Planning Association in South Africa. Some family planning workers were referred to me through the provincial managers of the ZNFPC, others I found by searching through FPAR papers for recurring names associated with certain places, and then matched these names to the Zimbabwe telephone directory for that location. Finally, some contacts referred me to others, former workmates and friends. Particularly in Harare, the social ties (usually church-based) among long-serving FPWs remained strong. Interviews were conducted in respondents' homes or in neutral locations like a café, and all but three respondents opted to use English rather than Shona. Interviews ran on average about two hours (with a range between 45 minutes and five hours) and were tape-recorded and transcribed verbatim.

My sample of respondents is likely to be biased toward those who loved their jobs, or who relished a chance to talk about their glory days as family planners with a stranger. The dilettantes and the disgruntled do not appear among my interviewees, as is shown by the missionary zeal with which many people talked about their work.[10] However, in reading through the records of the FPAR I found very little evidence that a high proportion of the FPWs were ever regarded as malcontents. This is particularly notable in comparison with the problems reported of managing the African employees of various government departments in the files of the Ministry of Native Affairs (later Internal Affairs), which employed African clerks and messengers. The FPWs were also comparatively well paid and worked under conditions that respected their professional autonomy more than was the case for most African workers in those days, which may also account for their relative contentment. This contentment with the past was also manifest in the self-confidence and self-assertion that they felt about the rightness of their work, and their conviction that they had been vindicated by history—the comrades and politicians who had opposed them had belatedly seen the light about family planning, and the Zimbabwean government had become one of the strongest proponents of family planning in Africa.

This sense of having been vindicated by history led to a reconstruction of the past in which victory was certain, despite all the very real difficulties that the FPWs experienced. FPWs presented the family planning movement as a case of successful meliorism, a crusade for the health and welfare of Zimbabwean families, and their own work as something that they consciously chose out of compassion and Christian altruism.

For instance, Mr. David Chibvongodze saw himself as one of these altruistic modernizers, initially unappreciated but later vindicated:

I still remember when I went to my home area . . . people were saying, "he is a murderer, he has come to stop our wives to have children." Even my wife was afraid when I took this job, but I said, "no, it's just like Jesus, when people were preaching about God many people didn't like to hear about God." Good things have always got opposition, but later people are accepting [family planning]. Now I am glad, even at my home they are practicing family planning. That time [when Mr. Chibvongodze was a FPW] they used to give me some names [insult or accuse him], they used to say we are soldiers of the Smith regime, so I just said, "it's okay, I know I am doing the good thing for the country, the good thing for our community." Now here we are; now they have accepted family planning.

*[handwritten margin note: Christian activism]*

Interviews are inevitably affected by what the people involved think about each other. In my self-presentation, I described myself to the interviewees as a student who was studying the beginning of the family planning movement in Rhodesia. My work in Zimbabwe was necessary for me to get my degree so that I could teach at a university. I said that it was well-known that Zimbabwe was a leader in Africa in terms of family planning, but that no one had ever studied the challenges that the family planning pioneers faced and how they overcame those challenges.

This approach contains its own bias: my assumption that the most appropriate entrée into the history of family planning was via a conflict paradigm that foregrounds issues of struggle and power differentials. This bias was signaled in interviews by my use of concepts such as challenges and problems. Nonetheless, a close look at my transcripts reveals that interviewees themselves tended to frame their experiences in terms of challenges or problems, even before I introduced those terms into the conversation. For example, in response to my initial question "How did you get involved in family planning?" Mr. Richard Chidakwa answered,

*[handwritten margin note: self awareness]*

> We were facing a lot of difficulties. Point number one, people really couldn't understand what family planning was. . . . The majority didn't understand at all what was family planning. It was difficult, but we managed. . . . There were some you couldn't spend even two minutes talking to them, they would just say, "We are not interested." They don't want to hear anything about what you are saying. So what are you going to do? Just go off to the next one.

I had some choice as to how I defined my mission while interviewing people; I had less control over how they perceived me and how it might affect the dynamics of the interviewing process (see Wolf 1996 for a summary of concerns over social location and methodology). I was clearly located differently from my interviewees in ways that derive from global inequalities and power differentials. I am white, North American, have many years of formal education, affiliated with powerful institutions such as the University of Zimbabwe and their former employer, the ZNFPC, and, even though my graduate student income might seem tiny to me, I was much wealthier than most of the people I interviewed. I was conscious that these power differentials existed and might affect what people said to me, even as I tried to avoid exploiting them by trying to ensure that people only spoke to me if they really wanted to; scheduling interviews at times and places recommended by interviewees; minimizing my association with the ZNFPC by not traveling with ZNFPC workers; making, as far as possible, my interview arrangements outside of ZNFPC channels of communication; and minimizing displays of the perks of being white, educated, and well connected, such as using public transport to go to the townships rather than a private car.

*[handwritten in margin: Positionality]*

Nonetheless, as a white, university-educated person attached to the ZNFPC, I was inevitably perceived as a bearer of modernity and development. This may have encouraged FPWs to synchronize their presentation with the way they perceived me, so that they may have been unwilling to discuss the concerns and hesitations that they had about family planning, or share some of their reservations about it. (However, ordinary Zimbabweans who were not FPWs did not hesitate to tell me or my research assistant that they thought family planning was bad or that, even if they supported it now, they had initially been strongly opposed to it.)

In many important ways, however, I was subordinate to the people I researched. I was younger than them by at least two-and-a-half decades, and I was a student, rather than a full adult. Many FPWs, in the course of our chit-chat before the interview, brought up their own children or younger relatives who attended or wanted to attend polytechnics and universities, or told me about younger relatives who they perceived to be about my age. In yet other respects, FPWs and I met on a plane of near-equality. In a way, we were fellow professionals, both conversant with the methods and concepts of modern family planning, both in command of a vocabulary and a body of knowledge that, while not esoteric, was not shared by the average person in either Zimbabwe or North America. We could thus talk about matters such as the problems and treatments of post-Depo amenorrhea or the combined pill versus low-dose pills, although the FPWs' experience clearly exceeded my own book-learning.

As a white woman studying social relationships in African communities, I must address the insider-outsider dilemma (Abu-Lughod 1988, Merton 1972). Given that I do not belong to the group that I am studying, can I claim any access to *verstehen* knowledge about that group? I believe that I can, even though I can't claim subjective or experiential knowledge of Shona communities. While a Shona researcher might have come up with different but equally reasonable conclusions about the culture of contraception, I have faith in my own conclusions. I base this belief on several foundations.

First, the literature on the insider-outsider dilemma suggests that outsiders are indeed capable of insightful research, provided they balance their knowledge claim with an acknowledgment of the limitations imposed on them by their outsider status (see Wolf 1996:15–19 for a review of this literature). My own experience has shown that outsider status may actually be helpful in some situations. Balanced against instances in which my lack of cultural fluency was a barrier between me and what I wanted to know (e.g., my slowness to understand what people meant when they talked about men's "weakness" caused by their wives' use of contraceptives in chapter 3) were instances in which my foreignness actually helped me to learn things, as when traditional healers in Wedza were willing to tell me more details about how traditional contraceptives were gathered and used because they knew I was not in a position to spread their "private business" through their community.

Second, I lived in rural Zimbabwe for three years, from 1990 to 1993, and had actively tried to learn about Shona life. This did not make me any kind of cultural savant, but it did mean that I was able to see connections between disparate practices in terms of the underlying values being expressed. Finally, in interviews, particularly with older and more assertive respondents, I would float hypotheses that I had developed from previous interviews and ask, "Do you think that this is true? Do you think I am understanding correctly or am I misunderstanding?" Within the research situation—I was a young person seeking knowledge about the past from a wiser older person, I was a student, and I was also an outsider seeking to understand *chivanhu* (our Shona culture)—this approach worked well.

In addition to FPWs, 77 people who had not been FPWs were also interviewed, mainly by my research assistant. These interviews took place in a set of small rural communities in Wedza district, about 80 miles southeast of Harare, with people who lived in the resettlement villages that had been established there after the war on former white commercial farmland. Not all my interviewees had grown up in the region as resettlers; they had come from other parts of the country, but generally from within a 100-mile radius of Wedza. In all, 45 women and 22 men, aged between 45 and 100 years old, were interviewed. These interviews were generally shorter than for the FPWs, ranging between 30 and 90 minutes.

This part of my research would not have been possible without Mrs. Nyaradzo Shayanewako. At the time of the research, Mrs. Shayanewako was the wife of the local headmaster at Magamba Secondary School and was related through her natal family or her in-laws to many of the largest families in the district. She had lived at Magamba with her husband and two children for eight years, and was well-known and well-respected by the older people in the area, despite her relative youth (she was 32 at the time of the interviews). Initially, she would set up appointments for me to meet and talk to local elders, but later, when she had mastered the questions I was interested in, she began doing interviews on her own, and proved to be much better than I was.

With Mrs. Shayanewako interviewing them, respondents were very willing to talk about the details of their own lives, rather than in idealized generalizations about OSC. When I was present for interviews, everyone I spoke to was very welcoming and very anxious that I, as an outsider, understand how things were done in Shona communities, how marriages were arranged, how families were planned, and various other sets of rules that were said to govern behavior.[11] While I appreciated the efforts and the time that people took with me, much of what I was hearing were idealized description of norms, which might or might not bear any relation to what people actually did in their lives. With Mrs. Shayanewako, however, knowledge about marriage and family practice could be assumed rather than explained, and the interviews focused more on how these norms were interpreted in the respondents' own lives. Elderly men and women talked quite freely about these issues, even about things said to be taboo.[12] The respondents spoke so freely, in fact, that I was concerned about the potential for embarrassment when this book made its way back to Wedza, so I decided to use pseudonyms for all the non-FPW respondents.

The selection of interview respondents was neither random nor truly representative, as Mrs. Shayanewako acted as a gatekeeper. However, because of her particular social location within the Wedza community, her gatekeeping afforded me access to a wide range of people in the community. As the headmaster's wife, she knew almost all the families in the area. However, because she had married into the Shayanewako family from elsewhere, she did not belong to any of the locally powerful clans, and so stood outside clan politics (her husband's clan, however, was one of the powerful ones). She also had no strong affiliation with any one of the numerous churches in the area, which imposed powerful cleavages on the community, so she was free to speak to members of all churches.

The interviews were influenced by two broader national trends in Zimbabwe in 1997, which encouraged people to idealize the past and to be cynical about the supposed benefits of modernization, including family planning. These two were the implementation of Zimbabwe's Economic Structural Adjustment Program (ESAP), introduced in the early 1990s, and the AIDS epidemic. ESAP made life more difficult in many different ways, including higher rates of inflation, increased user fees and declining quality in medical and health services, and the replacement of Zimbabwean products with more expensive imported ones. For many of the people in Wedza, despite being relatively financially secure, life was getting more arduous every year, and they worried about how their children would be able to afford to form respectable families and educate their own children. This concern led to pessimism about the future and a consequent tendency to present the past as a good time, particularly before Europeans and their money had corrupted the country.

The AIDS epidemic had struck every family that I spoke to in Wedza, and everyone had seen breadwinners in the prime of their lives killed by the disease. The omnipresence of AIDS led to frequent discussions of sexual morality (or lack thereof) and the patterns of sexual behavior that spread the disease.

The people of Wedza, particularly the older people, framed the AIDS problem as one of uncontrollable youths and women indulging in wanton and un-African sexual behavior, which had brought about a plague the likes of which they had never been seen before. This concern with the bad behavior of youth and women and their refusal to accept the rules laid down by elders and husbands may have led my interviewees to emphasize instances of disobedience and subversion in the past, so that the badness of certain people became a motif that ran through most of our conversations about new methods of fertility control. In terms of the effect of this concern on the finished form of this project, chapters 4 and 5 might have looked different had I interviewed people before AIDS and ESAP arrived. My interviewees might not have painted so conflictual a picture of the Shona social world, or concentrated so much on the issue of controlling women and youth.

## A ROADMAP FOR THIS BOOK

In the chapters that follow, I concentrate on fertility as a terrain of power, and contraceptives as conduits for that power. In doing so, I integrate three axes of conflict that run through much African social history—gender conflicts, tensions between generations, and nationalist or anticolonial struggles. I demonstrate the intricate connections between these different domains of social life: how ideas about gender-inflected nationalists' opposition to these new methods, for example, or how generational identity produced a range of different gender-specific stances toward the pill.

In chapter 2, I set the institutional context for the spread of contraceptives in Rhodesia, the efforts of the FPAR, and the white-led government. The formation of a population establishment in Rhodesia was spurred by white concerns about African overpopulation in the "designated African areas," triggering an attempt to apply a welfarist fix in the form of family planning. However, knowledge about Africans' reproductive habits and sexuality was not constructed objectively or neutrally; rather, it was the product of white Rhodesia's overarching project of defining and managing the African other. In this chapter, I bring out the world view of the white social engineers who launched modern family planning in colonial Rhodesia, and the racial conflicts that shaped their ideas about Africans and the nature of African fertility. I then describe the history of the FPAR, sketching out the programs that were implemented and the institutions within which the struggles described in following chapters took place.

In the third chapter, I turn to another body of knowledge that conditioned the way African men and women came to understand the pill and the injection: the indigenous ethnophysiology by which Shona men and women understood their bodies. In Western science, the individual body, as defined by the surface of the skin, is regarded as radically discontinuous from entities such as the body of society or the body politic. Indeed, such phrases are used as metaphors rather than as literal descriptions of reality. Shona ethnophysiology offers a different way of understanding the body—as part of a net of causes and effects, actions and consequences, which ripples back and forth between the embodied ego and a wide array of alters. This concept of the body, and of the far-reaching consequences of what an individual woman might decide to do with her body, had profound implications for the suspicion and anxieties roused by the new contraceptives. This idea of the unbounded female body in which sexual or reproductive choices by a woman affect the physical and spiritual health of others sheds some light on why the use of these new methods was so hotly contested.

Moving from the body into the wider social world, I demonstrate how the pill and the injection altered power relations between women and their sexual partners, especially their husbands. For years, men and women had argued and negotiated over domestic issues such as farming, money, and labor. However, the fact that women could use the pill or the injection without their husbands' knowledge or permission gave a new twist to these long-standing struggles. In addition to removing power over childbearing from men, the pill and the injection unleashed many other anxieties among men, such as fears of dangers of unleashed female sexuality and fears that men would lose their right to act as the interface between their wives and the world outside the domestic sphere.

These new devices, and the nurses and FPWs who gave them out, had the power to at least partially endow women with control over their fertility, beyond the vision of their husbands. Yet the fertility that was affected by those pills was not theirs alone, but was also claimed by their husbands as men's property. These domestic disputes over who should decide when wives should have children led women into paths of subterfuge and resistance. Both individually and collectively they sought out the forbidden pills, with the connivance of FPWs. The pill and the injection were thus the focus of male anxiety and fear, for their part in destabilizing the "natural" gender hierarchy within the home and, thereby, threatening the construct of masculinity that depended in part on control over family affairs. In the 1960s and 1970s, African men's power was being weakened by the colonial government on many different fronts, and in this context the appearance of a "white" pill, which could lead their wives astray, was particularly threatening.

In the fifth chapter, I show that contraceptives changed relations between the generations as well as between the genders. Elder women, who had historically acquired social power through being the gatekeepers of indigenous knowledge about fertility control, found themselves displaced by a new cadre of gatekeepers: the FPAR nurses and the clinic workers who dispensed pills and injections. These new gatekeepers would allegedly hand out pills to any young woman who wanted them, regardless of whether her in-laws approved,

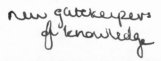
new gatekeepers of knowledge

and, worse, would actively encourage young women to disregard what the elders had taught them about childrearing and to rely on the clinics instead.

During the same time as the nurses and FPWs were threatening elders' power over the fertility of young women, the elders were also losing control over their youth in other spheres, as young men left home to seek wage-earning jobs on the white mines and plantation, as young men and women sought out marriages that were not brokered by elders, and as the influences of formal schooling and Christianity undercut the elders' spiritual authority. As a result, a second set of battle lines was drawn in the conflicts over the pill, cross-cutting the gender-based conflicts, between the old, who felt their influence over the young ebbing away, and the young, who wanted to pursue their own family formation and childbearing strategies independent from their elders.

From these struggles in marriages and families, the pill and the injection acquired connotations of disorder and danger, and in the sixth chapter I link these connotations to national political discourse. During the volatile decades of the 1950s, 1960s, and 1970s, Zimbabwean nationalists defined their nation partially in reaction to the colonial imposition of alien and dangerous practices, a category into which they put the pill and the injection. Some of these objections were demographic: the nationalists interpreted family planning as a threat to the building of a strong people's army, which could re-take the country from the white colonialists, and, afterwards, build a nation big enough to occupy and defend Zimbabwe forever.

Demographic arguments against the pill coexisted with deeper anxieties about what the pill was doing to African dignity and propriety, and about the symbolic significance of white men's tools in African women's bodies. Because the bodies that were "invaded" by pills and injections were female, this cultural threat had a gendered dimension, so that the destructive powers of the new methods of family planning were aimed against African men's rights to control "their" women. This gendered political objection is seen in the sex breakdown of those who voiced their objections: women, while they might be suspicious of the new methods for other reasons, did not regard them as a political danger. When the freedom fighters made opposition to family planning part of their platform, they were tapping into a pre-existing sense among men and elders that these new methods represented a threat to their patriarchal authority over female reproduction, as well as a widespread belief that these were genocidal technologies.

However, in their private lives, the nationalists held positions that were much more complex than simple rejection. Some denounced the contraceptives in public, as a way of appealing to disgruntled men and elders, while making use of injections in their private lives. In other cases, the issue of contraceptives was a bone of contention between women activists and their male counterparts.

In 1980, the first African-led government was elected in Zimbabwe. With this drastic change in the national political context, the social history of family planning also took a new turn. In the final chapter, I briefly survey the story of contraceptives since 1980, sketching out the radical about-face by the new government, which led to their embracement of these methods, and the consequent dramatic decline in the Zimbabwean birthrate.

I also draw out the challenges to current theory presented by the chapter of Zimbabwe's social history, which ended in 1980. I argue for the reality of gender as an always inflected category, in which social constructions such as age, communal identity, or family status combine in order to produce a proliferation of gendered identities and interests. I also call for sociologists to treat the body, particularly the generative female body, as not only a physiological identity but also as a socially constructed political artifact, and to attend to the cultural as well as demographic significance of changes in fertility behavior. Most fundamentally, I urge theorists to rethink their definitions of power, emancipation, and resistance in light of the nuances and the contradiction apparent in Zimbabwean women's use of these new technologies—as women "ran after pills" to enhance their independence from their husbands and their elders, while simultaneously submitting to the government's family planning projects and their not-so-covert agenda of controlling and domesticating the African people.

## NOTES

1. Such work may have the unintended consequence of undermining the entire project of creating grand theories of fertility decline with the power to predict cross-culturally when and how fertility declines will take place. As Greenhalgh (1990:85) puts it, "the closer we get to understanding specific fertility declines, the further we move from a general theory of fertility."

2. Because the war continues to be a difficult memory and a sensitive topic for many Zimbabweans, I have removed identifying material from family planning workers' accounts of the war era in chapter 6.

3. Guerrillas themselves were expected by their spiritual advisors to adhere to an ascetic code of conduct, which prohibited intoxicants, blasphemy, and sex while on operational maneuvers, as well as ritual prohibitions against certain foods or consumer items (Lan 1985, Kriger 1988, Staunton 1991). Unfortunately, much of this discipline slowly broke down by the end of the war (Ranger 1985, Staunton 1991, Nhongo-Simbanegavi 1998).

4. The other major ethnic group, the Ndebele, has not been the subject of as much attention as the Shona, and I am reluctant to generalize from the spotty information on Ndebele practices that I am able to find.

5. This struggle is still going on in Zimbabwe, particularly with respect to gender behavior. For example, sporadically since 1990, groups of young men at the University of Zimbabwe, such as the "University Bachelors' Association" or "Sangano Munhumutapa" (roughly, "the association to preserve Zimbabwe's past glory [Munhumutapa was the name of a major Shona kingdom before independence])" have challenged women students for wearing "immodest" and "untraditional" clothing such as trousers and short skirts, and for

being at the university at all, rather than staying in the domestic sphere where they belong. Women students have responded by organizing rallies at which they insist simultaneously that they have the right as modern people to go where they want and dress as they please, and also that they are as "Zimbabwean" as any of their accusers. Some women have also pointed out in letters to the newspaper that the real "traditional" dress for women consisted of a short woven apron and nothing else, which is surely as "immodest" if not more so than any contemporary skirts. Ergo, they conclude, the male students' campaign is not really about tradition, but it is being used as a pretext to make women students uncomfortable in higher education, and eventually to reserve that space (and the advantages of higher education) for men alone.

6. Mutambirwa identified five different types of contraceptive methods available to Shona women before the advent of nontraditional contraception (1979). These included

1. coitus interruptus—considered unreliable and a method of last resort;
2. continuous breastfeeding (which my interviewees considered unreliable);
3. *mishonga ye kunwa* (oral prescriptions);
4. *nyekupfeka* (insertions); and
5. *mhimvu* (belts of herbs with contraceptive powers absorbed through the skin).

7. The wages of FPWs can also be compared with representative monthly salaries for Africans in 1972:
Builder (grade eight education): $Rhodesian 144
Police sergeant (grade eight education): $Rhodesian 112
Teacher (female, grade eight education): $Rhodesian 80
Dressmaker (grade three education): $Rhodesian 40
Laborer (no education): $Rhodesian 25 (from Chavunduka 1978)

8. This differentiation was evident in the interviews I conducted, as the most senior FPWs generally were the most fluent in English, reflecting their origins in a socioeconomic group that could afford some education for its children. Interviewees who had joined the FPAR later in the 1960s and 1970s were less likely to speak English well, as their families had not been able to afford much education for them as children.

9. This faith in modernization does not mean that FPWs adhered to a dualistic world view in which "traditional" was opposed and inferior to "modernity." Many FPWs syncretized their belief in modernity with beliefs in local Shona concepts of physiology, gender, and social morality.

10. My observations of the FPWs lives today suggests that this crusading, socially engaged quality that they displayed in their accounts of their work may have been characteristic of the FPWs as people rather than of their family planning work. Most of the FPWs I interviewed, even the most elderly, fit Stack's (1992) definition of "centerwomen": dynamically involved in the affairs of everyone around them, both kin and neighbors; organizing and motivating the activities of various formal and informal community groups. This was evident in the lives of FPWs whom I visited at home—I had to schedule my interviews around Mrs. Elinor Dauya's activities with the mothers' league of her church, Mrs. Tendai Masvika gave me literature and frequent invitations to attend services at her Seventh-Day Adventist church; Mr. David Chibvongodze traveled regularly between Murehwa and Kambuzuma, outside Harare, in order to care for the affairs of sick relatives in town; and Mrs. Gladys Chitsungo was busy trying to organize a women's sewing cooperative in her area at the time I showed up. Walking with Mrs. Margaret Khumalo through Mufakose township, back to the commuter taxi that would take me back to Harare down-

town, we were greeted familiarly by literally almost every man, woman, and child that we passed (indeed, the FPWs were so well known locally that I never had difficulty finding their homes even in areas where I had never been before, since any passer-by would be able to direct me to the place I sought).

Although this tendency may be more pronounced in my sample, I believe this is fairly representative of the FPWs as a whole, because they were selected on this characteristic by the recruiters of the FPAR, who sought women and men who were well-known and well-reputed in their neighborhoods. My interviewees had maintained this behavior into the rest of their lives. However, almost all of this activity was directed into extended kin networks and benevolent or religious church groups—only one FPW had become involved in party politics after the war and very few had party cards.

11. This does not mean that interviewees always presented "Shona culture" in a positive or rosy light. Many women, especially in the youngest generation born at the time of World War II, were very critical of some customs such as the payment of *lobola* (bride-price) or polygamy, and were pleased that at least the latter custom seemed to be declining. However, even those practices that were disapproved of were presented in terms of generalizations, rather than particular events in particular people's lives.

12. In an interesting interpretation of "secrecy" and "taboo," several older women offered to show me (or Mrs. Shayanewako as my proxy) the "secret" herbs from which they made their contraceptive medicines. As described in chapters 3 and 5, knowledge about these herbs was said to be a closely guarded secret, as some traditional healers and elders obtained a measure of power from being the only gatekeepers for these methods. However, they said it would be all right for me, as a white person, to know their secrets, as long as I did not reveal it to any Africans. I concluded that either the herbs were not as "secret" as everyone said they were, or that being an outsider made me somehow exempt from some taboos that were based on preserving the power of knowledge in a small community.

# 2

# The Institutional History of Family Planning in Rhodesia, 1955 to 1980

## INTRODUCTION

While most of this book focuses on African communities, in this chapter, I visit the white community on the other side of the racial divide, and its project of modernizing Africans through family planning. This excursion is necessary for two reasons. First, the material and political constraints faced by the white founders of the Family Planning Association of Rhodesia (FPAR) and their allies (and opponents) within the white community affected not only the timing and tempo of the spread of Depo and the pill, but also the ways in which family planning was understood by those who were intended to be its beneficiaries.

Second, and perhaps more important, the story of the Rhodesian family planners demonstrates how political situations form what counts as knowledge about social life, especially knowledge about a group defined as "other." The Rhodesian social engineers and bureaucrats behind the family planning movement simultaneously drew on and contributed to the construction of frames concerning African fertility. Frames are shared ideas about the world, made up of unquestioned assumptions and "common sense" about phenomena and processes. Through relying on these frames, individuals and collectivities are able to "simplify and condense the 'world out there'" (Snow and Benford 1992:137). These frames gave shape to the ways that whites explained pat-

terns of fertility among the African population, how they defined these patterns as problematic, and how they allocated responsibility for solving the
problems. In the institutional history of FPAR, we see these ideas about
whites and blacks, and the contradictions and dependencies between the two
groups, being worked out on the territory of African women's bodies.

Concerns about African reproduction trends had been part of the intellectual
apparatus of colonialism in Rhodesia, whether framed as concerns about the
labor-supply implications of a too-low birthrate among Africans in the earlier
part of the twentieth century (Vaughan 1989), or as concerns about the political instability of a growing African population in the latter part of the century.
In this respect, Rhodesia was no different from any other society since the time
of Malthus, in which concerns about the dimensions of the underclass, the pro-
letariat, or other dominated groups have preoccupied politicians. By the 1960s
and 1970s, however, as political and racial tensions climbed, the notion of
excessive population growth among Africans became a matter of national
white interest, not only because of the threat it was thought to pose to white
political security, but also because of the challenge it presented to the benevolent white stewardship of a "backward" African population.

## WHITE RHODESIA: UNITY AND TENSIONS

While many white Rhodesians talked and worried about African overpopulation, they were never speaking with one voice. The contradictions among
different views of African fertility mirror the political tensions and contradictions in white Rhodesian society as a whole. White Rhodesia was not homog-
enous, although it was never as divided or stratified as in other white
oligarchies in southern Africa, especially South Africa. The split between
English-speaking and Afrikaan-speaking whites did not produce the same
schism in Rhodesia as it did to the south, because of the comparatively smaller
proportion of Afrikaners, who were mainly concentrated in ranching and
some commercial farming activities. The Rhodesian government was acutely
conscious of the specter of a "poor white problem" and fearful that a liminal
class of poor whites and "coloureds" would degrade the prestige of the white
race, leading to state-created mechanisms and programs to integrate even the
poorest of whites into a greater white society. The state provided support for
maintaining social and economic standards among whites, such as subsidies
for struggling white agricultural producers and a variety of charitable organizations to tend to the needs of the less wealthy, such as holiday trips to the sea-
side in South Africa. The high turnover among white Rhodesians also
militated against the entrenchment of schisms in the white community, as not
many white immigrants stayed around long enough to become deeply
invested in Rhodesian political institutions.[1]

Despite the evanescent nature of white settlement, the whites of Rhodesia developed a strong sense of identity and community, not just as whites, but specifically as Rhodesians, as a "white tribe" of Africa (Caute 1983, Godwin 1996). This communal identity reached its height during the latter years of the liberation war, when songs and slogans such as "Rhodesians Never Die,"[2] and public protestations of "Rhodesianness," such as letters to the editor in white newspapers, stressed the uniqueness of white Rhodesia and the pioneer toughness of the "white tribe" to which many new arrivals attached themselves. This collective identity was constructed in reaction to an imagined other—the African majority.

The white community had consensus on three points concerning the African population problem: first, African reproductive patterns were a problem; second, this problem was a danger not only to Africans but to the political and economic stability of the white population; and, finally, whites had a responsibility to intervene in African life so as to ameliorate this problem. It is to this white consensus on African population that I turn now.

## BENEVOLENT DEVELOPMENT IN A COLONIAL CONTEXT

In all colonies, human reproduction was a central problem of governance: "Colonial regimes had to come to grips with how people—colonizers and colonized—reproduced themselves, . . . where they did so, . . . with whom, . . . under whose eyes, . . . and with what degree of success" (Cooper and Stoler 1989:613). However, the terms in which most historians and other social scientists discuss reproduction are predominantly those of sexuality, the "when," "with whom," and "under whose eyes" of reproduction. This emphasis has produced many studies of concubinage, miscegenation, métis populations, and black, white, or yellow perils. By contrast, "with what degree of success"—that is, reproduction defined in biological terms, as the production of increasing numbers of human beings and the tensions that attend this process among colonizers and colonized alike—has not yet received this degree of attention.

The white response to fear of African overpopulation is part of a history of colonial projects intended to reshape African sexual and reproductive practices. Although the Rhodesian state provided very little in the way of health services for Africans, Rhodesia in the 1970s was heir to a history of programs, both governmental and nongovernmental, aimed at "socializ[ing] African women as biological reproducers" such as women's homecraft clubs and religious institutions (Hunt 1988:430, see also Kaler 1997). These, in turn, can be traced to the establishment of "scientific" programs to improve the practice of mothering and domestic hygiene in early twentieth-century Britain and the United States (Davin 1978). The existence of such projects was tied to wider waves of development, modernization, and rationalization of domestic life as they coincided, in the early and mid-twentieth century, with the time when home economics, nutrition, and child psychology were becoming scientific enterprises in Europe and North America.[3]

Such projects of domestication and persuasion included courses in child care, home economics, tailoring, and some home-based crafts, often run by Christian missionaries. While these projects might appear to be aimed at superficial changes, such as encouraging Africans to dress, wash, and cook like archetypal British matrons, the Comaroffs (1992) argue that there was a deeper intent—to urge Africans to adopt a moral, social, and economic order that was founded on European notions of gender-specific propriety and well-regulated sexual and reproductive relations. In Rhodesia, Schmidt argues that these projects were linked to efforts to create a suitable family life for an African elite modeled on Europeans. A well-regulated family was not merely an adjunct to a "civilized" Christian African man, but an essential part of his life. This necessitated the existence of wife-training courses at missions for women about to marry African Christians, and homecraft and women's clubs in rural areas to keep women abreast of new techniques for managing modern homes and families and to keep them cognizant of their position as part of the drive to recreate African home life in the European image (e.g., Ranchod-Nilssen and other contributors to Hansen 1992; Kaler 1997). Rhodesian efforts to introduce modern birth control fit into this trend toward organizing and rationalizing African family life.

White intellectuals and bureaucrats frequently engaged in efforts to define the other—the African—in such a way as to justify the perpetuation of benevolent white superiority. Within this discursive field, discussion of family planning took two forms. In the first variant, white family planners expressed concern for the development and betterment of both individual families and the nation as a multiracial whole and considered family planning as a matter of meliorism, the means to achieve a higher, more modern standard of living. This variant was linked to a generalized discourse of development, improvement, and modernization, which focused particularly on the problems of urban unemployment and ecological degradation in the Tribal Trust Lands (TTLs), where the majority of the African population lived.

However, the optimism of the idea that Africans could be "developed," "modernized," and generally improved contrasted with the second and more pessimistic theme in white talk about Africans and family planning. This second variant took the form of anxieties and fears for the survival of the racial hierarchy under the pressure of a growing African population. White Rhodesia could be submerged by the sheer mass of black bodies, or, calmer voices argued, African population growth could sharpen the pains created by the racially asymmetric economic organization of the country, and could thereby lead to a political crisis. Containing the African population was thus a matter of long-term political strategy, a consideration that coexisted with expressed concerns for the well-being of the African population.

## HOW DID RHODESIANS THINK ABOUT OVERPOPULATION?

Rhodesians used several conceptual frames to think and talk about population issues. Wilmoth and Ball (1992) identify five discursive frames, which predominated in the American popular media after the World War II, three of which can be detected in Rhodesian discourse on overpopulation in the same era. These include the "limits to growth" frame, according to which the danger of a high growth rate is that it threatens the ability of a nation's economy to absorb people, and the "overcrowding" frame, which focuses on the ways in which population growth and population density produce various forms of social pathologies, ranging from street crime to domestic violence and sexual deviance (640–41). However, their fifth frame, "race suicide," is most resonant with the ways in which African fecundity and fertility were viewed by the white elite:

> The central premise . . . is that population growth among some *other* group is too rapid in comparison with the growth of *our* group. However the notion of "us versus them" is defined, the argument deplores the fact that or perceived prospect that we are being outbred by them, or that they are invading, now or eventually, our space. Thus the arguments in this frame focus on differential fertility among sub-groups within a larger population, on migratory flows into or out of a population, or on the threat of dominance (military or otherwise) posed by the more rapid growth of a competing population. In all of these cases the argument builds on a perception that one population (or sub-population) is losing, or will lose, control over some vital aspect of social and political life because of its relative decrease in numbers. Within the race suicide frame, therefore, population growth is viewed favorably or unfavorably depending on the group experiencing it. (642)

These ideas about Africans, overpopulation, and contraception are found in the publications of highly educated white Rhodesians who worked for the government, the University of Rhodesia, and the FPAR. The fora in which they published their articles are both local and regional. Local journals such as the *Rhodesia Science News* and the *Rhodesian Journal of Economics* were intensely provincial in focus, written by and for the white intelligentsia. These Rhodesian publications drew on the same readership and writership as the national newspaper, *The Rhodesia Herald*, and the *Bulawayo Chronicle*. The people who wrote the opinion leaders and the letters-to-the-editor in *The Her-*

*ald* were also, in their academic and professional capacities, the contributors to the *Rhodesia Science News* and its fellow publications.

Papers dealing with Rhodesian overpopulation and family planning were also found in more specialized regional professional journals, especially the *Central African Journal of Medicine* and the *South African Medical Journal.* None of the Rhodesian experts published in standard international demographic journals, such as *Demography* or *Population and Development Review,* although their ideas show some affinities with ideas current in population journals in the rest of the world, as described in Watkins (1993) and Wilmoth and Ball (1992).

The topic of overpopulation was surrounded by a sense of urgency. On the level of the rhetoric emanating from the Ministry of Health, the FPAR, and white intellectuals within the University of Rhodesia, African overpopulation was defined as a massive problem (even though family planning programs never attracted the financial resources one might expect for a national priority). Consciousness of African fertility as a problem turned up in many unexpected places, suggesting a generalized concern among the white population. For example, a report on the birth of quadruplets in a township hospital concluded "while this sort of thing presents problems in its sudden contribution to the population explosion, it no doubt provided the hospital staff with an interesting exercise in pediatrics" (Annual Report of the Secretary of Health 1966:24). The *Rhodesia Science News* sponsored a school essay competition on the topic "What changes do you think might occur in this country as a result of increases in numbers of people? Do we have the natural resources to cope with four extra people per hundred of existing persons *every year?*"(*Rhodesia Science News* 1967:256. Emphasis in original.)

Rhodesian writing on population was also permeated with warnings of the growing urgency of the crisis, both domestically and internationally. On the domestic front, the leaders of the FPAR obviously had a great deal at stake in perpetuating this idea of impending national catastrophe,[4] and the tone of a 1971 article by Dr. Esther Sapire, the medical director of the FPAR, is typical:

> For many years there has been an ostrich-like attitude and an ominous silence about the population problem, but recently demographers, economists, world organisations and responsible governments have been uttering dire warnings about its consequences . . . The problems are vast and urgent, and to quote Dr. Roger Bernard, of the Pathfinder Find, Boston, who visited us recently after going to India: "In India the time has run out, but in Rhodesia you have five minutes more!" (Sapire 1971:104, 108)

Peter Dodds, the third director of the FPAR, contributed to this sense of emergency in 1977 by arguing that hormonal contraceptives should be available to African women without prescriptions or medical supervision, because the need to spread contraceptives as widely as possible overrode any minor health concerns (Dodds 1977:315). In a slightly different vein, Alfreda Geraty, a left-leaning research fellow attached to the FPAR, expressed concern that an exaggerated sense of crisis was warping Rhodesian population control efforts:

> An element of panic has crept into the situation which could defeat more carefully considered plans which take into account all the variables that influence dynamics in a multicultural society. (Geraty 1974:8)

Concern with excessive fertility among rural Africans intersected with concerns about ecological degradation and agricultural inadequacy in the TTLs. These lands, set aside for African occupation like the homelands of South Africa, held more than 60% of the African population, and were the most concentrated pockets of African poverty in Rhodesia, where "conditions are bad and deteriorating fast" (Gilmurray, Riddell, and Sanders 1979:18). In 1978, the average monthly household income was less than $Rhodesian 15, and real household income had fallen 40% since 1948. The TTLs included some of the poorest agricultural land in the country, yet "they carry over three times as many people as the land is safely able to carry, given current levels of capitalization" (8). Citing a report from 1969, Hanks noted that 57% of African land fell into the categories "overpopulated" and "grossly overpopulated" (Hanks 1975).

In 1969, 16% of African land was classified as "underpopulated," yet six years later virtually no land remained in that category (ibid.). The overcrowding of the TTLs was reflected in the declining nutritional status of the inhabitants. Gilmurray and colleagues estimated each peasant farmer to require 385 pounds of maize per year—but in 1962, 352 pounds of maize were available per person; by 1977, this amount had fallen to 231 pounds (Gilmurray et al. 1979:18).

The Natural Resources Board and the Ministry of Native Affairs had been wrestling with these statistics for years, concentrating their efforts on changing what they considered the "primitive and destructive methods of husbandry [which] have placed an intolerable burden on the soil, water, and vegetation resources of nearly half the land surface of Rhodesia" (Hanks 1975:173). Measures to regulate traditional land tenure and growing practices, such as the Land Husbandry Act of 1951, met with active resistance or noncompliance (Thompson 2000a). Given this concern about African agriculture among the development experts of Rhodesia, it is not surprising that, in the 1970s, fears about the food supply were adopted by the backers of family planning and integrated into the discourse of betterment and modernization of rural Rhodesia. Sister McCarthy, head of nursing for the FPAR, explicitly linked intervention in population matters with intervention in agricultural ones:

1975, say the experts, is the year when the Stork passes the Plough (i.e., when natural increase outstrips food production through cultivation). But I hope that over the next four years family planning will clip the wings of that overworked bird—and that scientific progress will push the plough faster. (McCarthy 1971:8)

Rhodesian policymakers agreed:

[T]here is eminent logic in a family planning programme being accompanied by extensive rural development schemes aimed at raising rural incomes. Early initiatives in this regard under the auspices of the Land Husbandry Act in 1951, the Community Development Policy initiated since 1965, lately through the Tribal Trust Land Development Corporation . . . have proven inadequate. (Clarke 1972:38)

They were inadequate, said Clarke, because they did not acknowledge that the existence of birthrates of 52 per 1,000 among Africans, "well above levels of 18 per 1,000 that are experienced in advanced countries and among economically advanced groups in developing countries," was an obstacle to the success of any rural improvement programs (ibid.).

When overpopulation was discussed in relation to urban settings, it was usually in relation to the specter of rising urban unemployment. Concerns about the uplifting of Africans dovetailed with fears for the stability of the racial hierarchy. Increasing population would exacerbate unemployment, especially urban unemployment.

Set against the background of existing rural poverty, relative stagnation of the economy in the period 1959–1968 in terms of income per head, low rates of growth in the modern sector of the economy . . . it will be readily apparent that population growth makes a negative contribution to the overall status of the African population and this predicament is likely to become increasingly severe in the future. (Clarke 1972:37)

The percentage of males aged 15 to 59 in some kind of waged employment had declined from 78% to 58% from 1956 to 1968, although the total number of employed African males had increased. At prevailing rates of employment and population growth, Clarke estimated that by the year 2000 only 29% of African males would be employed (Clarke 1971:14, 16). The consequences of this decline might be felt by Rhodesian society as a whole, as well as by the families of the men involved, as the number of idle young people, who could not be absorbed into the overcrowded TTLs or find employment, grew. Those who did not have a stake in the survival of the political and economic system, which a job might have provided, could easily become politically volatile.

## WHITE SECURITY AND RACIAL RATIOS

The political volatility of the black population and the possibility of being overrun by Africans were notes frequently sounded by the writers who framed the population explosion as a matter of national security for whites, threatening both their material standard of living and their culture. Discussions of overpopulation frequently turned to comparisons of racial birthrates, as opposed to discussions of absolute numbers or of the impact of both numbers and production/consumption patterns on the carrying capacity of Rhodesia.[5] For instance, in 1964, Paddy Spilhaus noted that "there were 19 African children born to one European child in Southern Rhodesia" ("14,000,000 Africans in Southern Rhodesia by 2000 A.D.," *The Rhodesia Herald,* [date unknown] 1964). Hooker's 1971 report for a series of American university field staff reports provides an example of this tendency to define population problems as problems of racial ratios. In 1969, only 4,004 white children had been born as opposed to about 215,000 Africans, so that "there are nearly as many African babies as there are Europeans in the entire country" (Hooker 1971:2). Even worse, of the 4.8 million Africans in Rhodesia, 52.6% were born after 1952, as opposed to only 38% of the Europeans, so that Africans were not only more numerous but were also younger and presumably stronger (1). Based on these ratios, Hooker went on to argue for a widespread program of birth control to limit African population growth. The framing of the overpopulation problem as a problem of racial ratios was also evident in the efforts by the FPAR to attract outside funding. General William Draper, head of the International Planned Parenthood Foundation, wrote in a 1966 press release that "[FPAR] needed much more outside financial help in order to meet the needs of the Bantus or Africans, who outnumber the whites in Rhodesia sixteen to one."

This concern with racial ratios can be understood in the context of the shift in overall black-white proportions. Most Rhodesians would have been very much aware, although they may not have known the exact figures, that the white share of the total population was shrinking. Until 1959, the white share had been slowly increasing because of white immigration; after 1960, especially after the Unilateral Declaration of Independence (UDI) and the war years, it shrank (Weinrich 1982:119).[6] The rate of natural increase among whites was also declining, in 1968, to "close to the levels experienced in economically advanced countries at 1% per annum" (Clarke 1971:13). Africans, who were nowhere near living in an economically advanced country, had a natural increase of around 3.6% per year (Hanks 1975:250). The release of the 1969 census, the first really accurate population estimate, confirmed to the white public that they were indeed a shrinking minority. Until this census was released, wrote Hooker, "most whites continued to tell themselves that the black people were peripheral to existence, that in time they would all go away on their own. Now [post-census] it is no longer possible to say this" (Hooker 1971:8).[7]

African population growth was clearly seen as both a political and a cultural threat. Van Rensburg, although writing about the region of southern Africa as a whole, depicted childbearing as a weapon in the hands of the black masses. He claimed that a black teacher told him:

> The only political weapon the African has got is numbers. We will never let it get out of our hands through family planning because it is the only means whereby we can reduce the whites to political impotence in this country [South Africa]. (van Rensburg 1972:102)

Consequently, "the only hope the Whites have of retaining their heritage for their children is to persuade the non-Whites to control the size of their families." The same note was struck in a letter to *The Rhodesia Herald* in 1971 from Ernest Mpofu:

> We, the silent majority, are not happily silent. We are instead busily producing more and more babies. That is our only weapon. We hope to flood this country with the black population by a huge percentage during the next decade or two. Nature is on our side. While the Government is busy screaming for more and more [white] immigrants, we are busy sending our pregnant women to the nearest clinics to give birth to future voices. (letter to the editor, *The Rhodesia Herald,* June 4, 1971)

Fears of exactly the situation described by Mpofu and by van Rensburg's informant was expressed by a white Rhodesian Front backbencher who introduced a (failed) private member's bill in 1966, urging a national campaign to reduce the African birthrate, including banning polygamy, heavily penalizing illegitimacy, and punitive tax rates for large African families, as well as aggressive promotion of family planning to Africans. One of his supporters contextualized the motion by denouncing "the appalling tendency on the part of the European to limit his family" and urged tax breaks for large white families (*Parliamentary Debates* vol.63, 1966, cited in West 1994:464).

Similar concerns were expressed in another letter to the editor of *The Rhodesia Herald* by Mrs. B.C. Gadd: "At present, [Europeans] are somewhat restricted by our own laws and customs and [are] losing out matching the African wife for wife and child for child, in order to secure a corresponding increase in population on the European side" (*The Rhodesia Herald,* July 2, 1970). The metaphor of a competition or population war between European and African was developed by J.J. Duvenage, chair of the Rhodesian Natural Resources Board (NRB) in 1970:

Mr. J.J. Duvenage . . . has hit the headlines with his statement that Rhodesians would lose their land "not to other nations but to the revenge of nature" . . . It is no doubt a disagreeable thought, but Rhodesia's future probably depends more on the launching and maintenance of a powerful national family planning campaign [among Africans] than on the resolution one way or another of the present political issues [i.e., the gathering political and military conflict between the apartheid-style Rhodesian Front, the ruling political party, and the African nationalist movement]. ("Rhodesians Must Face Up to Need to Check the 'Revenge of Nature,'" *The Rhodesia Herald,* August 28, 1970)[8]

During the 1960s and 1970s, these fears about the demographic threat posed by Africans were augmented by the gradual decline in numbers of the European population due to emigration. Net emigration figures were consistently reported in *The Rhodesia Herald* and *The Sunday Mail,* often on a monthly basis.[9] With a white population hovering at the quarter-million mark, a loss to emigration alone of 10,908 whites in one year could have a considerable psychological as well as demographic impact, especially as the whites most likely to emigrate were the young and affluent (*Sunday Mail,* January 22, 1978). This impact was shown in a feature article in *The Rhodesia Herald,* in 1977, titled "What Happens to Rhodesia's 'White Tribes'?" The author, Professor M.W. Murphree, argued that the outlook for the cultural survival of white Rhodesia was even worse than the demographic figures indicated, because many of the remaining whites were "sojourners" or "immigrants," rather than true "Euro-Africans" (*The Rhodesia Herald,* May 19, 1977). In a letter to the editor the next year, Mrs. C.I.M. Courtney asserted that

many Rhodesians have three or four generations living in this country. We are neither expatriates nor Europeans, we are white Africans. This is our home and that of our children, grandchildren, and great-grandchildren. They know no other. (*The Rhodesia Herald,* April 4, 1978)

## PATHOLOGICAL FERTILITY AND THE WHITE MAN'S BURDEN

The implications of African overpopulation for whites were clear—white society faced death by drowning in the sheer numbers of underfed, unemployed, politically angry African bodies. White intellectuals went on to ask themselves how things had gotten into such a parlous state. Why was white Rhodesia now being confronted with a demographic time bomb?

To answer this question, they constructed causal theories to attempt to explain why, in sociological terms, African fertility had increased to such alarming levels and, in ethical as well as pragmatic terms, why whites should do something about this. These theories relied heavily on shared common-sense understandings about the relations of whites to blacks and about the innate characteristics of Africans. The most important of these were two ideological constructs: (1) the idea of white responsibility, in the sense of both causal responsibility and a welfare responsibility for their less-developed African wards; and (2) the idea of a generic African personality and culture possessing subtle deficiencies that allowed unrestrained fertility to reach a crisis point.

They painted a picture of the population crisis as a white man's burden, one of the prices that Europeans had to pay as part of their altruistic effort to uplift the blacks.[10] In particular, they claimed the advent of white medicine and health services had bred a population explosion. White Rhodesians, facing a population explosion, were victims of their own compassion.

> White Rhodesians have been trapped, ironically, by their own civilization. Having built hospitals and clinics, they brought a standard of health to Rhodesia unknown among Africans north of the Zambezi. They eradicated or severely curtailed killing and wasting diseases . . . the authorities have underestimated the efficacy of their public health efforts . . . now that they have begun to understand, their consternation is both serious and apparent. (Hooker 1971:2)

> It is the health worker, with his information on elementary hygiene and his spray-pump of DDT, who has landed the world in its present state of overpopulation. (van Rensburg 1972:108)

> Even in the Tribal Trust Lands, there are strong indications that infant mortality has dropped by approximately one tenth of its previous level in 1963. Paradoxically, this success has provided Rhodesia with another intractable problem—that of overpopulation. (Hughes 1974:88)

Africans themselves are largely absent from these accounts of the genesis of the population crisis. They are the bodies on which the miracles of preventive health and medicine are worked, but they are not described as people actively seeking health. Like agricultural crops, they only respond to white medicine as to the application of new fertilizers or weed killers.

> Our problem is not in the birth rate, which has only risen from 45 per 1,000 to 52 per 1,000 since the turn of the century; the problem stems from the impact of preventive and curative medicine, which, over the same period of time, dropped the African death rate dramatically from 38 per 1,000 to 16 per 1,000. (Dodds 1977:314)

> Missionary activity, combined with the medical and welfare services of the state, prevented from dying a large proportion of the African population

which would normally have done so, yet they have taken no counter-measures to slow down the rate of reproduction. (Geraty 1974:14)[11]

The result of all these white interventions was said to be the creation of a society of African parasites, deprived of the need to take any responsibility for their own welfare. In an opinion piece for *The Rhodesia Herald,* one writer connected the alleged benevolence and kindness of white society in providing for all the needs of Africans with Africans' supposed propensity to procreate:

> Africans have developed the attitude that the consequences of having large families are not their problem. All their children will still receive the best that the country's social services[12] are able to provide at the same low rate that everybody else pays for their children. The real cost, for the moment, is somebody else's problem . . . The means by which family planning can be brought into action certainly exist, but under the comprehensive system of social welfare that the taxpayers sustain for the Africans, they have no incentive to use them. Unless the system is changed to ensure that Africans like Europeans feel the direct consequences of their own actions, this state of affairs will continue until the tax-paying capacity of the money economy has been bled to death by population growth. ("When Children Are Not a Blessing," June 14, 1973)

The image of a benevolent white colonialism was complemented by the construction of an African personality and culture that was uninhibited in its fulfillment of biological drives and essentially incompatible with white civilization. In its most benign form, this meant asserting the existence of a "cultural lag," according to which the Europeans had already made the "demographic transition," while the Africans, languishing in a historic stasis until colonialism jumpstarted their economic development, followed generations or centuries behind.

Paddy Spilhaus, the founder of the FPAR, ascribed fatalism, passivity, and a distorted sense of time to Africans in her account of the problems faced by the FPAR in its early years:

> How can we gain the co-operation of the African people with whom we are mainly concerned? I cannot over-emphasize the difficulty of this task. The African, through no fault of his own, has, even to-day, little consciousness of the forces at work beyond the limited sphere of his own interests. They are certainly unaware of global population pressures and the problems that confront the government due to rapidly increasing numbers. Generally speaking, these problems are beyond their comprehension . . . Also to be considered in some ways is the fatalism with which many of them take the so-rapid increase in their families. (Spilhaus 1961:4)[13]

Elizabeth Still attempted a slightly more sociologically nuanced explanation for these personality traits as they afflicted the unspoiled African who had not yet come into contact with white technology. Such a person was culturally conditioned to produce large numbers of children:

We have to understand, though, that people who have never known much more than a hand-to-mouth existence and are only now coming into contact with the rigors and possibilities of a cash economy have not looked on their lives as being other than "natural" and not of exceptional hardship. The climate is ideal, though droughts occur. The men hunt or clear the bush, but enjoy village life, go visiting, gossip, and drink home-brewed beer. It is difficult under such cultural circumstances to make rapid progress towards the acceptance of modern farming methods. I am told that if the maize crop is exceptionally good one year, the truly rural African sees no need to plant a similar acreage the following year. And he sees no reason to limit the number of children he has either. There is always enough to feed an extra mouth, the children are much loved and cosseted, especially while they are babies, and all the female members of the family help with their upbringing. (Still 1973:93)

This essentialist thinking enabled the overpopulation to be cast as a problem of African deficiency or pathology. Both the Ministry of Health and the FPAR subscribed to the idea that Africans, before the civilizing influence of Depo and the pill, were mindlessly driven to constantly increase their fecundity:

A propensity for procreation has always been a feature of primitive peoples and the reasons for this are well known. Yet it behooves the leaders of the African people of this country to recognize the direction in which we are heading . . . the extreme dangers in unlimited and uninhibited reproduction. (Annual Report of the Secretary for Health 1970)

Unsophisticated people, exposed to propaganda to encourage the adoption of birth control, have to make two decisions. The first decision is whether they accept or reject the concept of voluntary control of their own fertility. The second is whether to adopt modern methods of contraception. (Geraty 1975a:177)

This notion was part of a wider construction of an African personality and culture at odds with white values, white society, and white technology. Rhodesian intellectuals held that the cultural discontinuities between rural life in a subsistence economy and urban life in the orbit of the European cash economy generated psychological stress for individual Africans, which led to the production of socially undesirable phenomena, such as drunkenness, crime, and overpopulation. This belief led them to recast political problems of oppression and exploitation as cultural issues, generated by the collision of two unfortunately incompatible cultures.[14] This collision of cultures was said to produce many symptoms of pathology among Africans, such as anomie, family breakdown, and unregulated sexual activity. Urbanization and the recruitment of men into waged labor, while necessary for the growth of Rhodesian industry, produced another unintended consequences in the form of all manner of unhealthy phenomena in the area of reproduction:

> In no aspect of native culture have the effects of the part-time system [by which men left their villages for work in towns] been more deplorable than upon family life and morals. The frequent long absence of men from the reserves has led to a preponderance of one sex over the other in both the European and Native areas. In the European areas, the men turn to illicit and often impermanent unions, the offspring of which tend to grow up without discipline and in unsatisfactory surroundings. The situation in the Reserves is no more satisfactory. The absence of fathers makes for marital instability and deprives children of that necessary parental discipline and the wives of that help and support without which the family unit cannot be maintained. (Hooker 1971:4)

> They have relinquished the high moral standards of their own customs, they have given up the idea of ancestor worship, but they have found nothing to take the place of these foundation pillars of their society. This must surely be a lesson to those who seek to lead people into a new way of life. (Philpott 1969:13)

Pathological fertility was the byproduct of psychopathological anomie, produced by the collision between Africans and European ways of life. According to Hooker, for the African woman who lived in peri-urban areas,

> there is little of importance she can accomplish in town. Traditional village tasks, though perhaps performed in the new setting, are done so in a distorted form. There is a communal water tap rather than a distant stream; there is charcoal to buy instead of wood to be cut or gleaned. There is no stock to feed and so on—a litany of boredom. So little to do, and so much to buy. Having children in such circumstances might prove one's existence, might demonstrate that one does indeed have a job to do. Whatever is responsible, the babies are certainly produced. (Hooker 1971:6)

On the macro level, cultural incompatibility could be manifested as a population explosion.

> The incompatibility of traditional Black African values, concepts and institutions on the one hand and the way of life embodied in Western technology on the other is the cause of conflicts and problems of which we can only

perceive the outlines. The explosive rate at which the formerly stationary Black African populations are increasing today is a striking example of this incompatibility. (van Rensburg 1972:22)

Some commentators were aware of the instrumental reasons that Africans might choose to have many children, such as concern for old age security or the need to send more children out for wage work to compensate for declining agricultural productivity. However, even these reasons were described as purely cultural, thus robbing them of the justification of economic rationality. Geraty, one of the more liberal FPAR workers, acknowledged that "the man who can see security for his old age in the ground he is cultivating or in the job he is doing will not need to look to his children for old age support [and therefore will not have so many]" (1974:15). However she concluded in the same article that the main reason why Africans were not flocking to the FPAR clinics was that they were not "cognitively ready" to understand birth control (ibid.). Lack of a modern mindset, rather than the benefits of having many children, was the real reason for high African fertility, according to the accepted wisdom of white Rhodesia.

This view of African fertility as primarily a manifestation of cultural pathology, produced many silences in Rhodesian population talk. One of the most striking silences is the lack of interest in factors that by the 1970s were well known as determinants of fertility, such as the infant mortality rate. According to most mainstream thinking on population in the 1970s, obtaining such information was an essential precondition to a national family planning campaign. However, most Rhodesian social engineers showed remarkably little interest in finding such things out. If high fertility is the result of a primitive culture, pathology, and an uncontrolled biological imperative, then research into poverty and child death would be a waste of effort.

At the end of the decade, Gilmurray and colleagues deplored the lack of knowledge about child health in the TTLs and had to speculate that the infant mortality rate among Africans probably lay "between 120 and 220 per 1,000" (Gilmurray et al. 1979:22). He criticized the birth-control promoters of Rhodesia for failing to appreciate the significance of research demonstrating that "reduction in infant and child mortality is virtually a precondition for large reductions in fertility" (21).

Rhodesian family planners firmly concurred that it would not be necessarily to improve Africans' economic and political status in order to see the African birthrate drop. Two administrators of the FPAR explicitly stated that their work was intended to "challenge the hypothesis that only antecedent social and economic development can produce a decline in the birth rate" and then proceeded to do so through a survey of family planning clinic attendees (Castle and Sapire 1976:965). Dunlop (1975) concurred with this, describing as "positively dangerous" the findings of another social scientist, R.J.

Thiesen, that "there is a causal relationship between socioeconomic status and family size" (cited in Thiesen 1977:161). Peter Dodds, director of the FPAR, described Thiesen's findings and the beliefs of other development experts that "the best population policy is a development policy" as a "dangerous dogma" (Dodds 1977:314). He later warned that those who "urge the socio-economic prerequisite" (i.e., that birth rates will fall as a result of increased standards of living) are "harmful to Africa's future" and can undermine national family planning programs (Dodds 1978:162). This as also the opinion of Rowan Cronje, the Rhodesian Front Minister of Manpower, Social Affairs, Health, and Education, who stated that "economic development . . . is not going to help us control the birth rate" ("Rhodesia's Public Enemy No. 1," *The Rhodesia Herald*, May 20, 1978).

## THE BEGINNINGS OF THE FPAR

The promotion of family planning to Africans was in the hands of the FPAR. Ostensibly a nongovernmental organization, the FPAR received the bulk of its funding from the central government, which supplied 98% of the FPAR's income by 1979 (*Annual Report of the Family Planning Association of Rhodesia* 1979). However, this generous funding does not mean that the FPAR and the colonial apparatus worked smoothly together. The government was unwilling to be openly associated with family planning, fearing (correctly) that if family planning programs were associated with the white government, they would be tainted by African suspicions that family planning was a political tool to keep their numbers down or even kill them off.[15] The white regime alternated between promoting family planning, albeit with varying degrees of tentativeness, and keeping a distance from this controversial intervention into African culture and family life.

In this section, I focus on the FPAR, but also on the role of successive Rhodesian governments, through their Ministries of Health, and the sometimes difficult relations between the FPAR and the government. It is important to remember that, although the FPAR was a white-created organization, widely understood by both Africans and whites as an arm of state authority, it did not always pursue the same goals as the Rhodesian state, and often came into contradiction, if not outright conflict, with the state (particularly the Native Affairs Department [later the Internal Affairs Department]). The family planning movement in Rhodesia is not a case of a monolithic white force inserting itself into African sexual and reproductive practices, but rather a case of negotiation and occasional contradiction among institutions that sought to modernize Africans.

The tentative beginnings of the family planning movement go back to 1955 and the visit of a representative of the U.S.-funded Pathfinder Fund, Edith Gates, on a tour of African colonies. After stopping in Kenya to spark off the

THE RHODESIA HERALD, FRIDAY, MARCH 3, 1967

ANNING ASSOCIATION'S UPHILL STRUGGLE

s include lack of public

By Jill

Paddy Spilhaus (standing) and Joyce Wickstead, one of the first FPAR nurses. From *The Rhodesia Herald*, March 3, 1967. Source: Scrapbook kept by the Spilhaus family, kindly given to author.

creation of the Family Planning Association of Kenya, she proceeded to Rhodesia, where she addressed both black and white audiences in Bulawayo and Salisbury. Gates, described by her protégé Spilhaus as "a short, sturdy woman of missionary stock . . . family planning was her whole life," handed out some literature promoting the benefits of small families to patients in several African clinics (Spilhaus 1981:1). Her 1957 visit, with its suggestions that whites might get involved in African childbearing, touched off a storm of protest in African communities, as described in chapter 6.

After her first two visits, the first local organization devoted to the cause of family planning was founded in 1957. The Family Planning Association of Salisbury, was created by "a handful of European women struggling to establish a family planning clinic as a health service to European women in Rhodesia" (Geraty 1973:2). These women were led by the formidable Paddy

Spilhaus, the wife of an executive in a Rhodesian fertilizer company, who was persuaded to join the new committee by a friend who had heard Gates speak on her first visit to Rhodesia.[16]

The Family Planning Association (FPA) of Salisbury, and the offshoot Family Planning Associations of Bulawayo and several smaller centers, were initially established as segregated organizations serving whites only. The first clinics were held in the home of Joyce Wickstead, a nurse, who recruited her nursing colleagues to help, and her patients by word of mouth. Dr. Esther Sapire, who later became the medical director of the FPAR, remembered the first days of the white clinics:

> She [Wickstead] rang me one morning and asked if I could come and do the clinics that afternoon. I said no way would I come and do family planning, I don't know anything about it, we had done all of one hour of it in our medical training course . . . [Wickstead, who was only a nurse, offered to teach Sapire the basics, but insisted she had to have a doctor present for legal reasons] . . . She had three ladies lined up and the only method we could offer them was the cap, and we had to go down on our knees because it was in [Wickstead's] bedroom. (interview with Dr. Esther Sapire)

By the next year, 1958, the Bulawayo and Salisbury FPAs had managed to scrape together enough donations from private individuals to open clinics for whites in both cities. The Bulawayo branch also operated a clinic for the "coloured" population. However, even these modest initial endeavors faced opposition from the white commercial and political elite of the colony, who thought of contraception as an immoral endeavor. Local papers refused to accept advertisements from the clinics or even to print the dates and time when clinic services would be offered, landlords refused to rent space for clinics, and neighbors insisted that the clinics not put the name of the association on the front gate of the clinic premises, when premises were eventually found (Spilhaus 1981:10). Family planners faced hostility on a more personal level as well—Wickstead's fellow nurses called her "a disgrace to the profession" and refused to cooperate with her makeshift home-based clinic ("Family Planning Association's Uphill Struggle," *The Rhodesia Herald,* March 3, 1967; Spilhaus 1981:9). According to Sapire,

> It really wasn't acceptable. I remember my friends always said "What's a nice girl like you doing talking about something like that for?" I think it must be difficult for you to understand today [in 1997] when we do talk openly about sexuality and contraception and family planning—you can easily talk about it at dinner. But it really wasn't talked about [then] so to talk about affecting one's sexual behavior was really extraordinary. When we got up to give lectures we would talk about population and so on, and

inter alia say that one of the ways of dealing with it would be fertility control, family planning, contraception, and that was more acceptable to talk
about. Very socially conservative. (interview with Dr. Esther Sapire)

## FIRST APPROACHES BY AFRICAN WOMEN TO THE FPAR

In 1959, the Salisbury FPA first began to turn its attention to the African
population, partly at the prompting of Edith Gates and partly, according to the
veterans of Rhodesian family planning, in response to requests from African
women. According to Mrs. Margot Dobbin, an early education officer for the
FPAR, housemaids and nannies in the wealthy white suburbs were the first
black women to ask for family planning services, noticing that their employers had fewer children or had children at longer intervals than African women
did. White madams, when they came to the European clinics for their own
family planning services, asked the clinic staff if there was a place where their
"girls" could also get contraception. Mrs. Margaret Khumalo, who joined the
FPAR as an educator in 1964, worked as a nurse in a municipal clinic in an
African township. She said that even before family planning methods were
available to Africans, women among her patients in the 1950s had heard of the
new things being used by white women and wanted to know more about them:

> Before I worked for family planning I worked in the clinic in Mufakose so
> I used to know quite a lot of women, we would discuss things and they were
> wanting to know what they can do about family planning. Some would just
> come forward and say, "I have so many children, what can I do, and he [her
> husband] says he wants more children." Especially if you just have boys,
> boys, boys because then he will say, "I want girls for the *lobola*, [bride-
> price] so keep having pregnancies." So these were the problems that were
> occurring. We would talk about it at the clinic. There are dangers if you have
> too many children, if you have three your uterus can bear it, if you have five
> or six it will be expanding, when you have another baby it won't retract, you
> will bleed sometimes maybe to death. Some have seen it out in the *kraals*
> [in the rural areas] that when you have many babies when you have the last
> one you can die from bleeding. These were the problems women were hav-
> ing. (interview with Mrs. Margaret Khumalo)

According to Sapire,

> It [information about contraception] just spread through word of mouth, the
> black women came to us and they said—it wasn't a question of trying to
> proselytize, we didn't go to the townships, we felt that it was too politically
> sensitive, and then women came to us and, they said, "We hear and we see
> that you people [whites] do things to control the size of your families, will
> you help us?"[17] and then we felt that we were in business, that we could

actually do something. It needed to come from them, we didn't feel that we could impose it. I think it came through the church, I think it was church ladies. (interview with Dr. Esther Sapire)

At the same time, Spilhaus was receiving delegations at her European clinic from "some of the better educated African women, nurses and teachers" (Spilhaus 1981:18). She approached the secretary for health to ask for permission to hold a clinic for African women at Harari Hospital, the largest hospital for Africans in the country. Permission was granted, and the two-hour, twice-weekly clinic began in 1959, despite opposition from the white medical staff that ran the hospital (Spilhaus 1981:19).

In the late 1950s, according to the third director of the FPAR, "the Ministry of Health specifically forbade family planning and scientific contraception other than to the white population" (Dodds 1978:160). This hesitancy was the result of the strong negative reaction among African men and nationalists to early discussions of family planning for Africans, discussed in chapter 6, as well as the innate conservatism of Rhodesian white society noted by Sapire. At the end of 1959, the outgoing chair of the FPA, E.J. Whittaker, complained that "No co-operation or help is being given by the Salisbury municipal health authorities to people who seek assistance with family planning" ("Family Planning Assistance Urged for Salisbury," *The Rhodesia Herald*, July 7, 1960). Looking back on these years, Spilhaus recalled

> We had to fight for existence against terrific prejudice. Everybody shunned us, including welfare societies, Government and municipal officials, clergymen, and even the Red Cross. Nobody wanted to be seen dead cooperating with us. ("The 'Pill Queen' Calls it a Day," *Sunday Mail,* October 4, 1970)

The fledgling FPA persevered. By 1961, the Salisbury FPA had a staff of 16, including three African nurses who went door to door, spreading the word about the new services offered by the FPA, in the African townships around Salisbury ("Family Planning Group to Launch Branches for Africans," *Northern News,* October 19, 1961). They also had clinics operating in the towns of Umtali and Marandellas, as well as Salisbury and Bulawayo, and the municipal government of Bulawayo had agreed to take over the running of the Bulawayo clinic, a very different position from that of the hesitant Salisbury municipal government.

## THE ARRIVAL OF THE PILL

The first major innovation in contraceptive technology brought profound change to the work of the FPA: "In 1961 our fortunes did begin to turn. THE PILL arrived on the scene" (Spilhaus 1981:27). The pill quickly replaced the *sources: newspaper*

Volpar precoital foaming tablets, which had been the FPA's messy and inconvenient mainstay, and were much more popular than the intra-uterine devices
(IUDs) and diaphragms, which were also available through FPA clinics. The
first issue of the pill in Rhodesia was made in May 1961 to 60 white women,
amid press reports hailing the arrival of this new method, claiming that the pill
would not lead to promiscuity, but would actually help to stabilize marriages
by removing the stress of the fear of pregnancy from couples' sex lives ("A
Chemical Compound May Slash the Divorce Rate: Public Demand Grows for
1961 Blessing," *Sunday Mail,* November 12, 1961). Provision of the pill by
the FPA was later extended to women of all races. Despite problems with
reported side effects, and with finding a supplier who would be able to provide pills of consistently high quality, from the start, there was "tremendous
demand" for the pill, despite the relatively high cost, especially for African
women, of 14 shillings per month ("Rhodesia Should Adopt Free Birth Pill
Plan," *The Rhodesia Herald,* August 19, 1963). According to the 1963 annual
report of the International Planned Parenthood Foundation Regional Secretary for Europe, the Near East, and Africa,

> The agents for Anovular report that they are selling over 3,000 monthly
> doses. Many educated African women [in Rhodesia] are using it, but they
> do not wish for it to be known generally. (unpaged)

In the wake of the pill's success, the educational and clinical efforts of the
FPA began to move beyond the FPA's base in the urban and peri-urban townships. The first attempt to communicate with Africans outside the cities took
the form of a 1963 series of lectures by Spilhaus to Police Officers Wives
Clubs in various rural areas (Spilhaus 1981:45). The FPA also published its
first informational booklet "Family Planning: Why, How, Where . . . " that
year. Following a press advertisement for the pamphlet (the press having soft-
ened their attitude somewhat), the Association received letters of inquiry from
826 Europeans and 2,030 Africans[18] ("Family Planning Film a Hit," *African
Daily News,* July 3, 1961).

The FPA also made its first educational film for African audiences that year,
which was shown in township cinemas, after the sometimes difficult task of
obtaining the permission of white township supervisors, and later taken on
tour on the lecture circuit on commercial farms and African rural areas (see
table 2.2 for the growth of the FPA's ventures into film). Called "A Tale with
Two Endings," it followed two possible futures for a newly-married African
couple—a descent into squalor and the wife's death after the birth of eight
children, if the parents refused to plan their family, and an alternative future in
which the family prospered with only four children. The well-intentioned
amateurishness of the FPA, still a voluntary organization of liberal whites, is

evident from Spilhaus' description of the comedy of errors that attended the making of the film:

> There were some fearful discrepancies in the first section. It had evidently not been able to get the same group on different days and the ages and sexes of the children changed from scene to scene. In the second section where the young couple had gone to hear about family planning and how it was done, the part of the doctor had been taken by an engine driver and he did it very well but his hands and nails were engrained with dirt from his work and any doctor seeing the scene would have shuddered. (Spilhaus 1981:34)

By 1964, the FPAs were slowly beginning to gather steam in the urban areas. In Bulawayo, where the more active of the two municipal associations was located, a decrease in the African birthrate from 24.8 per 1,000 to 20.8 per 1,000 was attributed by the local press to the promotion of family planning ("Family Planning Paying Dividends," *The Bulawayo Chronicle,* [date unknown]). In Salisbury, eight clinics were running regularly for Africans as well as one for Europeans, and a branch was started in the Midlands, the agricultural heartland of the country. In the FPA's first venture into survey research, 15,000 African women in Salisbury townships were interviewed on their attitudes about family planning. According to the survey report, only 2,337 said they were not interested, 155 said they wanted more children, 473 were menopausal, and 98 were pregnant at the time. The Salisbury FPA estimated that approximately 10% of women of childbearing age in the Salisbury townships were using new family planning methods, predominantly the pill, in 1964 ("African Interest Growing in Family Planning," *The Rhodesia Herald,* December 27, 1964).

In 1964, the Bulawayo and Salisbury associations merged into a national association, the FPAR. Approaches were made to the International Planned Parenthood Foundation for financial support, which resulted in a first donation in 1965 and much-needed national and international legitimacy. Finally, after several years of lobbying by Spilhaus, "during 1964 the government began to take some interest in the progress of the Association" (Spilhaus 1981:58).

## UDI AND AN UPSURGE IN FPAR WORK

Despite the growing interest by African women, sparked mainly by the introduction of the pill, the FPA's work remained quite low-key until Ian Smith's Rhodesian Front regime declared its independence from Britain in 1965. In the Unilateral Declaration of Independence (UDI) period, freed from the constraints of British liberalism, the Rhodesian Front could move more aggressively to contain and manage the African population, expressing in concrete form their ongoing racial anxieties. The FPAR, throughout the 1960s and 1970s, became drawn into this strategy behind the face presented (rather unconvincingly) to the African population of concern for national development and the welfare of African families.

The militantly segregationist and racist UDI-era Rhodesian Front signaled its interest in keeping African birthrates down almost immediately. Although some voices within the government[19] opposed the promotion of contraception to the African majority, the Rhodesian Front government in general supported Spilhaus' endeavors. However, they did not share the benevolent motivations that led her and her colleagues to attempt to give African families a means to better health and happiness. The Rhodesian Front was explicitly concerned with family planning as a means toward the end of reducing a politically volatile and environmentally destructive surplus of African population. As early as December 31, 1965, just after the white minority of Rhodesia decided to go it alone without Great Britain, the Secretary of Information, Immigration, and Tourism K. B. McTavish wrote to his counterpart in the Ministry of Health and Internal Affairs:

> The Minister of Information, Immigration, and Tourism considers it vital that a propaganda campaign in the field of family planning among Africans be undertaken as soon as possible. . . . It would in my view be in the national interest for government to take active steps to reduce the ratio of Africans to Europeans. A reduction in the birth rate would considerably reduce the burden of the population explosion on the education and health budgets and the general economic development of the country. (National Archives of Zimbabwe [NAZ] B/137/3)

The Secretary for Health and Internal Affairs responded that

> Mrs. Spilhaus and her organization have been doing valuable work among the African population and so far as the Ministry of Health is concerned we have advised all our clinics to give Mrs. Spilhaus every assistance and Provincial Medical Officers are advising African women on how to get up-to-date information on family planning. (letter, January 4, 1966, NAZ B/137/3)

The Rhodesian government gave the FPAR a token sum of 300 pounds in 1973, which doubled and then quadrupled in the two subsequent years (see table 2.1). Despite government interest in the work being done by Spilhaus and her colleagues, voices within the government were wary of taking on what they viewed as a political hot potato such as the promotion of birth control among Africans. The Minister of Internal Affairs urged caution and discretion, if not outright secrecy, in disguising the government's interest in reducing the number of Africans. In a letter to the Prime Minister, Ian Smith, on April 15, 1966, Minister for Internal Affairs Roger Howman opined that

**Table 2.1**

**Income from the National Government as a Percentage of Total FPAR Income, 1965–80**

| Year | Total Income | Income from National Government | Government Income as Percentage of Total |
|------|--------------|---------------------------------|------------------------------------------|
| 1965 | 1,256 pounds | 150 pounds | 12% |
| 1966 | 3,964 pounds | 300 pounds | 8% |
| 1967 | 5,941 pounds | 1,200 pounds | 47% |
| 1968 | 27,053 pounds | 2,200 pounds | 8% |
| 1969 | 76,763[1] | NA | NA |
| 1970 | 85,499 | 4,700 | 5% |
| 1971 | 136,509 | 74,000 | 54% |
| 1972 | 280,162 | 80,802 | 29% |
| 1973 | 346,095 | 135,000 | 39% |
| 1974 | 494,285 | 250,000 | 51% |
| 1975 | 663,376 | 460,000 | 69% |
| 1976 | 818,886 | 650,600 | 79% |
| 1977 | 939,023 | 825,000 | 88% |
| 1978 | 1,076,713 | 1,021,000 | 95% |
| 1979 | 1,581,179 | 1,111,000 | 96% |
| 1980 | 1,196,801 | 1,150,000 | 96% |

All figures are for the FPAR's financial year, from 1 July to 30 June (e.g., figures from 1966 are for the period 1 July 1965 to 30 June 1966).
*Source:* 1965–1971: Chairman's Report at Annual General Meeting; 1972–1980 FPAR Annual Reports.
[1]All figures from 1969 onwards are given in Rhodesian dollars.

"to announce the [family planning] program is directed at the African population and not Europeans is to invite a recoil from Africans that would make destocking[20] look like a storm in a teacup and probably set the movement back for years" (NAZ B/137/3). The Secretary for Health concurred with this, writing to his counterpart in Internal Affairs that

> The attitude of this ministry has been to give advice where advice is sought and to give medical assistance where required . . . but for reasons which will be obvious to you not to indulge in any positive propaganda which we feel is better left to voluntary bodies . . . who are less likely to be blamed for indulging in this activity for political reasons. (letter, March 23, 1966, NAZ B/137/3)

The Secretary for Health zealously guarded the idea that family planning was to be presented to the African population as a nonracial, nonpolitical affair through scrutinizing the Ministry communiqués about family planning that went out to doctors and health workers in the provinces. While these circulars and pamphlets should reflect a positive view of child-spacing and family limitation, they should not give the impression that the Ministry wished to visit this on Africans as a racial group. In a letter to the Provincial Medical Officer of Health for Mashonaland, commenting on a circular concerning family planning that the medical officer had sent for revisions, he wrote

> I would like specific reference to Africans to be deleted from the circular . . . Will you therefore please delete the words "among Africans" in the 4th line of the first paragraph and the words "to the African" in the first line of the third paragraph. (letter, January 3, 1967, NAZ B/137/3)

The Minister of Health attended the first Annual General Meeting of the FPAR in 1965 and pledged his government's continuing support for family planning (Spilhaus 1981:60). Spilhaus noted, with restrained enthusiasm, that "the government has instructed their doctors to help where possible, and some of them do do a great deal" ("Government Medical Officers Give Family Planning Advice," *The Rhodesia Herald,* July 15, 1966). Although the government's financial contribution for 1966, 300 pounds, was minor compared with that of the International Planned Parenthood Foundation, which contributed 2,627 pounds, "the government was planning to give much more extensive help next year to further the Association's' work . . . [the 300 pounds] is a token sum, to indicate the government's support" ("Help Needed for Family Planning," *The Rhodesia Herald,* August [date unknown] 1966).

On the medical side, the forerunners of the mobile clinics were inaugurated. These mobiles played an important role in spreading information about new methods of contraception as well as providing medical services to African women who wanted contraception. "Clinics" was a bit of a misnomer, as they consisted of a medical kit in the trunk of the car of an FPAR doctor or nurse, who drove around first the commercial farms and then later the remote rural areas, inserting IUDs and screening women for use of the pill. Dr. Sapire, as the head of the FPAR's medical staff, first recalls that she began receiving a salary for her work in 1965, as the FPAR became more a professional and less a purely voluntary organization.

In a speech in Parliament on February 8, 1967, the Minister of Health, Labor, and Social Welfare committed the government to more aggressive support for family planning (see figure 2.1). The leading daily paper editorialized

> The Minister said the amounts for family planning which will appear on the estimates for the coming financial year "will be as large as we can possibly extract from the treasury" . . . All ministries were aware of the desirability of massive participation by the government, and the whole cabinet was agreed on the proposal. ("Aiding Family Planning," *The Rhodesia Herald,* March 17, 1967)

**Figure 2.1**
**Attendance at All FPAR Clinics, October 1976 to January 1980**

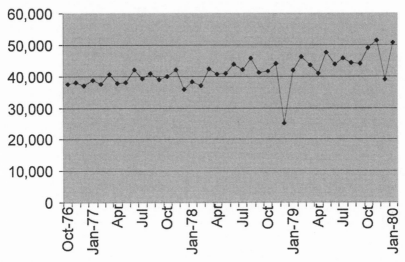

*Source:* Personal files of Peter Dodds, former director of the Family Planning Association of Rhodesia (FPAR).

## OUT OF THE CLINICS AND INTO THE VILLAGES: MOVIES AND EDUCATORS

As a result of increased government support, "our funds doubled in 1966 and more than doubled again in 1967" (Spilhaus 1981:98). (See table 2.2 regarding the steady increase, both in proportion and in absolute terms, in the percentage of FPAR funds provided by the central government.) With this infusion of funds, the FPAR was able to greatly increase its educational work. In 1966, they had received a grant from the International Planned Parenthood Foundation, which was used to set up a traveling film unit and produced two films in African languages (presumably Shona and Ndebele), and in 1967 the regime gave them money to set up two more regional film units based in Bulawayo and Umtali (now Mutare). These film production and distribution units were entirely administered by whites, although by 1971 mention was made of plans to involve Africans in the production and dissemination of culturally sensitive information. In 1967 four new family planning films were made, 75,000 pamphlets on family planning were distributed, and the number of film shows and educational lectures delivered by FPAR educators more than tripled over the previous year.[21] (See table 2.2 for the steady increase in the FPAR's educational work.)

**Table 2.2**
**Growth of the FPAR's Educational Outreach Work, 1966–79**

| Year | Number of Film Shows/Talks | Attendance at Film Shows/Talks | Pamphlets Distributed | Field Educators Employed | Home Visits by Field Educators |
|------|------|------|------|------|------|
| 1966 | 85 | 5,123 | 20,000 | 0 | 0 |
| 1967 | 252 | 16,960 | 75,000 | 0 | 0 |
| 1968 | 407 | 26,492 | 134,900 | 18 | 15,188 |
| 1969 | 748 | 52,633 | 197,934 | 32 | 20,063 |
| 1970 | 946 | 73,748 | 215,494 | 53 | 56,620 |
| 1971 | 1,434 | 41,888 | NA | 98 | 92,430 |
| 1972 | 4,416 | 234,536 | NA | 106 | 156,443 |
| 1973 | 3,417 | 128,866 | NA | 99 | 113,287 |
| 1974 | NA | NA | NA | 137 | NA |
| 1975 | NA | NA | NA | NA | NA |
| 1976 | NA | NA | NA | 173 | NA |
| 1977 | NA | NA | NA | 226 | NA |
| 1978 | NA | NA | NA | NA | NA |
| 1979 | NA | NA | NA | 246 | NA |

All figures are for the FPAR's financial year, from 1 July to 30 June (e.g., figures from 1966 are for the period 1 July 1965 to 30 June 1966).
*Source:* 1966–1971: Chairman's Report at Annual General Meeting. 1972–1979: *Annual Report and Accounts.*

Although the FPAR concentrated on educational and motivational work, it did expand its medical services through the creation of a mobile clinic service. These clinics, consisting of specially equipped vans, began by traveling through the white commercial farm areas, the nucleus of the FPAR's ventures outside the urban areas, and throughout the 1970s expanded their range to include visits to TTLs and rural population centers. The mobiles always included an educator as well as medical personnel, and frequently provided other minor medical services, such as dispensing aspirins or sticking-plasters.

Most important, in 1966, the FPAR inaugurated its corps of field educators with seven workers that year—men and women whose jobs consisted solely of traveling through the urban and rural areas spreading the word about family planning. Spilhaus described the decision to take on field educators:

The success of any family planning programme depends largely not only on how it is created but how it is sustained. The Education Unit could raise interest [through film shows and educational talks] but unless there was follow-up to sustain it, it was soon forgotten. So the committee decided to follow the example of India and train men and women who lived in an area and who could maintain permanent contact with the people. I gathered in nine men and four women, and this was our first class. Each candidate had been carefully vetted and the nature of the work explained to them, and though the whole idea was new to them they were willing to try, though they thought the title Field Worker, which is used in other countries, was not dignified and made them sound like farm labourers, so it was changed to Field Educator. (Spilhaus 1981:103–4)

The chosen educators spent one month being taught about global and national population growth, family economics in a cash economy, the history of the international family planning movement, and basic reproductive physiology. At the end of the month, they were given an exam, and the successful candidates were fitted out with a bicycle, a white uniform, a briefcase full of family planning literature, and a record book in which they would account for the home visits they made and then mail the record book back to the head office every month. The educators were then sent off to their home areas, and given a great deal of autonomy in arranging their work schedule in order to make as many home visits as possible. Their full-time job was to travel through the country, addressing public meetings and going door-to-door in African areas preaching the gospel of family limitation and child-spacing, and to maintain records of the families they spoke to, the converts they made, and the existence of any hostility to family planning. The missionary zeal that the field educators were expected to bring to their work is captured by their official motto, as printed on the cover of their field educators' notebook—"He who would kindle others must glow himself"—as well as in the religious metaphors employed by Senior Educator Mr. Richard Chikosi in a 1974 description of the work of the field educator:

Every field educator employed by the FPAR is attached to one or more clinics or hospitals. He/she paves the way and makes the path straight for the doctors, sisters, and nurses. As medical practicalities of family planning absorb the minds of the professionals at the clinics, the field educators constantly wield the sowing hand within the surrounding neighborhood. . . . In some places and with some people, only a little bla-bla-bla will do and you will find them at the clinic. In the majority of cases, however, the field educator has to talk and talk and talk, many times in vain: "It is good, it is safe, it makes the children and the mother healthy and strong," he/she will say to all and sundry. . . . The success of the field educator is measured in the number of new acceptors treated at his/her clinic per month and the number of old ones retained. Like a priest, he/she looks after his/her converts and endeavours to help them whenever they need further attention from the Association. Proficient field educators receive not only a pat on the back but also promotion with corresponding rise in pay. ("Field Educators' Corner," *Mhuri Inofara,* April 1974)

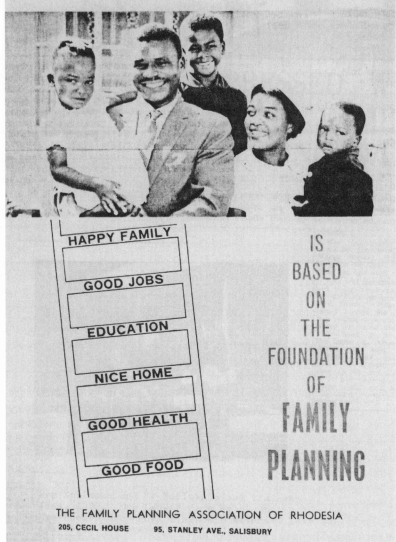

An advertisement for the services of the FPAR published in *Parade,* a magazine with a predominantly African readership, on April 8, 1970. Source: Scrapbook kept by the Spilhaus family, kindly given to author.

Paddy Spilhaus and Alec Ndhlukula training new educator recruits at Spilhaus Centre in March 1970. Source: Scrapbook kept by Spilhaus family, kindly given to author.

## THE FPAR AND THE RHODESIAN STATE: MONEY AT ARMS' LENGTH

With the inauguration of the field educator program, by 1967 the FPAR's involvement in national life, specifically rural as well as urban, had really begun. Although African nationalist leaders had claimed for years that whites wanted to reduce the African population, "there is little evidence, up to 1965, to support the notion of an officially sanctioned and co-ordinated policy to keep the African population in check" (West 1993:448). By 1966, however, the *Annual Report of the Secretary for Health* could report that

> The work of the Family Planning Association has been very much to the fore this year and has expanded very considerably ... The Ministry of Health intends to support the work of this association by making grants towards the costs of salaries of professional staff employed at family planning clinics ... and the Ministry itself is providing facilities through its own units. (Secretary for Health 1967:49)

This first mention of the FPAR in Ministry of Health annual reports set the framework for relations between the governmental and the nongovernmental body. The Ministry was to continue to both fund educational and medical work of the FPAR and to provide family planning services through its own clinics and hospitals. The maintenance of an apparent distinction between the FPAR and the state became a matter of great importance as the 1970s progressed, because the intensification of the nationalist liberation struggle led to increasingly repressive measures by the state, producing African antipathy toward the government and all its works. Spilhaus herself recognized this, saying in 1972 that "it is absolutely essential that family planning must be separated from politics even if government help is to be used. Our strength in Rhodesia, I have always said, is that we are not a government body" (quoted in van Rensburg 1972:187).

The Rhodesian Front government, although it took on more and more responsibility for family planning, was never wholeheartedly enthusiastic about assuming this role. The technocrats, white members of Parliament and social engineers in Salisbury, insisted that an African population explosion would spell disaster both in terms of national security and in terms of the potential for development of the Africans in the TTLs, but no one, except Spilhaus and friends, really wanted the responsibility for such a politically explosive issue as birth control for African women. Reports from the Ministry of Health are full of complaints that other government and nongovernmental bodies are refusing to pull their weight in providing contraceptive service to Africans. White civil servants who worked in the field, especially as advisors or supervisors of African political structures such as chiefship, were especially reluctant to be involved, despite the circulars from head offices urging them to promote family planning.

The correspondence between the FPAR administration and the Ministry of Health is full of complaints about local civil servants, both black and white, who refused to cooperate with the FPAR traveling film shows, and the field educators, because they feared a backlash from the local African authorities on whose goodwill they depended to maintain order in the district (NAZ B/137/3). Mr. T. J. Mugariri, an early family planning educator in the Gokwe region, described the opposition he met from the local District Commissioner (DC) who did not want Mr. Mugariri to stir up trouble among his chiefs:

> As I was coming here to look for a place to work I came with two letters [from the FPAR's headquarters], one for Dr. Ford [of the local Baptist mission] and one for the DC in Kadoma, the white man. The DC was hard to approach. He was just saying, "I don't think my chiefs will accept this, so I am going to write a letter to my chiefs so somebody will take you to my chiefs, and you will talk about your plan to them, if they accept you to come and work in

Sanyati they must write a letter accepting you." So he phoned his messenger in Sanyati rest camp to meet me at the bus stop and lead me to the two chiefs of Sanyati . . . [After a persuasive lecture on the benefits of family planning, both chiefs agreed to allow Mr. Mugariri to travel in their area teaching about family planning]. So they all agreed for me to work on family planning. When the DC came here to visit his chiefs, he interviewed them: "Did you really agree to accept family planning, you saw the family planning man here, did you really accept him?" He was suspicious. There was some friction. I think that DC was against family planning, so he wanted to know, "You chiefs, have you really accepted family planning?" I really worked hard, but I had a bad eye from the DC. (interview with Mr. T. J. Mugariri)

The FPAR focused on education and motivation in its early years, in keeping with the conventional wisdom that there was a large unmet need for birth control, which had to be prodded and stimulated in order to translate it into actual demand for contraceptives. This demand had to be reinforced by the message that small families were associated with individual and familial benefits, and nudged into action through the provision of information about the safety and availability of nontraditional contraception.

In 1968, family planning appears for the first time as a separate category in the Secretary for Health's annual reports (it had previously been restricted to a mention of the FPAR in the section on "Voluntary Organisations"). The dean of the Faculty of Medicine at the University College of Rhodesia addressed the Local Government Association that year, saying that the need for family planning in Rhodesia was "urgent and vital . . . the need in Rhodesia is for a vast local government and [national] Government sponsored educational programme" ("Family Planning Need Urgent, Vital in Rhodesia," *The Rhodesia Herald,* May 2, 1968).

In July 1968, white members of Parliament argued for the provision of more funding to the FPAR, describing the proposed grant for 1969 of 22,000 pounds as grossly inadequate. The Minister of Health appeared on Rhodesian television in a series of public-service messages to launch an appeal for funds to build a family planning clinic at Harari Hospital. The Secretary for Health, Dr. Mark Webster, told the Rhodesia International Medical Congress that "the limitation of the natural growth of the population" was the "first objective" of his Ministry ("Growth of Population is 'Frightening' Says Health Secretary," *The Rhodesia Herald,* August 21, 1968). Even a liberal opposition political organization, the Centre Group, took out a half-page advertisement in *The Rhodesia Herald* to advertise the seriousness of the problem of African population growth in Rhodesia, and Spilhaus reported a huge increase in inquiries from the European-dominated town councils as a result of this advertisement (Spilhaus 1981:124).

## DIRECT INVOLVEMENT BY THE STATE IN FAMILY PLANNING

The first direct governmental foray into organized family planning programs (aside from funding the FPAR) was the establishment of "well-baby" clinics in 1967. In addition to providing care and growth monitoring for infants and young children, the clinics were considered "the most advantageous means by which the Ministry [of Health] can advance knowledge and provide help in the field of family planning" and some other preventive health services (Secretary for Health 1968:24). Although the well-baby clinics came under some criticism from clinic users for the use of nurses rather than doctors to distribute pills, they continued to be a mainstay of the regime's family planning distribution network throughout the 1970s. The use of well-baby clinics for these purposes was based on the idea that these clinics drew clients to them, rather than government workers having to go out and get clients.[22] The clinics were lauded by doctors in the Rhodesian medical service, in terms that reveal the belief that Africans were unable to perceive the benefits of family planning or tame their reproductive drive without white help:

It is logical that family planning should form an integral part of these [pediatric] services, and that advice and facilities should readily be available. Constant exhortation is required to emphasise that married couples should plan to limit the size of their families. (Secretary for Health 1968:24)

By the end of 1968, the Secretary for Health was able to report that

Family planning advice and the supply of oral and intrauterine devices is [*sic*] now available at many of the Ministry's medical units as well as at the majority of Well Baby clinics . . . Regrettably, however, we must face the fact that so far we are only able to nibble at this massive problem. (Secretary for Health 1969:29)

Throughout 1969 numerous articles in the white press drew attention to the steady increase in the popularity of the pill in African areas. White opinion had evidently swung so far in favor of the pill that the editors of *The Rhodesia Herald* felt compelled to warn that

It is only in recent years that the idea of encouraging birth control as a response to the population explosion has become respectable here. It is now burgeoning into a cure for all our ills, present and future. ("Beware of Such Solutions," *The Rhodesia Herald,* May 8, 1969)

Meanwhile, the educational efforts of the FPAR were growing apart. More advertisements appeared in *Parade*, and 215,494 pamphlets were distributed in 1970 ("More Using Family Planning Clinics," *The Rhodesia Herald,* October 2, 1970). Their project of sending field educators out to African urban and rural areas, going door-to-door to spread the gospel of family planning, began at the end of 1967 with seven fieldworkers. By May 1971, they employed 68 fieldworkers, and claimed to have made 92,000 home visits in 1970 (Spilhaus cited in van Rensburg 1972:185) compared with 56,620 in 1970 and 42,527 in 1969 ("More Using Family Planning Clinics," *The Rhodesia Herald,* October 2, 1970). The FPAR reported a constant increase in the demand for the pill and for an intriguing new method, the Depo-Provera injection (which was soon to overtake the pill in popularity).

So many women turn up at the Highfield clinic, the largest of the Association's centres, that the sister in charge has to close the door at most clinic sessions after admitting the number of mothers our present staff can adequately cope with. (Joyce Wickstead cited in "Cost of Aids to Family Planning to be Reduced for Africans," *The Rhodesia Herald,* [date unknown] 1970)

In response to this demand, 1970 saw another important innovation in the work of the African cadres who had been trained as field educators. To facilitate the widest possible distribution network for the pill, some educators became educator-distributors, "responsible women who have small supplies of pills which can be sold to people providing they have a family planning card duly stamped entitling them to have pills for up to six months" (Spilhaus, letter to the editors "Easy to Get on the Pill," *Sunday Mail,* October [date unknown] 1970). In another milestone in the growth of the FPAR, in 1970, the Spilhaus Training Centre—to train nursing students, medical mission staff, and medical students in the theory and methods of birth control—opened in Salisbury.

The FPAR's budget in 1970 was Rhodesian$116,000 (of which $85,499 came in the form of donations), well over US$100,000 in 1970 dollars, but still not as high as might be expected, given the alleged prominence of family planning in national development. This shortfall irked the administration of the FPAR, who felt their contribution to national development and security was inadequately rewarded. However, the relatively small budget vote may have been the result of a compromise within the Rhodesian Front between those who viewed family planning as a protection against the political and economic catastrophe of a population explosion, and those who feared African backlash against it.

By the end of 1969, the Secretary for Health believed that

with regard to the expansion of family planning, there is no doubt that African women are eager for assistance in the regard, an eagerness which is shared by their husbands at the more educated and sophisticated levels . . . The Ministry of Health intends to employ considerable numbers of workers who will act as distributors of oral contraceptives. (Secretary for Health 1970:29)

This statement is worthy of note for two reasons: first, as a change from the rhetoric that Africans were unable to perceive the benefits of having smaller families, as discussed earlier in this chapter. The success of the family planning program had created a mood of optimism which re-inflected the construction of the African target group. This statement is also noteworthy for its acknowledgment of the gender differences in terms of attitudes toward nontraditional family planning. In discussing (again) the use of well-baby clinics as distribution points for contraceptives, Ministry reports focused on the figure of the mother as a persuadable acceptor of contraception, in contrast to earlier discussion that had focused on the unprogressive and unmodern African man as the locus of resistance to family planning.

> The mother and child welfare service is also logically the basis on which the family planning services of the Ministry have been developed. It makes very good sense to a mother of a recently born child when she is being taught the rudiments of . . . everything related to the health of a child that she should also realize that she can look after that child a great deal better if she does not have another one too soon. (Secretary for Health 1971:28)

## COMPARISON OF MINISTRY OF HEALTH AND FPAR EFFORTS

Complete details of Ministry of Health family planning efforts appear for the first time in the Annual Report for 1971. A total of 17,636 women attended their clinics that year (Secretary for Health 1972:42–43). The Ministry operated 81 dispensing clinics, of which 40 were located in the TTLs; yet these TTL clinics accounted for only 4,739 attendees, suggesting that opposition to the pill and Depo, as well as the practical obstacles to clinic attendance, ran higher in the impoverished rural areas.

In the same year, the FPAR's Spilhaus Centre in Salisbury saw an average of 1,808 clients per month and introduced mobile clinics to the Mrewa, Shamva, and Bindura commercial farming regions north of Salisbury, as well as produced a weekly radio program in Shona and Ndebele, inaugurated six more mobile film units, and provided staff and educational programs to eleven agricultural shows, including seven in the TTLs, with apparent success. In additions, they began supplying selected women in the TTLs, beginning with an experimental group of 200, with six-month supplies of contraceptive pills to dispense to their neighbors, who had been given medical clearance to use them (Geraty 1973:63; Spilhaus cited in van Rensburg

1972:186). The medical director of the FPAR stated triumphantly that "at first many sceptics told us that the whole thing was a white elephant, as African women would never walk through that gate which so boldly advertised that it was a family planning clinic . . . we now feel that our confidence has been justified" (Sapire 1971:106).

The contrast between the performance of the Ministry of Health and the voluntary organization suggests that the FPAR, less tainted by the suspicion of destocking and anti-African motives, was more socially acceptable. This hypothesis is borne out by the recorded reactions of Africans to family planning programs and by the report by FPAR fieldworkers that their largest single obstacle in the field was that they were frequently mistaken for regime employees.

The FPAR and the Rhodesian Ministry of Health continued to expand their work throughout the early and mid-1970s, and melded their efforts more and more closely, while retaining the crucial distinction of the FPAR's nominally nongovernmental status. In 1974, Hughes wrote that "[t]here has been a very considerable expansion in the work of this organisation [FPAR]. Training of nurses and other paramedical personnel in the theory and application of family planning methods is being undertaken in conjunction with the Ministry of Health" (Hughes 1974:95). In 1973, the Ministry of Health set up a university program to train a new category of community nurses "whose role will be the extension of mother and child welfare services, and family planning services" (Secretary for Health 1974:9). In the mid-1970s, the FPAR gave out free supplies of contraceptives of an unspecified type to government employees; members of the police, army, and air force; and African employees of major industries, and, by 1977, nearly 25% of the Ministry of Health's grants to outside agencies went to the FPAR (Secretary for Health 1978:47; Weinrich 1982:121). Other contraceptive-providing organizations, such as the Salisbury City Health Department, also adopted a policy of providing free pills for Africans ("Free Pill is Applauded," *The Rhodesia Herald,* January 17, 1974). This move, however, was not universally applauded within the FPAR. Some staff members, Dr. Sapire among them, were opposed to the issue of free pills on the grounds that this degraded the perceived value of the pill, and fueled rumors that birth control pills were a white plot to reduce the African population, as no other form of medical treatment was free to Africans at the time (interview with Dr. Sapire).

## CONTRADICTIONS AMONG WHITES

However, even as the work of family planning grew, the internal contradictions among different factions of the white establishment, including the ruling Rhodesian Front, with respect to promoting family planning to Africans also grew. On one hand, the Rhodesian Front faced pressures from its members to do something about African overpopulation. As the nationalist liberation struggle accelerated into a shooting war, white anxieties about the African political threat were displaced onto a perceived African demographic threat. These fears were articulated by Rhodesian Front members of Parliament in parliamentary debate and by the rank-and-file membership alike. Overpopulation fears were present at both the highest policymaking levels of the Rhodesian Front—as when rumors circulated that a "comprehensive plan to combat the population explosion" had been agreed on by cabinet ministers in a confidential session at a Rhodesian Front congress ("Plan Details, Please," *The Rhodesia Herald,* September 25, 1973)—and at the party grassroots, as in this letter from the secretary of the Sabi Valley branch of the Rhodesian Front:

> This branch is most distressed with the present population explosion and appreciates that your department is doing all it can with regard to family planning. It appears however that the average African is not at all perturbed with the situation and shows no interest in family planning. In fact we would go further and say that they are using the population explosion as a weapon against the future of the European in this country. We are most anxious to know whether your department has any further plans in mind for alleviating the situation and if so would be grateful if you could give us some idea of what you have in mid. We as a branch of the Rhodesian Front are eager to help your department in any way possible. (letter to Mark Webster, Secretary for Health, September 24, 1973 [NAZ B/137/5]).[23]

Supporters of the Rhodesian Front outside the party structures also put pressure on the party to aggressively work to contain the African population. For example, the head of the Salisbury branch of the Natural Resources Society—an important think-tank in an economy heavily dependent on mining and other forms of extraction—found it "disappointing that the recent Rhodesian Front congress had only thought in terms of warnings [about African overpopulation] rather than of immediate positive action . . . The Family Planning Association has a budget of only 23 cents a head [per African]—the price of one beer!" ("Cent-a-Pill Plea to Curb Births," *The Rhodesia Herald,* October 22, 1973).

However, at the same time, civil servants and officials of the government often refused to promote family planning, fearing a backlash from the Africans who were their responsibility. Margaret Westwater, the Provincial Medical Officer of Health for Mashonaland and a strong proponent of family planning, complained about noncooperation, not from African nationalists or irate African husbands, but from within her own ranks in the government:

> There are many thousands of African women [in Mashonaland] who are willing and anxious to accept family planning advice but are unable to

obtain it. Many government hospitals not only do no active family planning, they do not even discuss family planning with the patients nor are they able to tell them where to obtain advice. We do talk to nurses and nursing sisters but they seem not to be interested. . . . I am offered the film "Road to Health" [an FPAR-produced pro-family planning film] . . . when I advised that it should be given to the Ministry of Information to be shown on their film units [which toured the country presenting educational films on a variety of subjects] I was informed that they will not show it because it contains information about family planning. If the head of the Ministry of Information was the pope in Rome, he could not be more implacably opposed to the dissemination of information about family planning. If we had sufficient staff and the backing of a good information not propaganda service, we could have thousands of African women on a three monthly routine of Depo Provera and make a real impact on the soaring birth rate, what we are doing now is a drop in the ocean. (letter to Mark Webster, Secretary for Health, August 13, 1971, NAZ F/118/3)

Westwater complained further that

The time to discuss family planning behind closed doors is past. Ministry of Information please note. One of their officers very recently informed me that they don't discuss family planning because during the Federal days [before the Rhodesian Front's 1965 Unilateral Declaration of Independence] their image was so bad and they are desperately trying to restore it and talking about family planning might ruin it again . . . We do not want blatant political propaganda from the Ministry of Information but they could just drop their opposition to anything that even mentions the subject. (letter to Mark Webster, Secretary for Health, September 18, 1972, NAZ B/137/5)

Dr. Pugh, the Provincial Medical Officer of Health for Matabeleland and a strong supporter of the FPAR, reported the same problems in his corner of the country:

The Ministry of Information has been too terrified of the subject to allow their mobile cinema units to show family planning films or to use family planning articles in the *African Times* [the broadsheet for Africans produced by Internal Affairs]. (letter to Mark Webster, Secretary for Health, September 18, 1972, NAZ B/137/5)

For the staff of Internal Affairs, the government's policy of "community development" in African areas came into conflict with the promotion of family planning. Community development was a cornerstone of the white regime's dealings with Africans. This policy provided for the shoring up (and the creation, if necessary) of traditional authorities, allowing the white regime indirect rule through chiefs and headmen and, in the process, cutting out an age cohort of younger, less conservative and more politically dangerous men. As a result, community development brought "relatively elderly men to positions of authority, and in many cases such persons through tradition, inherited conservatism, religion, or for other reasons, are hostile to the pressing need for family planning and are reluctant to promote its cause to their communities" (Clarke 1972:45).

Within the Ministry of Health, Webster himself had to intervene to pressure recalcitrant medical officers into accepting family planning as part of their work, or even tolerating the presence of FPAR personnel in their institutions. In 1973, the Provincial Medical Officer of Health for Victoria province balked at allowing FPAR personnel to hold mobile clinics at rural clinics in the province, on the grounds that no "respectable" Africans wished to be seen in the vicinity of a family planning clinic, and that the presence of family planning would deter people from coming to the clinic for any kind of medical attention.[24] Webster responded sharply:

> I understand that you take the view that perhaps the presence of family planning people may keep women away from the clinic. I cannot accept this view and I should be grateful if you would in future see your way to collaborating with the family planning personnel. (letter, July 26, 1973, NAZ B/137/5)

He took a similarly hard line with clinics run by Catholic missionaries that did not wish to permit family planning in their clinics, telling them that the continuation of their government grant was dependent on their falling into line. There was to be no more financial support for Catholic clinics that did not "fully co-operate" with the Ministry of Health's agenda for family planning (letter from Mark Webster to the Secretary of the Archdiocese of Salisbury, September 19, 1973, NAZ B/137/5).[25]

## THE FPAR'S GROWING PAINS AND THE "NEW BROOM"

In the first year of its existence, the FPAR's budget was $Rhodesian 200. By 1972, it had an annual operating budget of $Rhodesian 280,162 of which 29% came from the Rhodesian regime. As Webster put it in his speech to the 1972 Annual General Meeting of the FPAR, "the Family Planning Association is now big business" (NAZ B/137/8). As "big business," it developed its own share of internal problems. These included personal rivalries between the founders of the FPAR and the more recently recruited administrators, and allegations of financial and sexual impropriety. In 1970, Mrs. Spilhaus resigned (unconnected to any of these scandals) but did not bow out of family planning affairs altogether. The various crises led to a change of leadership and the arrival of Mr. Peter Dodds, an "outsider" from Kenya who was recruited through the personal friendship network of the honorary treasurer Eric Henderson to be a new broom (interview with Mr. Peter Dodds).

These problems within the FPAR were watched closely by the Ministry of Health. Mark Webster kept his Minister, Ian McLean, up to date on the unfolding of the gossip emanating from within the FPAR. Webster urged McLean to seek more direct state control over the FPAR, pointing out that "this organization [FPAR] which is now commanding very considerable sums of public money should be kept under more close control than it is at the present time" (letter, September 17, 1971, NAZ B/137/8). Webster and McLean wanted the Minister of Health to be represented ex officio on the executive committee of the FPAR and for all FPAR staff appointments to be subject to the Minister's approval. The FPAR executive was divided as to whether this represented an inexcusable interference with their autonomy as a nonpartisan welfare organization, or whether the request was reasonable in light of the Ministry's promise to fund them at an even greater level. This controversy led to the resignation of at least one member of the executive committee, Dr. Timothy Stamps, in 1974. Dr. Stamps, who later became Minister for Health and Child Welfare in Zimbabwe, considered the other members of the executive "inexcusably naïve" to think that they could permit increased government involvement in the daily operations of the FPAR without, at the same time, politicizing the humanitarian practice of family planning, under the sign of the Rhodesian Front (interview with Dr. Stamps).

After this period of chaos, the new director, Peter Dodds, viewed his new mission not just as a clean-up operation but as a chance to re-orient the FPAR away from its preoccupation with education and motivation and toward being more directly involved in giving out contraceptives:

I had a number of bodies in the field simply chatting and passing on the good word, but the motivational effort was wasted because there were no opportunities [to actually obtain the contraceptives]—opportunities that did exist were at medical facilities which were at a great distance from everybody. So Paddy's work was to create a motivated populace but the motivation was slowly dying away . . . So what we did as a first task was to draw up a program for what we termed educator-distributors. The purpose was to get a person with the capacity to convey a message and the confidence of the society in which he lived to pass on after the message the means. There was a directional change. Instead of just recruiting people in Salisbury who pitched up and said, "I'd like to be a family planner," I got my personnel deliberately out to look for the right person. The intention was to lift them out of their environment, train them in motivational methods and supply, then having trained these personnel put them back where they lived. (interview with Mr. Peter Dodds)

Peter Dodds, director of the FPAR from
1973 until its demise after independence.
Source: *FPAR 1978,* a promotional brochure
published by the FPAR.

The educator/distributor program further refined the mission of the FPAR,
and slowly weaned the organization off its dependence on the facilities of the
Ministry of Health. The work of educator/distributors gradually grew from
providing pills to women who had already been vetted by a clinic, to going
through a checklist and assessing a woman's suitability for pills themselves,
to giving women Depo-Provera injections.

Dodds also created the position of senior educator in 1972. The senior educators were a cadre of experienced African men who had come up through the
ranks of the educator and were available for supervision of the junior educators, troubleshooting, and occasions where a more prestigious representative
than a mere field educator was required, such as audiences with chiefs.
Although the senior educator posts were all filled by men, under Dodds, the
gender composition of the field staff began to shift away from being predominantly male. By the end of the 1970s, the majority of all educators and edu-
cator/distributors were women.

The second major change for family planning in the early 1970s was the
emergence of the Depo-Provera injection as the dominant method. Although

**Table 2.3**
**Distribution of the Pill and Depo-Provera Through Salisbury [Harare] Municipal Clinics, 1973–78**

| Year | Pills (packets) | Depo-Provera (ampoules) | Estimated Woman-Years of Contraception[1] |
|---|---|---|---|
| 1973 | 43,254 | 13,279 | 6,668 |
| 1974 | 21,425 | 23,000 | 7,398 |
| 1975 | 28,866 | 32,037 | 10,299 |
| 1976 | 32,995 | 40,905 | 12,764 |
| 1977 | 40,123 | 48,941 | 15,322 |
| 1978 | 49,889 | 45,336 | 15,172 |

*Source: Annual Report of the [Salisbury] City Health Department 1973–1978.*

[1]Calculated as total number of pill packets divided by 13 (each packet provides four weeks of contraceptive protection) plus total numbr of Depo-Provera ampoules divided by 4 (each ampoule provides 13 weeks of contraceptive protection).

the injection had been available through the FPAR since 1969, and had been popular since its inception,[26] by the early 1970s it was clearly ascendant over the pill as the method of choice for African women (see table 2.3 for a comparison of the popularity of the injection and the pill in Salisbury). This led to the creation of the post of educator/distributor-injectible to train FPAR workers to administer the drug. The dominance of Depo had strong repercussions for the conflicts between the genders, which surrounded the use of family planning at the grassroots, discussed in chapter 4.

In the mid-1970s, Dodds also steered the FPAR to greater cooperation with the commercial and industrial structures of Rhodesia. Although FPAR educators had always cooperated with the management of factories and commercial farms to give educational talks and show films, from 1974 onward Dodds and his colleagues persuaded industries to shoulder some of the costs of providing family planning to their workforce by providing clinics and accommodation to family planning workers, both clinical and educational. These FPAR clinics became permanent presences on some of the largest industrial concerns of the country, such as the Triangle Sugar Estates, the Wankie Colliery, and the Rhodesian Iron and Steel Corporation, as well as establishing permanent clinics on commercial farm land in the Bindura district north of Salisbury, augmenting the free distribution of condoms to protect their largely male workforce from the dangers to productivity posed by sexually transmitted diseases (The Family Planning Association of Rhodesia [FPAR] 1978:44). The presence of these clinics also had the effect of further cementing the uneasy alliance between the FPAR and the white establishment, both white government and white capital.

## THE FPAR AS A NOT-QUITE-RESPECTABLE CORPORATE CITIZEN

Despite the quantitative success of the FPAR's clinical services during the 1970s, (see figure 2.2) and the growth of educational outreach work (see figure 2.3), the FPAR was not always accepted by white society as a good corporate citizen. In addition to difficulties with different branches of government, the actions of the FPAR and the attitudes of its leaders continued to generate controversy within Rhodesian society, as had surrounded family planning since its inception in the 1950s. FPAR leaders often displayed enthusiasms that were quite out of the mainstream in the politically and sexually conservative white establishment. Many of the white administrators of the FPAR were considered political as well as sexual liberals, by the standards of white Rhodesia, including Spilhaus, who reportedly tolerated her senior African staff's involvement with the legal wings of the national liberation movement (interview with Mr. Enoch Chikutu).[27] Alfreda Geraty, a FPAR Research Fellow, was an ardent admirer of the birth control policies of communist China at the same time as China was supplying arms and ideas to the guerrillas (e.g., Geraty 1975b:428).

Peter Dodds, the third director of the FPAR, was a zealous crusader for vasectomy and tubal ligation, and lamented that "much that the Association would do is regulated and restricted by the social mores of the white community" (Dodds 1978:162). He campaigned for the creation of a national scheme for free surgical sterilization, only to be defeated by the refusal of the Salisbury City Council, which refused to lend the operating theaters of its hospitals because they did not want to "become involved with such a hot potato as surgical sterilization" (FPAR 1978:44). Dodds was particularly vocal about the opposition "from the [church] pulpit" to sterilization and to his plans for national distribution of free condoms (ibid.).

Leaders of the FPAR also took relatively radical positions, in their individual capacity, on the question of abortion, which was being addressed by a parliamentary inquiry into the laws governing the termination of pregnancy, then legal only if the mother's life was in danger. Spilhaus called for abortion to be the decision of a woman alone, on the grounds that "women should not be forced to have children which they do not want" ("Let Women Decide on Abortions," *The Rhodesia Herald,* March 2, 1973).

The FPAR under Dodds also involved itself in advocating sex education in Rhodesian schools. Dodds complained that "secondary schoolchildren leave school knowing more about the reproduction of the cockroach than about their own bodies"("Sex and the Teenager," *The Rhodesia Herald,* July 14, 1978). This remark set off a minor controversy in the letters column of *The Herald,* in which correspondents accused the FPAR of trying to usurp parents' prerogatives. Dr. M. Ewart Smith, director of student health at the University of Rhodesia, described the FPAR as a renegade organization, opposed to "the

**Figure 2.2**
**Rhodesian Government Appropriations to Fund FPAR, 1971–80, in Rhodesian Dollars**

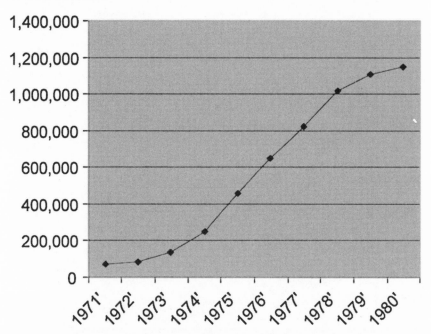

*Sources:* 1965: From minutes of the First National General Meeting of the FPAR, July 3, 1965. 1966: From the Balance Sheet of the FPAR, June 30, 1966. 1967: From the Balance Sheet of the FPAR, June 30, 1967. 1968: From Spilhaus 1981:134. 1969: From the Balance Sheet of the FPAR, June 29, 1970. 1970–73: From minutes of meetings of the Executive Committee of the FPAR (NAZ B/137/8, Minutes and Agendas of All Meetings of the Family Planning Association). 1974–80: From *Annual Report of the Family Planning Association of Rhodesia*, 1974-1980.

majority of authorities in the vast literature on the subject, few of whom would agree with the policy [on sex education] which is at present being so militantly pursued by, among others, the FPAR" (letter to the editor, *The Rhodesia Herald,* July 22, 1978).[28]

Of all these tempests in teapots, the most seriously controversial issue that the FPAR faced was that of compulsory birth control. Some Rhodesian Front politicians, carried away by both the specter of ecological apocalypse from overpopulation and their fear of the political consequences of an increasing African birthrate, urged that birth control should be enforced on some sectors of the population, namely blacks. The FPAR, whose educators spent a good part of their time attempting to defuse rumors among Africans that the whites were attempting to force Africans to cut down their numbers, found them-

**Figure 2.3**
**Growth in Number of Fieldworkers Employed by FPAR, 1968–79**

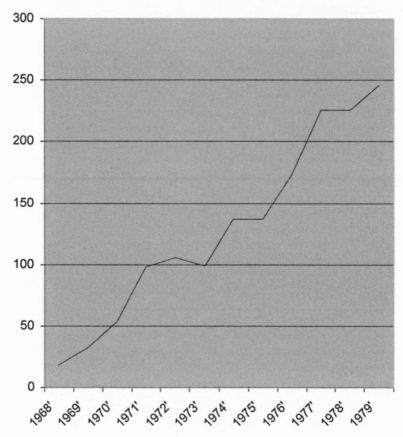

*Source: Annual Report of the [Salisbury] City Health Department, 1973–78.*

selves having to fend off whites who wanted to enforce contraception. In 1976, for example, Mr. Gordon Handover, a member of the Natural Resources Board of Rhodesia, told the annual meeting of the Natural Resources Society that one of the most important tasks facing Rhodesia was to

> impress on our population the dangers of uncontrolled and irresponsible proliferation. Population can be controlled and it must be. If it is not done voluntarily then I can envisage the time that it may have to be done by regulation. ("Compulsory Birth Control Hint for Rhodesia," *The Rhodesia Herald,* May 18, 1976)

This brought an immediate response from Dodds, who stated the next day that "compulsion can play no part in Rhodesia's birth control program" ("Birth Control Must Be Voluntary," *The Rhodesia Herald,* May 19, 1976).

## INDICATORS OF FPAR ACCOMPLISHMENTS

By the mid-1970s, it was possible to evaluate the effect of the FPAR and the Ministry of Health on knowledge and use of the new methods of contraception. By the end of 1974 in Gwelo (now Gweru), Rhodesia's third largest city, about 15% of African women of childbearing age were said to be regular family planners. As a result, the African birthrate in Gwelo was said to have dropped from 57 per 1,000 in 1973 to 52 per 1,000 in 1974 ("Africans Use Birth Control Despite Politics," *The Rhodesia Herald,* November 15, 1974). In Salisbury as well, 15% of African women of childbearing age were said to be on contraception, as the Depo injection overtook the pill in popularity ("Jab Takes Over from the Pill," *The Sunday Mail,* December 15, 1974). The next year, Dodds claimed that nationwide 1 out of every 11 fertile African women was using one of the new methods ("Time to Get Rid of Birth Bogeys," *The Rhodesia Herald,* August 21, 1975). Dodds also claimed that the efforts of the FPAR were having a measurable demographic effect, in that the annual growth rate for Rhodesia had dropped from 3.8% at the beginning of the decade to 3.4% by 1976 ("New Trend Encourages Family Planners," *The Rhodesia Herald,* January 3, 1977). In 1976, according to the chair of the FPAR, the organization prevented 25,000 births ("25,000 Cut in Births Claimed," *The Rhodesia Herald,* September 28, 1973). The FPAR exceeded its target of achieving 40,000 clients per month by August 1977, and Dodds announced that its new target was 48,000, or 20% of all fertile women ("The Day an Outcry Was Good News," *The Sunday Mail,* August 21, 1977).

The medical staff of the FPAR attempted, through sampling attendance at various clinics, to assess how many women were regularly using the new methods. Castle estimated that 20% of urban women, though only 2.7% of rural women, in Mashonaland in the 15 to 49 age-group were "reliably" using these methods of contraception in 1974 (Castle and Sapire 1976:966). This urban-rural differential may reflect both greater rural conservatism in sexual and familial matters as well as the increasingly dangerous conditions for field educators as the guerrilla war, centered in the rural areas, progressed.

In a more detailed and generalizable study, Weinrich found that, in 1974, 34% of rural women had heard of the new methods of contraception, although only 4% had actually used it. Of those who had heard of it, 56% had learned of it through a FPAR field educator (Weinrich 1982:125). Among women living on white-owned farms and mines who had heard of it, 95% had heard of it through a field educator, reflecting the FPAR's ability to penetrate the captive audience of commercial farmworkers, as well as the interest of white land-holders in keeping the number of their tenants low.

## THE SHOOTING WAR

In the 1970s, the increasing political tensions between the Rhodesian Front government and the insurgent African nationalist organizations gradually turned into a shooting war, as nationalist guerrillas began to harry white farmers in rural areas and waged equally potent battles for the "hearts and minds" of the African peasant population. As this guerrilla war spread, the FPAR found a new arena for its efforts. Just as they had initially concentrated on commercial farms, where the African population was subject to a high degree of white control, and hence assumed to be more receptive to messages about small families, during the war, the FPAR concentrated on the protected villages (PVs) or keeps. These PVs were cramped, barren, guarded enclosures into which rural peasants were herded to prevent them from aiding the guerrillas who were advancing from Mozambique and Zambia south and west through the countryside and were, in some ways, the ideal setting for family planning work. Inhabitants were under acute pressure for living space, they could not absorb increasing numbers of children into impoverished families, they were uprooted from traditional social relationships that might have exerted pronatal pressures, and they were under government surveillance, making easier for FPAR educators and distributors to move around.

Starting in 1976 with the PVs in Chiweshe TTL, the FPAR mounted a special campaign to convert the "soft targets" in the PVs to modern contraception (Weinrich 1982:123). The FPAR and the regime claimed great success among the women in the PVs, who were not as exposed to nationalist influence as the women outside the enclosures, implicitly laying the blame for rejection of family planning at the feet of the guerrillas. Weinrich suggests that the PV women's desire to use contraception was due to the overcrowding, chaos, and threat of sexual assault that prevailed in the PVs, but the Ministry of Health expressed pride in their workers' ability to motivate women:

> My [family planning] staff can get the willing co-operation of the illiterate and primitive women in the resettlement camps in the northern border areas, where one would not be surprised to find opposition both because of traditional beliefs and possibly because of resentment because of their changed way of life. On the contrary, we have had nothing but co-operation . . . we now arrive early in the morning by air and the leprosy patients, the family planners, the babies for measles vaccinations, and so on are dealt with efficiently and systematically. (Secretary for Health 1974:16)

Outside the PVs, although harassment of government family planning workers escalated, the number of women seeking family planning did not decrease. Reports from the mid- to late-1970s juxtapose accounts of the hazards faced by family planning workers with evidence that demand for the pill and Depo continued to exist:

> The supervision of family planning agents has become quite a problem as has their pay and supplies distribution. They have not escaped the attention of the terrorists but have managed to continue their activities, albeit in a less open fashion. The fact that they managed to increase their numbers [of women accepting contraception] slightly is, in the circumstances, highly commendable. . . . Even keeping existing services going is a triumph under the present circumstances, but when one reads that in some areas maternal and child health and family planning figures have actually increased . . . I feel that a great deal of admiration is due to our staff. (Secretary for Health 1978:37–8)

In many cases, women employed by the FPAR to distribute contraceptive pills took over the work of government family planning workers:

> These women [pill agents] have performed invaluable service as they provide the only family planning service in many areas [in Victoria province]. They have ensured the continual interest of the mothers in areas where neither our nurses nor Family Planning Association [regular] staff can visit. They also give advice on hygiene and infant care and simple home remedies, as well as escorting mothers to the nearest centre to receive Depo-Provera injections. (Secretary for Health 1979:37)

> The activities of the Family Planning Association have been reduced throughout the province [Matabeleland] because of the security situation, and it is very dangerous for the Educators and Distributors in some parts of the province . . . Not only have the vast majority of our African Council clinic outlets been closed, but our services through family planning agents have been severely strained or curtailed because of intimidation and an inability by our agents to travel unmolested about their business. It is indeed surprising, in the circumstances prevailing at present, that the number of acceptors has not diminished to an even greater extent. (Secretary for Health 1979:36)

The pattern that emerges is one of simultaneous intense opposition to the activities of family planning educators and continuing interest from women in the pills and injections the educators and distributors brought with them. This contradiction, which points to differentiated responses to family planning among Africans, is taken up in the following chapters.

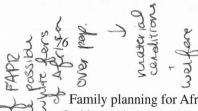

*Growth of FPAR made possible from white fears of over pop. in Africa*

*material conditions ↓ + welfare*

## CONCLUSION

Family planning for Africans emerged at the confluence of several streams of white anxieties. As I have shown, the growth of the FPAR was made possible by white fears of African overpopulation. This concern had two main sources. First, changes in the material circumstances of Rhodesia, particularly the increases in overcrowding in the TTLs and urban unemployment among Africans, and the disappearance of whites through emigration. The second source was the idea of a welfare responsibility on the part of benevolent white overseers to protect and guide Africans. The provision of family planning to Africans, and the growth of the FPAR, addressed both of these issues. While some whites were queasy about using contraceptives to address these issues, the emergence of family planning and population control within the rhetoric and practices of white Rhodesians was probably overdetermined, given the particular historic situation.

However, even if these initiatives were overdetermined, they were not monolithic. Through the words of different white interest groups, and the comments of Africans observing this arguments among these white groups, we see the wide variety of ways in which people understood birth control—as a humanitarian measure, as a way of effecting the modernization of atavistic Africans, and as a way of neutralizing a demographic threat to white rule.

*different ideas of B.C.*

### NOTES

1. Dr. Esther Sapire, the medical director of the FPAR during most of its history, was unusual among whites in Rhodesia in that she was a "born-Rhodesia," who grew up in Salisbury. Peter Dodds, the executive director during the FPAR's period of greatest expansion was a more typical Rhodesian. He and his family had come from England to Kenya, left Kenya after its independence, went to South Africa briefly, and eventually landed in Salisbury. After Zimbabwe's independence, they went back to South Africa.

2. Clem Tholet's song of this title became an unofficial anthem of white Rhodesia:

> We'll preserve this nation
> > For our children's children.
> > Once you're a Rhodesian, no other land will do
> > We will stand tall in the sunshine
> > With truth on our side
> > And if we have to go it alone
> > We'll go alone with pride.
> > We're all Rhodesians
> > And we'll fight through thick and thin
> > We'll keep our land a free land
> > Stop the enemy from coming in
> > . . . And this mighty land will prosper
> > For Rhodesians never die. (quoted in Frederikse 1984:51)

3. On the colonial scene, the advent of projects designed to reshape African women as biological reproducers coincided with similar projects directed at men, aimed at escorting

them into the rational world of modern scientific agriculture, again in imitation of foreign models. Scientific agriculture and domestication represent respectively the public and private faces of attempts to modernize Africans.

4. Within the leadership of the FPAR, this tendency toward catastrophism coexisted with a belief in the efficacy of social engineering and a meliorist view of human evolution, under the stewardship of benign technocrats. Peter Dodds, the charismatic director of the FPAR in the mid- and late-1970s, had to walk a line in his public pronouncements between pessimism and optimism, propounding the idea that the population crisis was indeed a looming disaster, but that the means—family planning—existed to avert it, and that therefore all that was needed was a commitment of will and resources by the white public:

> [In the wake of the Club of Rome report "Limits to Growth" and the dire proclamations of International Population Year in 1974] It may well be that the failure of so many sectors of Rhodesian life to respond to the plea for involvement in family planning stemmed from inherent pessimism, but a pessimism founded not on fact but in theory. Today we can question the validity of that pessimism. . . . The Club of Rome, from their computerized heights, have cause for optimism—how much more so have we in Rhodesia when we can derive first hand satisfaction and encouragement when we see our concern for people manifesting itself daily in the improvement of the human condition. ("Let the Population Pessimists Beware," *The Rhodesia Herald,* 27 December 1974)

5. In 1969, "on average each European family has two servants, 76% of European homes have telephones and 97% have refrigerators." Whites had universal free education up to secondary IV, and had a death rate of 8.2 per 1,000 (compared with 11.2 per 1,000 in the United Kingdom) and an infant mortality rate of 17 per 1,000 (compared with 16 per 1,000 in the United Kingdom [Gilmurray et al. 1979:14–15]).

6. Ratio of black to white population:

```
1904—46:1
1911—31:1
1941—20:1
1959—12:1
1966—17:1
1975—22:1
1977—25:1
(Weinrich 1982:119)
```

7. Hooker overstates the case somewhat in implying that white Rhodesians had been oblivious to Africans before the census—the long history of attempts to regulate African life, including its domestic and sexual aspects, belies this. But he is correct in saying that the census provided irrefutable proof that Africans were increasing in numbers and were advancing on the margins of white society.

8. The interest of Duvenage and other Rhodesian Front backers was an awkward issue for the FPAR to handle and contain. While white support for family planning was essential for the continued existence of the FPAR, white enthusiasm for reducing the number of Africans could be an embarrassment when trying to present family planning to the African majority as a disinterested health and welfare measure. In public discourse, this embarrassment had to be muted, but Dodds did allow himself to grumble that "we could well have done without the contributions of certain politicians who chose to involve them-

selves" ("Let the Population Pessimists Beware," *The Rhodesia Herald,* December 27, 1974). In my interviews with former FPAR education workers, both black and white, this discomfort with the enthusiasm for family planning from some sectors of the white community, particularly the commercial farmers and the Rhodesian Front, was frequently expressed. The sentiment that family planning made strange bedfellows (or more bluntly, that with friends like these, family planning didn't need enemies) was evident whenever former FPAR staff talked about the 1970s.

9. They were faithfully reprinted in the official organ of the Zimbabwe African People's Union (ZAPU, one of the two major national liberation organizations), as evidence that the war was being won by Africans.

10. A letter to the editor from "Hopeful" in Umtali: " . . . the whites of Rhodesia are not on trial, the whites are not the ones needing to respond. . . . They have already proved themselves. Rhodesia is their proof. The whites are responsible for keeping the peace between the various black tribes, and through their integrity are responsible for the country's orderly development, which has been brought about by the predominance of sound judgment, honest endeavor, goodwill and leadership based on Christian values" (*The Rhodesia Herald,* April 8, 1978).

11. Other aspects of white colonialism, in addition to preventive health care, shared the blame for creating an African overpopulation problem. Missionaries, who promoted monogamy instead of polygamy, are blamed for increasing the number of children per woman, as are urban development policies, which reserved urban African housing for married couples, thus forcing men to marry and have children in order to live in town (Geraty 1974:14; Hooker 1971:6).

12. Almost all Africans, as well as most objective outside observers, would certainly take issue with Robertson's assertion that Africans received "the best that the country's social services are able to offer." Enormous racial discrepancies in health, life expectancy, and education, as well as income and standard of living, were recorded for Rhodesia in the 1970s, as they were for South Africa a decade later prior to its own democratic transformation.

13. The construction of "the African" as being absent from historical time and having little sense of causality pervaded Rhodesian popular anthropology. In this excerpt from *The Man and His Ways,* a booklet put out by the Rhodesian Ministry of Information in 1975 to encourage "understanding between the races" and to help whites relate better to their servants and employed, the following description of African "timelessness" is tinged with amused benevolence:

> During generations of endurance, he [the African] has acquired a passive fatalism . . . There was nothing he could do to avoid it [misfortune], so he gave no thought for tomorrow. He conserved his energies and blamed everything bad on something else. How often do we hear "I was failed by the examination" rather than "I failed!" . . . The African loves laughter. His needs are few and when he has satisfied them he is inclined to sit back. After all, time is given to men for nothing. It has no value, so why do today what can be put off to tomorrow? Land and water have also been put here for the free use of mankind, so they, like time, can be wasted. Let tomorrow take care of itself! . . . How then should we deal with this man? We should remember his background and treat him with patience and courtesy. (Rhodesia Ministry of Information 1975:4–5).

14. An example of the public health response to the idea of an essential disjuncture between Africans and more advanced white society:

> An urgent need is the provision of additional accommodation for mental
> patients, especially Africans, among whom the incidence of mental distur-
> bance is increasing each year as more and more of this community are caught
> up in the intricate web of urban and industrial society. (Ministry of Health of
> Rhodesia 1966:19)

15. Rhodesia was not unique in this—in colonial Kenya, for many years before the white government refused to consider setting up state-sponsored family planning clinics for Africans on the grounds that such clinics would be too controversial with the African population, who would assume that the clinics had been established so that Africans would be fewer than Europeans, who would then be able to take over the land (Susan Watkins, personal communication). However, more research is needed to establish the extent to which the ways in which population issues were framed, and the operational understandings about the indigenous population, differed among different colonial regimes.

16. Homage was paid to Spilhaus throughout white debate on family planning for several decades to come, and who was described in 1973 by an admirer as "a wonderful pioneering woman who created family planning virtually single-handedly [in Rhodesia] and has brought it to a level of effectiveness that makes Rhodesia an outstanding example in the field" (van Rensburg 1972:141).

17. When the first clinic for Africans was established at Harari Hospital, Spilhaus gave informational lectures about family planning to mothers recovering from delivery in the postnatal wards. She recounts that she tried to pass this duty on to her interpreter, who knew the material of the talk as well as Spilhaus did, but this plan failed because "the women wanted to hear the 'white woman's secret' from a white woman" (Spilhaus 1981:19).

18. Given the very low rates of African literacy of the time, this written show of interest is more impressive than the numbers might suggest.

19. Especially those within Internal Affairs who feared a backlash from African men opposed to giving their wives the means to promiscuity.

20. Destocking was the practice of forcing Africans to reduce their holdings of cattle, in the name of environmental protection. This move by the government was wildly unpopular with Africans (see Thompson 2000).

21. In addition, the Christmas issue of *Parade,* the largest-circulation English language monthly aimed at Africans with a circulation of 20,000, contained an insert supplied by the FPAR entitled "Questions and Answers on Family Planning."

22. The decision to use pediatric clinics, the site of irreproachable motherhood, as cover for the distribution of contraceptives, shows that the Ministry of Health was aware of the domestic conflicts associated with the encroachment of contraceptives into African homes, as discussed in chapters 4 and 5.

23. The Sabi Valley branch received in reply a bland statement that the Ministry of Health thanked them for their interest in national affairs, and was very interested in promoting the health of all Rhodesians.

24. Granger's concern that the presence of family planning would taint his clinic is borne out by reports from other provinces, where that did indeed happen. For example, in Victoria province

> there has been a marked falling off in attendance at a number of well-baby
> clinics after the family planning mobile clinic had been present. In Gutu, at
> one clinic attendance fell from 280 to 17. Another from 170 to 0 following an

incident in which one woman was beaten up for practicing family planning. A number of women have asked the health nurse if they may go to her home to see her as they do not wish to be seen by the mother-in-law to be visiting the mobile health clinic. There has been a disturbing decline in overall attendance at nearly every well-baby clinic in Gutu. We are having to close clinics. ("Work Done May/June/July 1973":6. NAZ F/118/6)

The following year

in February and March family planning educators visited European farms [in Chatsworth area]. In March after the educator had been there the attendances were not only nil for family planning but also for baby clinics. Once family planning had been singled out even those who had quietly supported it followed the trend and repudiated it. (Report by the Provincial Medical Officer of Health, "Work Done March/April/May 1974":3. NAZ F/118/6)

25. I was unable to discover whether the Ministry ever carried through on this threat and cut off funds to Catholic clinics that did not encourage family planning.

26. The Chairman's Report at the 1969 Annual General Meeting noted that the new injection "is popular and is being asked for increasingly widely" (4).

27. The same was not as true of Peter Dodds, who despite his clashes with both the socially conservative and stridently racist elements in the Rhodesian Front—the first group did not want to upset African men by distributing family planning to their wives, and the second group wanted birth control to be compulsory—had much stronger personal and professional connections with the Rhodesian Front than his predecessors.

28. The reaction of Dr. Smith and others has interesting parallels with the attitudes of some African men, who accused the FPAR of usurping men's prerogative of controlling their wives' and daughters' fertility. The anxieties produced by perceptions of change in the locus of control over fertility and sexuality appear to reverberate similarly in very different cultural spaces.

# 3

# BLOOD AND
# BOUNDARIES:
# LOCAL KNOWLEDGE OF
# PHYSIOLOGY AND
# THE BODY

## INTRODUCTION

This chapter is about the bodies that were quite literally at the center of the struggles over family planning. Local Shona ideas about female bodies and reproduction were not merely different from the biomedical premises that the Family Planning Association of Rhodesia (FPAR) worked from, they were also part of a conceptually coherent, if not always consistent, whole. At the same time, the stock of Shona body knowledge was not static but evolved over time, as new elements entered the realm of what "everyone knows" about the workings of their bodies, and older elements faded away. Despite this evolution, body knowledge contained several persistent themes—the vulnerability of the reproductive system, the importance of reversibility for medicine to be safe, and, above all, the notion of the body as an entity bounded not entirely by skin, but by social ties and relationships, so that the things that one person did with his or her body could radiate out to affect others in different bodies. All of these ideas shaped the ways that women and men reacted to the pills and injections that filtered into their communities.

Local body knowledge also shaped the ways that side effects were understood and handled. Women all over the world have found the headaches, weight gain, and circulatory problems associated with the pill troublesome, but when the pill and the injection were introduced in Rhodesia, all of these side effects were overshadowed by women's anxiety about disruptions to menstrual processes. These anxieties were rooted in the belief that menstruation fulfilled a crucial cleaning and regulatory role for the entire body, and that menstrual irregularities were not only inconvenient but positively dangerous. Men, even though they did not take pills and injections themselves, also feared their side effects—in the form of rumors that attributed impotence to wives who used the pill.

Local knowledge did not only manifest itself in fears and anxieties. Many women found creative and unusual uses for contraceptives, in addition to using them for their ability to prevent conception. Contraceptives were used to preserve and to end marriages, to enable some types of sexual activity, and to hide the signs of others. These "off-label" uses for contraceptives bring us back to one of the central themes of this book: men and women as agents rather than objects of reproductive change, who weave new resources into the evolution of their relationships with others, in order to secure their own goals.

## THE MEDICAL LOGIC OF "DOING TRADITIONAL"

In the earlier part of the twentieth century, before the arrival of the new contraceptives, Shona women used various herbs and devices to prevent conception. While the technical and operational aspects of these methods were not known by everyone—indeed, access to the details that made the methods work was supposed to be a closely guarded secret—the principles on which they worked were generally well known in Shona communities. Everyone had heard of the methods, although they might not know where to get the correct ingredients from, or how to make the methods work.[1]

This body of knowledge was not handed down intact from generation to generation. New information and new resources were incorporated into the models of the body's working and into the practices that derived from these models over the decades of white rule. For example, women told me about practices involving *chirungu* goods such as safety pins or Panadol (a painkiller), and described them as "traditional medicine." The safety pin could be used to cause an unfaithful wife to be "pinned" to her extramarital lover, so that they would not be able to separate their bodies and could thus be caught in flagrante delicto; the Panadol could be doctored so that a wife could use it to compel her husband's fidelity to her. Nonetheless, despite innovations and variations in traditional[2] medicine, some general principles about the body and its workings hold constant.

Traditional methods were used for spacing pregnancies, not for stopping childbearing.[3] Four traditional methods[4] were ubiquitous in Zimbabwe, with many local variations. The first was withdrawal (*kurasira panze*), which was universally known.[5] The next three methods were all female-dependent (although not necessarily controlled by the woman who used them). They all operated by closing or stopping up the entrance to the womb, so that the sperm never reached the uterus.[6] The first female-dependent method is *mishonga yekupfeka*—medicine that is worn—which had a vast number of variations. It took the form of belts worn around women's waists, although the belts might be made of specially treated strings or beads or bark from certain trees, and items might be hung from the belt, including beads, leaves, roots, sticks, soil from a termite hill, or small pieces of cloth. As long as the belt was tied around the woman's waist, the womb was also "tied," so that sperm could not enter it.

The second method was *mishonga yekunwa*—medicine for drinking—which usually took the form of teas made from herbs or roots. The frequency with which it was drunk varied from once a day to once a year, as did the quantity to be consumed. This was considered the most potentially dangerous of the traditional methods, as the concentrations of the active ingredient in the teas could vary from plant to plant and could inadvertently induce permanent sterility.

The third method was the practice of jumping over certain shrubs or trees in order that passing the entrance of the womb over the special powers of the trees would seal it (*kudarika gwenzi*). A woman jumped once over the shrub or tree to seal the womb, and once again in order to re-open it. This jumping had to be accomplished in the context of different rituals involving the direction the woman was facing, what she was wearing, and how she behaved on her way to and from the tree, which varied from place to place. (A fourth category of method, which was not so commonly known as the others, was the use of clay pots that were inverted, buried, or otherwise sealed up to "close" the womb and then re-opened to open it again).

Women also practiced long periods of breastfeeding, up to two years, often in combination with postpartum sexual abstinence between husband and wife. However, most of the women I spoke to regarded breastfeeding as an unreliable method of child-spacing, less reliable than other traditional methods.[7] These periods were regulated by older female in-laws who would give permission to resume sexual relations when they judged that an adequate spacing between births had been reached. I treat this practice of prohibiting sex in following chapters rather than here, as it was primarily a manifestation of social relations between generations and genders, rather than a source of insight into Shona medical logic.

These methods (in particular the use of *mishonga yekunwa* and *mishonga yekupfeka*) were embedded in wider cycles of medical practices within women's lives, unified by the common goal of securing happy and socially acceptable sexual and reproductive lives. Women used belts of different types (*mitimwi*) at different stages of their reproductive lives—as children, to ward off evil; as young women, to attract boyfriends; as young wives, to conceive (especially to conceive a boy); and during pregnancy, to protect the growing baby. They also took different kinds of *mishonga yekunwa* at different times in their marital lives—to conceive, to have a successful pregnancy, and then to recover from pregnancy. The oldest women I interviewed told me that adherence to these traditional practices throughout the reproductive lifecycle not only benefited women physiologically but also benefited them morally, while the modern methods destroyed their moral character. Mrs. Nyamera,[8] and 87 year old, described modern methods as "prostitution for our culture" and added

> We used traditional herbs from pregnancy until she gave birth [and the births were easy]. Now they [women in labor] are being operated on because you ignore our culture and just rush to the hospitals, so you die. (tr. NS[9])

Traditional medicine was not only for promoting happy married lives. Alongside these medicines for women who wanted to bear children happily and healthily was a range of other practices that were not so benign and that overlapped conceptually with witchcraft. These were medicines that women could use to gain control over their husband or other men, specifically in sexual matters, and bind him to them. Known collectively as "love potions," they could make a man unable to have sex with anyone but the woman who had given him the potion, or find her so desirable that he would be unable to refuse anything she might ask for. In Wedza, at the time of my interviews, the use of "love potions" by women was a much-discussed community scandal. My research assistant Mrs. Shayanewako described vividly men's concerns about "husband-taming herbs," which would turn a husband into a "yes man," who would then say yes to any request from his wife. The prevalence of husband-taming herbs was even discussed at District Council meetings in the late 1990s, and men demanded that some way be found to determine where the women were getting these herbs from and that they be stopped (Goebel, personal communication). Husband-taming herbs were also implicated in bad relations between the generations, as older women blamed their daughters-in-law for feeding them to the older women's sons, causing the sons to devote all their energy to the wife and neglect his parents. Most women that I spoke to regarded husband-taming herbs as an inherently amusing topic and joked about going off to get some or giving me some as a present, but no one ever said that she did not believe in them.[10]

Even when traditional medicine was used benignly, to enhance the laudable goals of marriage and pregnancy, it carried risks. In particular, sterility was always a potential risk because of the unpredictable potency of the herbs or beads. While very few women actually reported becoming or knowing someone who became sterile inadvertently because of using traditional methods, every woman who had used these methods knew that sterility was a remote, yet frightening possibility, and discussions of the risk of sterility and the social consequences of being an infertile woman were woven throughout all our discussions of traditional methods. Sterility had strong symbolic connotations, and fear of sterility is woven through the history of child-spacing, with political, spiritual, and psychological aspects, even though Zimbabwe is not in the "sterility belt" of central Africa in which as many as one in five women is unable to have children.[11]

To avoid this fate, the medical logic of traditional methods required that special processes had to be used to reverse the contraceptive effects of the beads, herbs, or tree-jumping. The womb, once closed, could not re-open itself without some action on the part of the woman affected. If she was unable to conceive as a result of a curse put on her, the womb could not re-open without remedial action by the person who placed the curse or by a similarly skilled traditional healer or *n'anga*. If she took one herb to prevent conception, she had to take another herb to undo the effects of the contraceptive. If she jumped over a bush one way, she had to jump over the bush another way to conceive again. Even *mishonga yekupfeka* could require a counteracting agent or ritual—a woman could not assume that the powers of the *mishonga* around her waist would simply wear off as time went by.[12]

This need for an antidote was a crucial difference between traditional methods and the methods brought by the family planning workers (FPWs). FPWs told people that the effects of the pill and the Depo injection would simply wear off over time, and that no action needed to be taken in order to bring back fertility. (The intrauterine device [IUD], of course, needed to be removed, but the IUD was the choice of only a small minority). These new methods, which did not require an antidote, were alien to the medical logic of the traditional methods.

In addition to the issue of antidotes, the new methods were also alien in a more profound sense, one that is difficult to express except in the most abstract terms. Traditional methods were described as "*kwechivanhu*" or "*kwechiShona*"—things of the people or things of the Shona. They were part of a specifically Shona totality, in which cultural and material factors conjoined to produce a mentally, morally, and physically healthy Shona body and mind. For example, the herbs used in *mishonga yekunwa* and *mishonga yekupfeka* and the shrubs used for *kudarika gwenzi* had to be found in specific sites in the neighborhood, just as certain sites were used only for burial grounds and certain sites for divining and other religious practices. Knowing where the herbs and shrubs came from and who had obtained them was crucial to their functioning—foreign items could not be trusted the same way. However, during the 1960s and 1970s this relationship between certain medicines and certain specific places was beginning to break down through urbanization, as more and more "Shona medicine" became commodified and sold in town markets.

Indeed, the idea that foreign items and devices—be they contraceptives, medicine, foodstuffs, or other things—could "go along with" (*kuwirirana*)

Shona bodies was greeted with suspicion by some of the oldest people that I interviewed (see also Watkins, Luke, and Warriner forthcoming). They argued that Shona foods and medicines produced healthy Shona bodies and that foreign interventions, especially dietary ones, led to illness and distress, particularly in reproductive matters.[13] Sugar and black tea (as distinct from infusions of roots or herbs) were singled out as especially dangerous, and also addictive, to African bodies.[14] In interviews, questions about childbearing practices in the respondent's youth often led to discussion of changes in diet, to the detriment of the Shona, or of the superiority of all the traditional medicines used throughout the reproductive lifecycle:

> [NS: Did people in the old days have problems with childbearing?] No, they didn't have that, what I know is that they had children until their old age. These old people, they say sugar [a colonial-era import] is the one which causes the problems, because in their time nothing was a problem. They were strong, giving birth today and going to the fields tomorrow. Nothing was a problem. (interview with Mr. Jenya, tr. NS)

> At that time there were no health problems like now. We just bore our children, no matter that they were without clothing, their health was perfect. They ate *sadza* [the staple maize porridge] with beer and peanut butter, we cooked sour porridge . . . we cooked without sugar, with peanut butter only. (interview with Mrs. Gukutwa, tr. NS)

> [NS: Did people in the old days have problems with childbearing?] No, they spaced their children well. Health problems were good. No problems, because [illnesses] were few. I think now diseases are so many because we are rushing to eat Western foods—that's why mothers fail to push their children [give birth safely], and end up with operations in the clinics. (interview with Mr. Mbiti, tr. NS)[15]

By arguing that Shona diet, culture, medicine, and health made up a philosophical and medical unity, I am not claiming that "traditional" and "modern" practices were mutually exclusive. The dichotomy between ethnophysiology and biomedicine is "more distinct in [its] institutional representation than as experienced by people in the course of their daily lives" (Paxson 1997:1). The new contraceptives and their effects on the body were integrated into Shona ideas and practices about physiology by means of a pragmatic syncretism, in which "traditional" and "modern" ideas and practices combined. See, for example, Mrs. Dzoma's account of using traditional herbs to "wash out" the effects of the Depo-Provera shot below. Other examples of this syncretism include Mrs. Marjoree Mugwagwa's account of being approached by women who had been "doing traditional" and who sought clinical help to undo the effects of inadvertent sterilization caused by improper use of the medicine; the experiences of Mrs. Ivy Mhlanga and Mr. Alec Ndhlukula, who separately encountered traditional healers who were willing to perform rituals to make Western contraceptives acceptable to their followers in the same way that traditional medicines were acceptable; and accounts of women who used "modern" and "traditional" contraceptive methods simultaneously.

Even though the new methods could be syncretized with older practices, the pills and injections came out of an entirely different knowledge context, that of clinical northern biomedicine. In clinical biomedicine, individual physiological processes are thought to have their own internal logic, operating autonomously from the intentions or the moral character of the person who lives in the body, or any of that person's associates. Moreover, the body is always becoming more and more knowable, as its mechanics are constantly opened up by scientific study. FPWs were steeped in this twentieth-century European knowledge system as part of their training. They became effectively bilingual—fluent in biomedicine as well as in the local physiological knowledge with which they grew up.

FPWs were also encouraged by their employers, the modernizers of Rhodesia, to identify themselves with the projects and institutions of biomedicine as part of an overall project of modernization. My interviews suggest that that they did so identify themselves, albeit without scorning their relatives and neighbors who did not share their belief in biomedicine. Many of the early FPWs had received nursing training in the 1950s before joining the FPAR, and for those who were not nurses, their training as FPWs from the 1960s onward included several weeks on reproductive anatomy and physiology (Spilhaus 1981).

In addition to exposure to biomedical knowledge about reproduction, FPWs were encouraged to regard themselves as part of a national team that was bringing health and enlightenment to the masses. In a striking combination of religious and medical rhetoric, FPWs were reminded by Mr. Richard Chikosi, the senior educator in the April 1974 issue of their newsletter that

> every field educator employed by the FPAR is attached to one or more clinics or hospitals. He/she paves the way and makes the path straight for the doctors, sisters, and nurses. As the medical practicalities absorb the minds of the professionals in the clinics, the field educator continually wields the sowing hand within the surrounding neighbourhood . . . the success of the field educator is apparent in the number of new acceptors treated at his/her clinic per month and the number of old ones retrained. (*Mhuri Inofara,* April 1974:12)

In my interviews, several FPWs remembered with pride how they were mistaken for nurses or doctors (and indeed their uniforms were very similar to those worn by government medical staff) and how they were asked for medicines or treatments by their clients, who believed that they were actually trained medical professionals.[16]

FPWs were keenly aware of local Shona ideas about the body, but referred to them as "myths" that had to be "rectified." Their accounts of encounters with ethnophysiology usually took the form of stories of how they had corrected the myth or presented an alternative "scientific" explanation. Interestingly, though, their identification with biomedicine did not lead them to dismiss traditional medicines as worthless. Even in their interviews with me, a white foreigner presumably with favorable attitudes to biomedicine, not one FPW said that he or she thought *mishonga yekunwa* and the other traditional methods were useless.[17]

## SIDE EFFECTS

Many women complained of the side effects that have been reported universally as problems with the pill and Depo, especially the high-dose versions common before the 1980s, such as headaches and weight gain. However, the most distressing side effects were those that affected women's reproductive and sexual anatomy. These side effects were particularly troubling because women's sexual organs were the sites in which female morality and virtue was grounded. Physical changes in these areas had implications for individual and collective morality.

One of the most common concerns about Depo and the pill was that these medicines caused women's vaginal secretions to increase. This particular side effect has not been recorded in clinical studies in North America or Europe. However, in Rhodesia, women complained about becoming "watery," with bad consequences for the husband.[18] His pleasure in intercourse might be diminished, or his very health might be threatened, as his wife's vaginal secretions became toxic to him. According to Mrs. Imelda Mudarikiri, a wife's use of family planning threatened her husband's enjoyment: "They say that when you take pills, it makes you watery and so the husband won't enjoy. We had to stamp out that rumor." Mrs. Ennet Mudzimwa concurred, saying, "They said about the pill, both men and women, that if a woman is using the pill she discharges too much watery discharges."

The problem of excess vaginal secretions[19] strengthened the link between women's use of contraceptives, female sexual immorality, and danger to men. Many FPWs reported confusion between side effects of contraceptives and symptoms of sexually transmitted diseases (STDs). Some men assumed that their wives were infected because their vaginal secretions had increased or changed (Mrs. Marjoree Mugwagwa: "there was sort of confusion between the family planning and the STDs, there was confusion between the types of discharges"); or thought that the use of contraceptives might actually cause a woman to develop an STD (Mrs. Shamiso Kudakwashe: "Some thought the woman might have a sexually transmitted disease from family planning, various reasons for refusing [to allow their wives to use pills or Depo] . . . ").[20]

The link between a woman's sexual activities and the health of her intimate family members is also evident in stories about how a mother's infidelity would confer sickness on her children. Children are part of the father's rather than the mother's lineage, so that an injury to the children is also an injury to the husband's lineage and ancestors—a very dangerous thing for a wife to risk. During my interviews, I heard that a woman who attended well-baby clinics could be suspected of trying to cover up evidence of her adultery by using Western medicines to cure her child of sicknesses brought on by her misbehavior. Ministry of Health reports from the 1970s contain mention of resistance to measles vaccinations on the grounds that this would enable adulterous women to cover up the telltale signs in their children:

Opposition to vaccinations comes . . . from men who allege that if a child is prevented from getting measles they will not know if their wives have been unfaithful, the belief being that the wife's infidelity is revealed by the child becoming seriously ill or dying. (Secretary for Health 1972:17)

Mr. Tsuro told me that both men and women could have their guilt revealed through the illness of their child:

Men must say the truth in cases of adultery when the child is sick, especially measles, both parents will say the truth so that the pain will go early or the measles will take [only a] few days. There is no problem if the wife is perfect [in her marital fidelity]. (tr. NS)

Mr. Shorechena concurred, saying that in the early part of the twentieth century, before these curative medicines became widely available, "many children died due to prostitution and adultery of their parents" (tr. NS).

This link between a woman's body and the health of her family members came up repeatedly in reports from the FPWs. In some cases men would appear at clinics, convinced from their own symptoms of ill-health that their wife must be using contraception secretly. According to Mrs. Stella Padoro,

Some [husbands] were complaining, "I have abdominal pains because my wife is getting contraceptives," he doesn't take contraceptives but he is getting pains because of the pills which the wife is taking. They say, "I have lower abdominal pains and I went to the doctor and he told me that it was my wife taking family planning pills." We had to convince them that it is not a venereal disease that can spread from one person to another. You can't eat food today and expect your wife to have abdominal pains tomorrow because of the food you ate today.

Abdominal pains might be inconvenient, but what men feared most was impotence, which was mentioned by almost all the FPWs I spoke to. I interpret this fear of impotence as both a literal fear of having a nonfunctional penis, and as a metaphor for the loss of power in other spheres. On a symbolic level, impotence could be read as the loss of power in the marital relationship when one's wife, armed with the new "invisible" contraceptives, could take more responsibility determining when and if the couple would have children, and as surrender to the white pushers of contraception who could take away some of a man's control over his family.

The quote below from Mrs. Gladys Chitsungo shows that impotence carried connotations of emasculation by the colonial state. However, it is also clear that the fear of impotence was also an actual physiological fear, mediated through very specific channels such as the vaginal secretions of the woman, as well as a domestic and national political metaphor. Before my interview with her, I had heard from many different people that men feared they would become weak if their wives used the pill or the injection. I had taken "weak" as referring to one of the unspecified abdominal ailments said to attend sexual impropriety in Shona society; however, Mrs. Chitsungo set me straight:

> Some of the men used to say when a woman takes pills a man would feel weak. That was a belief to men. They thought they would be weak. They [women] were told by their men, "Now you are going to make me weak, you are killing me like witchcraft." It was very much said by the men. And even up to today there are some men who are talking like that. [AK:[21] They thought that the man would be sick if his wife was taking the pills?] No, he doesn't become sick exactly, he says he will not be strong to meet [have sex with] his wife. They say a man will not feel like making intercourse, he won't be able to. (Makes limp-wrist gesture of flaccidity, laughs.) As it was during the wartime, people were really afraid, they didn't know which was which, they thought it was the way of decreasing the tribe of Africans, they thought all that was going to come to men if women took the pills, men would be weak so that they could not do intercourse, the could not make any more babies.

This concern with impotence can also be interpreted as male fears of women's sexual autonomy. This concern is related to frequently expressed concerns about witchcraft or curses directed against husbands by wives (see Goebel 1998). Despite being constrained, in theory, within the framework of the patriarchal household, women had the power to wreak havoc on their husbands through sex, if they were so inclined.

All of these concerns—the dangers of vaginal secretions, fears of abdominal pain, and impotence—that swirled around the effects of Depo and the pill point to a foundational element of Shona bodies and Shona social relations. The body, especially the female body, with all its complicated processes and its systems of causes and effects, is not bounded by the physical surface of the individual body or contained within the skin. Changes in the activities of a woman's sexual or reproductive systems, such as those occasioned by the use of contraceptives or by illicit activities such as adultery, could radiate out from her own body to affect the bodies of others, such as husbands and children. This is, of course, a radically different understanding of the body from that held by the biomedical doctors and nurses in the clinics, and by the administrators of the FPAR. The contradictions between these two forms of body knowledge contributed to the suspicion with which the FPAR's activities were regarded by many Africans.

In addition to this basic difference between Shona knowledge and the FPAR's knowledge of bodies, some side effects of the new contraceptives were particularly troubling. I turn now to the two most common of these side effects.

### Menstrual Disruptions

The most common problem was disruption to the menstrual cycle, reported by every FPW as a drawback of the pill and Depo. Both men and women disliked this, not only because of the inconvenience it caused or because of the threat of anemia if the bleeding was heavy, but also because of what it signified in terms of women's sexual behavior and availability. The women who abandoned the pill and Depo because of menstrual irregularity were not only spurred by physical discomfort and ill-health, but also by the implications of changes in the menstrual cycle within Shona body knowledge.[22]

FPWs were scolded by angry and frightened women and their husbands, when the pill or the injection produced either too much bleeding or not enough.[23]

"You gave me the pill to take, now I have missed my period. . . . What am I going to say to my husband?" And sometimes when they forget in between they will have withdrawal bleeding. "You made me have a period before my time!" It was quite difficult to train these people. (interview with Mrs. Elinor Dauya)

Most of the men they know that if somebody is bleeding without your knowledge . . . it's part of the family planning . . . Some [women] were beaten to hell and going back to the educators crying, and they [husbands] still want to beat the educator also, so it was really troublesome. They said to us, "You are the one who has given my wife this injection, I want this bleeding to stop now now now!" We could just say, "Give me a little while so that I can examine what is happening," then we examine the mother, then we show the husband how to take the pill to stop the bleeding, the combined pill. So that was where problems come from, if there is a side effect the educator is also in trouble, the nurse is also in trouble. (interview with Mrs. Marjoree Mugwagwa)

Why should disruption of menstrual patterns cause such concern? The answer lies in the ways in which menstruation and menstrual blood were understood. Menstruation was regarded as a form of purification, cleaning the female body of accumulated toxins.

> Many people used to stay about six months, a year without menses and it was worrying the women . . . they didn't like it, they prefer to have the period because the period cleans. They said if you flow the menses you are cleaning inside the womb. That was a tradition. And some even thought if you do your intercourse, even those who were a bit older [i.e., menopausal], if you don't flow the menses the dirt [semen] doesn't come out, the *tsvina* [unwanted matter]. (interview with Mrs. Gladys Chitsungo)[24]

Menstrual blood carried the flotsam and debris produced by the whole body, maintaining a woman in a state of overall good health, extending beyond her reproductive organs. Releasing blood during menstruation could regulate body temperature, keeping a woman from getting too hot, and could carry off any toxins a woman might have inadvertently swallowed (Cornwall 1990:28).

A woman who does not menstruate, such as one who is pregnant, lactating, menopausal, or amenorrheic because of contraception does not have this means of cleaning and protecting herself, and must be careful about the foreign substances she takes into her body. Male sperm is potentially harmful to a female body, and so one consequence of this belief was a set of loosely-observed taboos against intercourse with nonmenstruating women (i.e., women who were pregnant, nursing, or menopausal[25]). This was not only for the protection of the woman, to prevent more foreign agents from being introduced into her body, but also for the protection of the man, so he does not risk illness through sexual contact with a woman who is unable to purify herself regularly.[26] Women who feared losing the cleansing protection of the menstrual period might believe they were unable to function as a normal wife:

> Some side effects, they say they have had amenorrhea for years and years and are now just acting like a man[27] [i.e., no longer a real woman] "because I don't have a period." They believe that women who don't have a period are just as good as a man in the house. Their belief is that "When I am not having a period where does the sperm goes? The sperm will stay in you. That's why I am getting too fat. My tummy would be so big from all the sperm." (interview with Mrs. Elinor Dauya)

Menstruation was also said to keep the uterus in good shape, to keep it in a state of *chinyoro,* which means "freshness, moistness, and general well-being" (Cornwall 1990:27).

The menstrual cycle and menstrual blood itself was also a locus of ill-will expressed through evil magic perpetrated by hostile acquaintances or by dissatisfied ancestral spirits (Cornwall 1990:25). Daneel (1971:48) records that if a husband was remiss in showing the proper respect to his wife's relatives, her ancestors could "steal the menstrual blood of the granddaughter," stopping her periods and causing infertility, thereby depriving the husband of his potential offspring. Similarly, amenorrhea could be induced as punishment for an adulterous woman, either by an angry husband or by others wishing to bring the woman's transgressions to public knowledge (Daneel 1971; Gelfand 1980:30). *N'angas* were reputed to be able to stop menstruation at will, or to use the by-products of menstruation to induce barrenness (Crawford 1967:95).

Men also objected to their wives' amenorrhea or irregular menstruation, fearing that either their wives or they themselves would become sick through it:

> The husbands were against the taking of pills or injections just because their belief was of saying that when a woman is pregnant or breastfeeding a baby [i.e., not menstruating], no husband ever admires her [wants to have sex with her]. She will never be proposed love by anybody because she will not be having her time to clean herself. No husband loves a dirty woman. (correspondence with Mrs. Mutede)

This was corroborated by the clinical experience of FPWs:

> Some men believe that "If I meet [have sex with] a woman who is not menstruating, whether on family planning or old age, I will become sick." So you have that time to explain. If you really know anatomy and physiology, it's not like that. . . . The sperm is something that is invisible, you can't even see it, it is just taken by your blood and goes into your body then your body just stays with it well. (interview with Mrs. Elinor Dauya)

The alien substances like sperm or pills that accumulated in women's abdomens could produce both overt and subtle changes in women. The pills added to the accumulation of unwanted substances, known collectively as *tsvina,* within the stomach. *Tsvina* was normally expelled through menstruation, and if it was not expelled could lead to illness. Many women feared a condition called *chimimba mteko,* abdominal bloating and illness, caused by the accumulation of foreign matter and unexpelled menstrual fluid, in the stomach. "Some said, 'If we take pills every day, where do they go? They will make a heap in my stomach'" (correspondence from Mrs. P. Marufu).

> Some said that when you are on Depo-Provera and you are not menstruating you will have this big tummy, that was very, very common. Also with the pill, all the pills that you take are piled up in the corner, so eventually you will just blow up. (interview with Mrs. Shamiso Kudakwashe)

They said . . . that after taking the pill for a long time you will become ill because there will be many pills in your body and you will have a big tummy. I had to explain that no, think of people who have chronic diseases like TB, they take these pills for a long time but do they have big tummies, no. That is the urine we pass. Anything not wanted by the body is excreted out. . . . if a patient is a diabetic patient he has to take the pills or the injection, it doesn't do any effect to your body because your body will be working using that medicine, so there is nothing to fear. (interview with Mrs. Dorothy Dzuda)

## Risks of Sterility

Although menstrual disruptions were the most frequent cause of anxiety about the new methods, no side effect was feared more than the possibility of permanent sterility. All the people that I talked to, FPWs and non-FPWs, reported that concern about being rendered infertile followed the introduction of pills and injections all over the country.[28]

Fear of sterility was augmented by two features of the new contraceptives—they often did inhibit the return of normal menstruation even after a woman stopped using them, a distressing thing in itself, as noted above, and they were introduced by whites during the war, a historic moment that led many to suspect that the devices were a Trojan horse, introduced by the white government as a way of sterilizing Africans.[29]

This fear affected not only the women who took the pills and injections, but also their husbands and relatives within the extended family:

> People had a lot of rumors and misconceptions. People thought that if someone is on family planning it means you are sterilized, you will not have any more children. Some thought that if a woman is on family planning she is not going to be normal, she is not going to have normal children in the future. . . . Some of the husbands they thought, "If my wife is on family planning she is going to be sterile. What will I do among the relatives, I will be shy [ashamed, because of not having many children]." . . . it was accepted not well because everyone has got his own ideas. People were just thinking that we are going to be sterilized, we are no longer going to have any children. (interview with Mrs. Rita Masara)

> I started using the Depo injection in 1973 when I was 21 years old, after I gave birth to my first born. I [then] tried traditional [methods] when I was afraid to use the injection because I was given an injection for three months but it lasted for three years and some months. I used traditional herbs to wash out the injection, and then I became pregnant again. (interview with Mrs. Dzoma, tr. NS)

The biggest problem was that when you were injected the injections takes a long time, maybe two or three years but the nurses say a month. I was injected privately [without the knowledge of her husband] and the injection lasted three years instead of three months. It was a problem with our husbands. Some of us were divorced [because our husbands thought we were infertile] . . . My husband wanted me to have more children, but I was now old. (interview with Mrs. Jongwe, tr. NS)

FPWs emphasized that they could not dismiss fears of infertility casually, because they knew that "it really did happen"—that use of the pill or the injection really did result in delayed fertility—unlike some of the rumored other detrimental side effects of the hormonal contraceptives, which could be dismissed as just gossip.

On Depo-Provera there were some women who were having a problem of having babies because of the delayed fertility. And some people were actually divorced because of that, it was a big problem. It can be a year or more. Some of these people they have post-pill amenorrhea after taking the pill, then if someone comes in at three years or five years [of not menstruating] we just reassure, reassure, [saying] "No problem," but knowing that we have already done the damage to the person through family planning. (interview with Mrs. Marjoree Mugwagwa)

Mr. Timothy Nzuma said that he thought very few cases of secondary infertility could be genuinely laid at the door of the pill, but that pill use could be a convenient scapegoat when a couple failed to have the number of children they wanted. He stressed that FPWs had to explain the pill very precisely and carefully to their prospective clients, to distinguish between the normal unpredictability of conception and the effects of a wife's use of the pill or the injection:

They were suspicious that it was causing permanent sterility . . . We would refer back, we would ask them in your community do you all have the same family size? You find some have ten, some have five, some have one and they are just staying with one. Were they on family planning? But what caused it? So you can see a child is God given, isn't it? . . . Don't say it doesn't happen because it really does happen, sometimes you are only to have one child, then you are on family planning, you want a second baby, you don't get a second baby, you say it is the pill. But if you were not on the pill, what would you say? Sympathize with them, don't say that it doesn't happen because it does happen, but it will not have been caused by the pill. (interview with Mr. Timothy Nzuma)

For many FPWs, the fear that they might be accused of causing infertility haunted their working life. They recalled the accusations that they had

bewitched and crippled women who did not return to a normal menstrual
cycle soon after stopping the pill or the injection.

> Now the problem comes, sometimes infertility will be prolonged, she will
> come straight back to you and say, "When I delivered my first children and
> so forth, after weaning my baby I will have my period straightaway. Now
> what has happened this time?" And they think they are no more going to
> have a baby. (interview with Mrs. Elinor Dauya)

## ALTERNATE USES FOR HORMONAL CONTRACEPTIVES

Family planning clients and their families did not just fret and worry over the
side effects of contraceptives. Many women (and some men) wove these side
effects into their own agendas for their sex lives and marriages, to further their
own agendas in domestic relations. Rather than simply absorbing received
beliefs about bodies and sex, women were using the new methods to further their
own agendas, effectively making of the female body an instrument of power.

Most histories of family planning concentrate on the manifest use of contraception—to prevent births. However, people use contraceptives for many
other purposes, using the technologies as they want to, rather than as they are
"supposed" to.[30]

Bledsoe and colleagues (1994) have demonstrated that, in the Gambia, men
and women use new contraceptive methods for purposes other than the cur-
tailment of fertility, specifically that "rural women . . . are using Western contraceptives . . . in order to resume sexual relations early [after the birth of a
child] while achieving . . . goals of maintaining breastfeeding and 'decent'
birth intervals" (85). Bledsoe and her colleagues conclude that

> whether people adopt contraceptive technologies and how they use them is
> mediated less by the original Western formulations of these technologies
> than by local cultural perceptions . . . [O]ur terminology is admittedly inad-
> equate. "Western" is inappropriate . . . because people quickly assimilate
> the meaning and usage of Western contraceptives into local practices. (86)

Benefo (1997) refers to the process whereby contraceptives become
employed for other purposes and other goals than their manifest ones as
"hybridization," according to which "people generally transform borrowed
ideas and technologies so that they fit the existing cultural environment and
enable them to secure their own goals" (4). The contraceptives are thus
imbued with new utilitarian possibilities, as well as taking on new connotations as a result of these new uses. Both FPWs and non-FPWs frequently
talked about what clients hoped to achieve by using contraceptives, in addition to preventing the FPAR-sanctioned goals of spacing births. The most fre-

quently (indeed, universally) mentioned other goals were those associated with unsanctioned sexual activities by women, whether premarital sex by unmarried girls or extramarital sex by wives.

We have no way to know whether women really did use the new contraceptive to facilitate prostitution or casual alliances to the extent that they were represented as doing so in rumor and gossip about the contraceptives. The FPWs insisted that the accusations of prostitution were wildly overblown by fearful men. Nonetheless, one of the earliest FPWs, who worked in the townships and peri-urban areas of Salisbury (Harare) during the late 1950s recalled that her first and most enthusiastic customers were "the ladies in Pioneer Street" (Salisbury's red-light district). Another FPW, Mrs. Elizabeth Utete, who worked on the commercial farms surrounding Marandellas (Marondera), reported that the women who "did *mapoto*" (moved from one short-term liaison to another, as a means of securing a place to live in the farmworkers' quarters) were more enthusiastic about the new contraceptives than were the "real wives." Mrs. Utete saw this use of contraceptives as a good thing, rather than a sign of encroaching immorality, because of the high rates of domestic violence on the commercial farms. If a woman was protected from conception, it was easier for her to leave an abusive situation and move on to a better man, because the abusive man would have fewer claims on her if she was not carrying "his" child.

In addition to using contraceptive to facilitate "immorality," some women used them in order to have more children, rather than fewer. Mrs. Winnie Pasipanodya had been plagued with a succession of stillbirths, until she decided to use the pill in order to spend time building up her strength without the stress of yet another failed pregnancy on her body:

> I wanted family planning when one child died. . . . when I delivered I bled and then my husband and I plus the doctor thought it was good that I could just rest and get some blood in me, some more strength, so that I could start afresh. What happened when I started afresh? I have got a baby . . . I had a stillbirth and so from there that's when I started liking family planning because from there I started practicing stopping [waiting for a long interval before becoming pregnant] and having another one and the following one I got safely.

She used her own experience as a talking point for convincing suspicious community members that family planning was not only for stopping births but also for ensuring that more healthy children were born, and reported that other women who had been unable to carry a pregnancy to term were able to have healthy babies after taking the opportunity to "rest" between conception, which the pill provided.

Other women assumed that the power of the new methods to prevent pregnancy meant that it could also be used to interrupt an ongoing pregnancy. "She will like to take the pill, thinking the pill will remove pregnancy. They did that:

'If I take the pill maybe the pregnancy will come out,' and yet no [it didn't]. They would be trying to abort, but it would be no good" (interview with Mrs. Regina Chokwenda). Mrs. Tendai Masvika said that, in her experience inserting IUDs, many women would lie, saying they had just finished their period and were coming, as instructed, at the end of their menstrual cycle, while in reality they had not menstruated for a month or more. These women feared they were pregnant and hoped that the IUD would interrupt the pregnancy. This use of the IUD became known to the nurses at the Spilhaus clinic, when the women would return to the clinic the following month, complaining that the IUD was ineffective and they had become pregnant. They were told that they must carry the baby to term, and then "when you deliver you come here [to the family planning clinic] straightaway and we will help you." Mrs. Masvika said she realized from the dates when the women arrived at the clinic with their newborn babies that they must have already been pregnant on their first visit.

Many FPWs reported that women tried to procure new contraceptives, particularly the IUD and the pill, to induce abortion. This may have been based on belief that the methods acted to interrupt existing pregnancies, which were latent in a woman's stomach, rather than by preventing a pregnancy from starting. Mrs. Tendai Masvika reported being told by opponents of family planning, "Do not do that job, you are killing our children in the stomach! We want our children to come out." Mrs. Salina Mumbengegwi said that, in her experience, people believed that "you have to give birth to children until the [children] are finished, as if they are lined up in there, number 1 to 12," and that the use of contraception would kill an unborn child awaiting its time to come out.[31]

Mrs. Gladys Chitsungo reported that

> They do say you are killing [unborn babies], but when you started explaining you find that most of the educated people can understand that it is an egg that is being—what can we say—that egg is being discouraged to grow, then they could understand. But those who didn't know how the egg goes and the fertility system goes, it's a problem. We were really explaining that we were discouraging your egg to grow so that it can make a baby, so it doesn't grow, some eventually understood it. They thought it was abortion really, but there is a big, big difference.

The "big, big difference" between family planning and abortion may have disappointed some women, even as it reassured others.

While some women feared becoming sterile because of the pill, other women wanted to create an illusion of infertility, which the pill could give them. They included young widows who wanted to escape being inherited by their late husband's brother, a practice which was widespread in some communities. If a woman was believed to be infertile, she would not be a desirable wife for her brother-in-law and might be released to return to her natal family.

If there is a widow, they [her in-laws] say she mustn't take the pills because she must be inherited by the young brother or the cousin. But if that woman is clever enough she will come [to my house] hiding [secretly], saying, "I don't want this inheritance . . . they are forcing me." But if they find out that she is not becoming pregnant, why should she stay with the brother? [The brother will say] "She can't have children? I don't want." Then she can go back to her family. They would come to us because it was appropriate for them to do this because they are widows with six children and they still force you to go and get married to somebody else, or they take everything from you while you have a small child, and it is far much better that you go back to your parents. You can go to your parents if you are not having more children. (interview with Mrs. Elinor Dauya)

Mr. Chikorera concurred:

In our culture we have some women who were forced to marry, so these women were happy [to use the new methods] because the man will chase her away after she fails to have children. I think these women were the ones who were happy [with the new "invisible" contraceptives]. (tr. NS)

Women in particular types of marriages found "invisible" family planning methods especially useful, such as those unwillingly married to elderly polygamists:

Women liked it [the pill and the injection] because some of them were forced to marry an old man due to [the teachings of their] church or due to poverty of the family, maybe the old man was rich . . . [they are] forced to marry him, but to have many children, maybe he has 10 wives, so those that are clever, they have to prevent [pregnancy, because the husband cannot care for all his wives and their children]. When the old man dies it will be the woman's problem to look after all the children. (interview with Mrs. Nyati, tr. NS)

or those contending with domestic violence:

Some [men] they beat their wives no matter that [i.e., especially when] they are pregnant, so they were happy to have secret prevention. (interview with Mrs. Hwata, tr. NS)

Women with adult daughters also got contraceptives for their daughters, in order to avoid being blamed as a bad mother if the daughter became pregnant. While young women had their own reasons for not wanting their sexual activity to become known through an unwanted pregnancy, their mothers also had a vested interest in keeping the daughter's activities secret. Most of the women I knew spoke of cases where mothers and daughters had been expelled together from their home if the daughter was found to be pregnant, as husbands and in-laws assumed that the daughter had learned her "bad behavior" from her mother. Some mothers resorted to criminal and potentially fatal abortifacients, not only to preserve her daughter's future but also to protect her own. FPWs agreed that it was much better that such mothers give their daughters contraceptives secretly, rather than endanger their health. To avoid having her own security jeopardized, a mother who had reason to doubt her daughter's chastity would do well to give pills to her daughter:

> You know with the African culture once a daughter is pregnant the blame goes to the mother. "Why, what happened?" So the mother will just hide the pill. Some of the mothers, the blame was that she will go behind the husband to go and do criminal abortions, and some children died, in such cases. Some were Women's Association women, going to church and putting on uniforms, "I am a preacher [in church], what will people say when they see my daughter becoming pregnant, what will I say to other people. So she must take off [get rid of] the pregnancy. So if she can hide to take the pill and not become pregnant, nobody will know she is a bitch [a promiscuous woman], and I her mother am in the Mother's Union [the church women's association]. She can still have a white wedding." When you are a mother there are so many problems that arise from families and you really don't know what to do and in most cases all the blame will come to the mother. When you are married if anything goes wrong with your family your in-laws will blame you. The blame will go to your own mother—she was not well-taught, well brought up, she can't cook. . . . So they don't blame just one person, but the mother most specially, it is better that that daughter will have family planning and she [the mother] is safe. (interview with Mrs. Elinor Dauya)

Contraceptives could be used to end marriages, as well as to preserve them. I heard of cases where husbands who wanted to divorce their wives planted evidence that the wife was using family planning without her husband's permission as evidence of her disobedience and thus as a pretext for divorcing her.[32]

> The women [who came to the FPAR's Salisbury clinic] used to tell us that they were in separation, that she is staying with her own parents, the husband has divorced her because she was found with family planning. Then the husband would be contacted in writing by the director [of the FPAR]. . . . The director would just write a letter to say come and see us, we would get the message that they were divorcing because of this family planning. Then they [the disgruntled husbands] start changing [their story], they say that this woman is having boyfriends and whatever, he has seen the boyfriend. He would change the subject. It is not really the family planning.

Then we would understand that this is a domestic problem, it is not a family planning problem. The fact of the matter was that it was not family planning which has caused the divorce. (interview with Mrs. Annah Musarurwa)

Extramarital girlfriends also used these strategies to displace the legitimate wife. Some girlfriends accused the wife of "secret use" in order to disgrace her with her husband; while others urged the husband to make a false accusation against his wife in order to have legitimate grounds for divorcing her. As Mrs. Annah Musarurwa put it, "Really honestly, there were some women who wanted to destroy people's marriage." Most of the stories I heard about the use of family planning to destroy marriages had the quality of well-worn fables about the untrustworthiness of men or the perfidy of female friends, suggesting that these were idealized versions of actual incidents.

Mrs. Tendai Masvika's story is typical. She told me about a woman who married when she was eight months pregnant, whose best friend was conducting an affair with her husband. The husband had refused his wife permission to use family planning but wanted the girlfriend to use it. The girlfriend wanted to marry the husband so she encouraged the wife to use family planning secretly and urged the wife to go to Spilhaus Centre, the main family planning clinic, with her. At the same time the girlfriend told the husband to come to Spilhaus at a certain time and he could find his wife disobeying him. The man found his wife in the clinic waiting room. The wife said at first that she was just accompanying her friend, but later admitted she had come to get pills. That evening the man packed up all her things and took her with her daughter to her uncle in Highfields and gave the uncle *gupuro* (a small monetary token of repudiation) because "*akaenda kuzotora matablets* (she has gone and taken pills)." The next day, the wife came crying to the staff at Spilhaus and accused them of collusion with the husband and girlfriend. Mrs. Masvika convinced the administration that they had a responsibility to help this woman, who had come to grief because of family planning, and the FPAR undertook to supply the woman with two kilos of Lactogen (powdered milk) per week for the child. The man married his girlfriend, but they had to leave the township where they lived because everyone knew how the girlfriend had tricked the wife. The man later died, and his second wife had had no child, which Mrs. Masvika felt was a just retribution for the second wife's treachery toward her friend. Mrs. Masvika pointed out that family planning was used by the husband and the girlfriend to engineer the end of the marriage because "the husband was not opposed to pills because he was getting some for his girlfriend. He told us at the clinic that he divorced his wife because he was anti-family planning but that was not the reason."

Women also made use of other properties of birth control methods, in addition to their contraceptive effects, to attain their own goals in marriages. In the early days of family planning, before the pill arrived in 1961, women valued the ability of the Volpar foaming tablets to kill sperm and draw out *tsvina,* even when pregnancy was not a possibility. Several FPWs reported that menopausal women in their areas would refrain from sex, because they believed that, if sperm that entered their body were not washed out by menstruation, they would become sick. However, if the sperm were killed through contraceptive foam, menopausal women could continue to have sex and remain healthy—and decrease the likelihood that their husband would marry a younger second wife in order to have a sexual partner. Mrs. Phoebe Mpezeni was at first puzzled by the number of women clearly past childbearing age who came looking for contraception, and who insisted they wanted the otherwise-unpopular Volpar tablets. Later, she realized that they believed that "the foam will just take away the man's seed, and she will be okay."

Side effects specific to hormonal contraceptives, specifically the changes in vaginal secretions, which were believed to accompany the use of the pill or Depo-Provera, were also used to achieve certain specific outcomes. Throughout both interviews and written accounts, FPWs and non-FPWs stressed the similarities between the vaginal discharge believed to be produced by the hormonal contraceptives and that believed to be a symptom of a sexually transmitted disease (STD). Mrs. Marjoree Mugwagwa reported that some women who were using the pill with their husbands' knowledge would use this side effect as a "cover" for the symptoms of an STD contracted through extramarital sex.[33] Any excess vaginal discharge could be explained away as a result of the pill:

> There was a sort of misunderstanding between family planning and the STDs. You find the estrogen pill causes these watery discharges, there was confusion between the types of discharge. But if they [women] have STD, they can still say, "It is a discharge I have been warned about. They say when we practice family planning women are going to have this watery discharge." Women were having an advantage through that. They wanted to rule out the STD [i.e., to argue to their husband that they did not have STDs] because of the pill.

Similarly, the libido-suppressant effects of the pill could be used by women as an excuse for not wanting sexual relations with their husbands, when (according to the FPWs) the real reason for avoiding sex lay deeper in the marital relationship. Hormonal contraceptives could be used to explain a problem internal to the marriage. According to Mrs. Imelda Mudarikiri,

> [Clients were] saying that if you are on Depo or the pill there is loss of libido. But after trying to find out the cause of that libido most of the time we discovered that they are not in good books with their husbands, so that would be loss of libido.

Men could also use the idea that the pill lessened libido to explain away their wives' dissatisfaction with the husbands' sexual prowess, or lack thereof. Mrs. Judith Rasika said that husbands would use the wife's use of the pill as an explanation for her "coldness," when the real explanation lay in their own shortcomings as lovers.[34] She offered advice to the wives:

> It was said that when you take the pill you will have a loss of libido, and we used to ask them [women who complained of this] if their husband romances them before having sex. Then they would say, "No, we don't do anything romantic when we have sex, he just wants it right away." So we could tell them no, you must begin making love with foreplay and caresses. Then you see that you should continue like this, but if loss of libido contin-ues even when you do this, then you can go to the clinic. People were say-ing that the pill causes loss of libido. (tr. AK)

## CONCLUSION

In this chapter, I have discussed how knowledge about the body and its workings affected what women and men did with Depo and the pill and how that knowledge differed between clinical biomedicine and local Shona ethno-physiology. In particular, I believe that the idea of the unbounded female body, in which the effects of contraceptive use or other sexual or reproductive choices by a woman affect the physical and spiritual health of others, sheds light on the debates and contestations over these new methods.

In Western medicine, or Western science in general, the individual body is defined by the surface of the skin and is regarded as radically discontinuous from such entities as "the body of society" or "the body politic." The relation between an individual body and the social world in which it is embedded is assumed to be one-way—our bodies can be injured by stress or damaged by the health consequences of the social relations in which we are involved (as through work-related injuries or domestic violence), yet the consequences of what we choose to do with our bodies do not transmit themselves so easily back to the social world. Shona body knowledge offers a different way of understanding the body—as part of a net of causes and effects, actions and consequences, which ripples back and forth between the embodied ego and a wide array of alters. The alters most affected are those connected through sex-ual or reproductive links, such as marriage partners or children.

However, while people's knowledge about their bodies is crucial to the way they use reproductive technologies, I do not want to give the impression that people are "cultural dupes" with respect to what they know about their bodies. In the latter part of this chapter, I have shown how both women and men could use what was known about family planning and other bodily processes as new resources for them to achieve their own ends, be it the resumption of a sexual life after menopause, the concealment of an STD, or the end of a marriage. The pill and Depo were meant for spacing or limiting births, but they could be put into the service of very different personal agendas.

## NOTES

1. In deference to the wishes of the people I interviewed for this section, I will not describe the precise details of how and where to obtain the ingredients for traditional methods of birth control. See chapter 5 for some thoughts as to why they did not want me to make the details widely known.

2. I use the term "traditional" although I am aware that making a distinction between "traditional" and "modern" practices is analytically difficult, if not pointless. My informants, both FPWs and non-FPWs, however, made a strong distinction in their discussions of fertility control. These methods I discuss here were referred to in English as "traditional methods," or "doing traditional," in Shona as "*kuronga mhuri kwekarekare*" or "*kuronga mhuri kwechiShona/kwechivanhu*" ("family planning of long ago" or "family planning of the way of the Shona/of the way of the people"). The newer contraceptive methods such as pills and injections were referred to as "*kuronga mhuri kwemazuva ano*" or "*kuronga mhuri kwechirungu*" ("family planning of nowadays" or "of white people"), or by use of the English term "family planning" or "planning." In English interviews, these were universally called "modern methods."

3. I did hear one reference to "traditional" ways of rendering oneself sterile (as distinct from being cursed with infertility by an enemy). Mrs. Marjoree Mugwagwa said that some people in her area had deliberately sterilized themselves with herbal concoctions—but she went on to say that these women later regretted their decision and came to her clinic asking her to "undo" the sterilization, which she was unable to do.

4. See also Cornwall 1990 for an alternate classification of the methods I call "traditional" (80–88). Cornwall reports that the use of these methods was much less common than my respondents claimed.

5. Interestingly, no one that I talked to shared the belief common in many European societies that coitus interruptus could be harmful for the man. Instead, the ability to practice withdrawal was seen as a sign of strength and self-control, and many elderly women praised the men of their generation, saying that they were able to use withdrawal alone to space their children, as part of their general ability to practice *kuzvibata* (exercise self-control or self-mastery), an ability that has been lost since the encroachment of *chirungu* practices, particularly the adoption of *chirungu* diets.

6. The fact that menstruation did not always stop when women used these methods was not inconsistent, as menstrual blood was thought to be the product of many things besides the lining of the womb, including sperm left over from intercourse, blood from other parts of the body, excess vaginal secretions, and generic dirt produced by everyday living.

7. This is corroborated by Mhloyi (1991) who concluded that periods of breastfeeding had been declining from generation to generation and that lactational amenorrhea was not a significant means of child-spacing in Zimbabwe, as compared with West Africa.

8. "Mrs. Nyamera" is a pseudonym for a respondent from Wedza, who was not a family planning worker. All respondents from Wedza have pseudonyms and are identified only by title and family name, unlike family planning worker respondents, who are identified by title, first name, and family name (e.g., Mrs. Gladys Chitsungo).

9. Translated from Shona by Nyaradzo Shayanewako, my research assistant.

10. Another form of ethnomedicine that might be considered part of the same class of medicines as the love potions were the vaginal tightening and drying agents used by women in the belief that these made sex more pleasurable to their male partners, and thereby gave the women an advantage over their husbands. Mrs. Tendai Masvika used these agents to illustrate her statement that "we women, we know how to do these things. We hide so many things form our husbands."

11. For a discussion of the relationships between persistent concerns about infertility and the use of "modern" contraceptives in a different African context, see Benefo 1997.

12. My information about how to reverse *mishonga yekupfeka* is not as clear as it is for the other methods—it seems that to use the method "properly" a woman had to follow specific rituals when removing the belts. However, many women simply cut them or took them off on their own, although this could lay them open to reproductive mishaps.

13. Diet was also brought up by elderly people as a sign of the cleavage between generations, and food was often brought up in interview contexts in which we were discussing the difference between the past and the present. They said that young people (who could be any age from early teens to their fifties) ate *chirungu* diets, including bread, cake, tea, sugar, and Cokes, while older people prided themselves on sticking to "true" Shona diets (in theory if not always in practice, because I met many old men and women who liked tea and other *chirungu* commodities).

14. In Thompson's (2000) interviews with elderly women in Madziwa Communal Land about the ways that *chirungu* commodities had affected their lives, the women described sugar as a fascinating, powerfully attractive, but ultimately destructive substance, and mimed uncontrollable appetite when acting out the ways that they cooked with or consumed sugar. The desire for sugar caused their menfolk to leave off traditional Shona farming and hunting in order to enter into wage relationships with whites, to earn the money to buy sugar for their demanding families. The parallels with cocaine—another pernicious white powdery substance—are striking.

15. The importance of harmony between one's cultural allegiance, be it to "Shona culture" or to *chirungu,* and the things one puts in one's body is corroborated by Percival (1989) who reported, in her survey of family practices of Zimbabwean women in the 1980s, that young women who were periodically "possessed" by ancestral spirits as a means of communication with their living descendants and were advised to abstain from using the pill or other "Western" birth control methods. According to Percival's informants, the disjuncture between the *chirungu*-ness of the methods and the Shona-ness of the ancestral spirits, who episodically used these young women as their channel, was so profound that the women would experience severe physical side effects from the pill, beyond what their non-spirit-possessed peers would undergo. The ancestral spirits and the *chirungu* medicines could not coexist peacefully in the same body.

16. See Kaler and Watkins 2001 for similar accounts by FPWs in Kenya.

17. Some FPWs did re-interpret "traditional" within a biomedical context, telling me for example that tying beads around one's waist worked because it created a strong psychological block against pregnancy, not because the beads were effective in themselves.

18. This side effect could also be hazardous for the woman, as it could be a way for the husband to discover that his wife was using contraceptives: "He is going to ask what has happened to you [if your vaginal secretions vary in quantity or consistency], because you know with our African husbands they like this dry vagina and that is a true fact" (interview with Mrs. Phoebe Mpezeni).

19. Similar objections from men are being voiced in pilot studies of the acceptability of the new "female condom" or "femidom" in Zimbabwe. The lubricant supplied with the

female condom is reportedly suspiciously similar to excess vaginal secretions (Ray et al. 1995).

20. The use of contraceptives, beginning in the1970s, is also linked to the emergence of AIDS in the 1980s."Many Africans are now saying that that [family planning] is what is presently causing AIDS" (correspondence with Mrs. Bhenge, tr. AK [translated by Amy Kaler]). Respondents made the link between family planning and STDs through the medium of increased prostitution, which is made possible when women can indulge in sex without the fear of illicit pregnancies: "When there is a lot of prostitution, some people just say, 'Let [us] take passports [and go abroad]' That is how AIDS has come, coming from the white people of South Africa" (correspondence with Mrs. Mugodhi, tr. AK).

21. Question asked by Amy Kaler.

22. See Cornwall (1990:32) for accounts of women who stopped using contraceptives because they feared that their already irregular menstrual periods would stop altogether.

23. Menstrual disruption could also inform a man that his wife was using family planning without his consent, as her amenorrhea or continuous bleeding betrayed her secret. Women who were "private acceptors" invested much time and energy in finding strategies to hide the menstrual side effects of the new methods. See chapter 4 for a full discussion of how these side effects were managed by private acceptors.

24. Mrs. Chitsungo describes regular menstruation as "tradition," a word also used to identify marriage rituals, respectful greetings, dances, and other manifestations of "our Shona culture." The use of tradition with respect to a bodily process suggests to me another example of the strong identification between Shona bodies and Shona-ness, or Shona culture.

25. These taboos have reportedly largely lost their force, and were never observed as strictly as similar taboos further north in Africa (Mhloyi 1991).

26. Similar dangers are said to attend a man who has sex with a woman who has had sex with another man since her last period, so that the first man's semen has not yet been washed out by menstruation. In a recent study on the acceptability of the female condom in Zimbabwe, Ray and colleagues (1995) found that men complained about the lubricants provided with the female condoms (as well as vaginal secretions) on the grounds that they indicated that another man might have been there in the recent past. However, the proliferation of casual commercialized sex and of multiple partners in Zimbabwe suggests that this belief, like many others, may affect people's ideas about sex and sexual technologies, but does not determine actual practices.

27. I was unable to find out exactly what "acting like a man" meant in the context of amenorrhea, although this would be a fascinating topic to pursue.

28. In Wedza and other places, fears of infertility took the form of believing that the effects of Depo would be measured in years rather than the months that the FPWs claimed they would last—for example, that an injection would be effective for three years rather than three months.

29. Suspicions of the government's interest in African sterility dated back to the 1940s; see chapter 6.

30. For more Zimbabwean examples of how commodities acquire new meanings and new uses, see Burke's (1996) fascinating work on the accretion of local meanings by Western commodities such as new types of soaps, cosmetics, or blankets in Zimbabwe.

31. See Cornwall (1990) for an account of the Shona notion of *mafundo,* pre-embryonic entities in women's abdomen, which are present in finite numbers from birth and which all ought to be brought into the world. Once all the *mafundo* have been born, a woman enters menopause. See Bledsoe (1998) for a more general discussion of the ramifications of the

notion that embryos are immanent in women's bodies and that each woman has a set number to bring into the world.

32. The FPWs' interpretation that family planning was merely the pretext for the divorce, rather than the real reason, is open to question. As mentioned above, FPWs had a vested interest in absolving their new methods from any suggestion that they led to adultery or promiscuity. Thus, it would be consistent for them to argue that husbands or jealous rivals simply seized on the evidence of family planning as the quickest way to manufacture grounds for a divorce, rather than that the wife might actually have been involved in adultery with the aid of the pills.

33. Even for women who were not involved in extramarital liaisons, the frequent confusion between the side effects of the hormonal contraceptives and the symptoms of STDs was a source of embarrassment, as health workers assumed their complaints were because of STDs. Mrs. Mbira reported indignantly that when she went to a clinic with complaints about painful side effects from her contraceptive method, the clinic workers assumed that she had contracted a sexually transmitted disease from extramarital affairs:

> Those people [at the clinic] they are rough, they are rude. I used an injection
> but now I am suffering from uterus problems. They said I had an STD but they
> didn't even check the problem! I am married, me and my husband we are
> faithful! The workers are rough, they are rude, they treated me badly. (tr. NS)

34. Once again, FPWs had a professional interest in exonerating the pill from charges against it, including charges that it destroyed libido. This professional interest may explain why Mrs. Rasika and others said that the pill was being used as a convenient explanation for a deteriorating sexual relationship but did not actually cause the deterioration.

# 4

# CONTRACEPTION AS SUBVERSION: GENDER AND POWER IN MARITAL RELATIONSHIPS, 1960S AND 1970S

## INTRODUCTION

Pills and injections gave women a new way to choose when and whether children would be born. Yet the children whose births were delayed or prevented were not theirs alone, but were also claimed by the men who had married the women. Differences of opinion between husbands and wives about how many children to have and when to have them could kindle into outright conflict, now that women had the pill to help them get their own way.

Conflicts flared not only over the manifest purpose of contraceptives—to prevent conception—but also over issues of female sexuality and male power, which were linked to the growing availability of family planning. Male anger about the pill and injection was also imbued with years of disempowerment and degradation at the hands of the white state. By the time contraceptives came to African communities in the late 1960s, African men had already faced the loss of their economic and spiritual wealth to the forced destocking of their cattle and reduction of their agricultural lands in the 1940s and 1950s; the alienation of their labor in order to raise cash to pay head taxes since virtually the beginning of white rule; and the symbolic emasculation of being constantly reminded of their inferior status.

Thus, the arrival of family planning methods meant not only that men worried about what their wives were up to, but that they were also at risk of losing control over childbearing matters to the forces of white settlement. With these pills and injections proffered by the whites, men were not only at risk of losing some of their domestic power—they were also losing it to a culturally alien force, strongly associated with the malevolent designs of white colonialism. Male hostility toward these new methods, frequently expressed as fears that these methods gave women too much sexual and reproductive freedom, was born out of a complicated mix of gender politics in both their homes and their nation.

Depo and the pill are hardly unique in their ability to spark conflict between husband and wife. In Rhodesia, as everywhere else, marital relations were fraught with struggles over who shall control what resource, be it money, food, land, or labor. The arrival of these new contraceptives meant that fertility was added to this list of contested resources in the late 1960s. However, struggles over the contraception rarely turned into outright battle. Because the pill, and to an even greater extent the Depo injection, could be hidden from husbands, these conflicts were played out through secrecy and evasion, rather than confrontation. Women talked of "hiding" or "stealing" to describe how they kept their contraceptive use out of the reach of their husbands, even as the husbands in turn sought to "catch" their evasive, escaping wives.

## THE HOUSEHOLD AS A SITE OF CONFLICT OVER RESOURCES

In all cultures, the household and the family are idealized as the site of harmony and cooperation, set apart from the harsher exigencies of the market or the polity. However, studies of African families, as well as families in other places, has produced a more ambiguous vision of what really happens in families. Households, and specifically the relations between husband and wife, are instead sites of struggle between genders over production and consumption of resources (e.g., Geisler 1993, Guyer 1988, Haddad and Hoddinott 1991, Kennedy and Peters 1992, Kongstedt and Monsted 1980, Munachonga 1988, Pankhurst and Jacobs 1988).

For example, Fapohunda (1978, 1988) has demonstrated that Yoruba men and women have their own gender-specific patterns of production and consumption, and guard the details of their income from their spouses with great secrecy. This secrecy enables them to protect their ability to buy the goods that are appropriate and necessary for each gender—such as the purchase of children's clothing for the women, or the purchase of large article of furniture for the men—and to prevent their spouses from capturing income. What economists like Fapohunda have done for income streams, anthropologists like Vaughan and Moore (1994, especially chapters 3, 7, and 8) have done for the circulation of foodstuffs, emphasizing how the struggles to capture women's agricultural labor for market production comes to the fore in peasant agriculture. These struggles have direct implications for the health of the woman, and of her children, as poor women come into conflict with their husbands over the use of her resources of time, labor, money, and her body itself, which she needs to "produce" the health of herself and her present and future children (MacCormack 1998).

In most cases, men's success in capturing women's labor power and resources is not matched by women's success in diverting their husbands' resources of labor and money into their own projects. Men usually have a store of customary norms and ideologies that emphasize patriarchal control over women and land, which they can use to legitimate their claims. Although norms may exist that guarantee to women the right to a plot of land or to expect subsistence from the husband, these have unfortunately proven quite fragile when faced with opportunities for men to profit by usurping the resources of their wives. Geisler (1993) suggests that changes like the advent of cash crops have enhanced men's abilities to capture women's time and labor to direct it into their own male consumption patterns. In her Zambian study, as a result of changes in the market structure for crops, family agricultural practices increasingly deviated from villagers' professed ideals of complementarity and mutual responsibility between husbands and wives for the welfare of the family:

Wives ... by virtue of being identified with the household sphere had been increasingly burdened with the provision of consumer goods and other cash requirements for household needs. Male interests determined the conceptual boundaries between cash and food crops. . . . While husbands could divert part of their wives' crops from household consumption, wives themselves, far from being able to do this, could not even ensure that their husband' crops remained within the household. Married women generally had little control over "their" production. (Geisler 1993:1971)

In addition, the selective reinforcement of patriarchal structures by colonial and postcolonial governments enhanced men's power in the household at the expense of the women's, increasing their ability to appropriate their wives' labor and other resources (for the Zimbabwean context, see Courville 1993, Goebel 1998, and Schmidt 1992).[1] Nonetheless, the balance of power in the household can be tipped to favor women under certain circumstances, as "positions of superiority and subordination are neither eternal nor unchangeable" (Silberschmidt 1992:238).

Silberschmidt provides an example of this changing balance in a district of Kenya. In the 1980s, this district was affected by crises of proletarianization and land pressure, which adversely affected men's ability to live their identities as providers and household heads, and which denied them opportunities to act out these identities. Because of economic changes that had a negative impact on men's life chances, from which women were relatively more insulated, their wives were able to assert control over their own labor and resources. This assertion, however, came at great cost in terms of poor marital relations, violence, and verbal abuse from their frustrated and bitter husbands.

The area that is most marked by gender struggle over resources is reproduction. Other types of resources, such as agricultural labor or cash, can (in theory at least) slide from man to woman according to individual interest and the social structure in which the man or woman lives—women as well as men can work for money, grow crops, and so on. Whether or not they do so is the result of social structures and pressures, which are at least to some degree malleable. However, reproduction is not even potentially gender-neutral. If a man wishes to have children whom he can claim as his, he *must* come to some sort of arrangement with some woman to bear them for him. The getting of children, unlike the getting of money, food, or labor, must always be mediated through a woman. Wealth or social status does not change this essential relationship— fertility is always, inevitably, the subject of negotiation between men and the women they need in order to have children. Contraception, therefore, emerges over and over again as an area of conflict between husbands and wives.

## MARITAL STRUGGLES OVER RESOURCES IN ZIMBABWE

In 1994, Cecilia Manyame and Tsitsi Kuuya of the Zimbabwe Women's Resource Centre and Network (ZWRCN) held large focus group meetings with rural women in eight sites across Zimbabwe. The intent of the meetings was to explore, in the words of Manyame and Kuuya, the ways in which women perceive "their culture" as an obstacle or an asset to local economic development and to encourage the women to "critically analyze culture" (1). Although the women in the studies did not issue blanket condemnations of their men, or issue ringing manifestoes against patriarchy, the behavior of men in trying to capture or control their wives' time and labor came in for constant criticism.

This criticism should not be interpreted as a totalizing statement about the unpleasantness of all Zimbabwean men. Like everywhere in the world, individual marriages and families show great idiosyncratic variations in the ways in which patriarchy is manifested. It would be wrong to extrapolate from this survey that all Zimbabwean marriages are battlefields—as I show later in this chapter, many men and women did manage to come to mutually agreeable arrangements about how to manage wives' fertility. Some women were content to follow their husband's lead in this area, and other women were able to negotiate and discuss the process of family building with him. However, women's descriptions of their lives are rife with stories of opposition to and attempts at subversion of their husbands' claims on their bodies and their resources, suggesting that this kind of conflict is, if not ubiquitous, at least well-known. Secrecy and evasion were the most common strategies women used. As Mrs. Tendai Masvika put it, speaking not only about taking pills but about a whole range of activities that women kept secret from their husbands, "We are women, we know how to do these things. We hide so many things from our husbands."[2]

In the ZWRCN interviews, the major source of complaints was male appropriation of women's contributions to agriculture, to the productivity and fertility of the land. Several examples from ZWRCN's 1994 report follow:

- The disposition of crops grown by women on land owned by men was a sore spot for most of the women interviews. In its most extreme form, this led to suicide.[3] In one of the interview sites, wives' unhappiness at the appropriation of their labor by their husbands was manifested by "on average not less than 10 suicides every post-harvest because some men squandered the family's hard-earned income. The women said they worked hard in the field spending the little income they had on pesticides, seeds, and labor. After the harvest, the men took all the money and used it as they saw fit. In order to "fix" the men, some of the women used pesticides to kill themselves" (8).

- The alienation of land, known in Shona as *tsewu,* which women had used for "their" crops (usually used for subsistence and informal marketing to buy household needs such as cooking oil or soap) in order to plant "men's" crops (usually sold to the parastatal marketing boards, with the income remaining under the control of the men).

- The use of women's credit record by men to obtain loans from the Agricultural Finance Corporation, the state-run body that provides loans to small-scale farmers, when the husband's credit record was poor or when he had outstanding loans.

- The need for women to keep control of the income they earned from making pots, weaving mats, or brewing beer, by secrecy if necessary, to prevent it being taken by husbands and used for beer-drinking, sometimes linked to the proliferation of women's clubs or women's revolving credit schemes. Similarly, women spoke of men's practices of hiding their money from their wives, often by burying it the ground. "The wife was not told where the money had been kept. This was for her own protection from possible harm should someone want to steal the money and blackmail the woman in the process. But it was also believed the women could not keep secrets" (41).

Throughout focus group meetings, women repeatedly cautioned one another to keep their plans and their knowledge secret from men, and not to tell the men what they had learned about their rights under civil law, potential access to new sources of credit, and other resources that could be interpreted as a threat to their husbands' control. When the researchers asked the women what they would say to their husbands when the husbands asked what their wives had been doing at the focus group meeting,

> At Bonda, women said that they would tell their husband that they were discussing women's development, they cautioned each other against telling the men that they had discussed women's oppression by men or empowerment of women, or even mention the Civil Marriages Act [which gives women more rights to marital property than "customary" marriage regimes] as this would make men suspicious. (23)

> What would they say they had been discussing at the women's meeting? A few women said that they would tell their families that they had been discussing life in Nemangwe [district]. An elderly woman stood up and said, "if we go back and say that we were discussing oppression of women by men we will bring trouble on ourselves, instead we shall say that we were discussing [income generating] projects." The women clapped and ululated to that. Another woman stood up and added that the women should tell the men what they wanted to hear, for example, that "we were being reminded how to look after our men properly." This suggestion was also received with glee, clapping, and ululation. (49)

> [In Marenga district] What would they tell their families? They would say that they had been discussing "how to look after our homes and how to look after our men." The older ones cautioned against telling the men that the meeting had anything to do with the empowerment of women, arguing that after all women have always been one step ahead of their men, that clever women never revealed all their secrets and strategies to men. (55)

Secrecy and evasion were common among married Zimbabwean women and, moreover, were quite acceptable and justifiable by the women themselves (although they might only be acknowledged in all-women gatherings). The ubiquity and acceptability of secrecy can explain how quickly women caught on to the idea of hiding their pill and Depo use from their husbands.

## THE "PRIVATE ACCEPTOR ISSUE"

In this chapter, I focus on the experiences of those family planning clients known euphemistically as "private acceptors" or "private planners"—married women who used the pill, the Depo-Provera contraceptive injection, and the intrauterine device (IUD) without the consent or knowledge of their husbands in the 1960s and 1970s. The exact number of these women is impossible to know, as very few of the Family Planning Association of Rhodesia's (FPAR's) records survive, and those that do survive are erratic and unreliable. My interviews with both family planning workers (FPWs) and ordinary men and women are probably the best source yet of information about private acceptors, even though quantitative information is lacking.

In discussing private acceptance, I run the risk of presenting Zimbabwean men as a monolithic group bent on controlling their wives' fertility, oblivious to their wives' interests in spacing or limiting births, and unwilling to listen to reason from women or FPWs. My experience living and working in Zimbabwe has convinced me that Zimbabwean men cannot be categorized so neatly, and that they are no more oafs or ogres than any other men in any other situation. Many men—including the male FPWs interviewed here—thought and acted in ways that were not dictated by an obsession with patriarchal norms, or with proving their authority at the expense of their wife. As Mr. Tsinza of Buhera said, "We men are also human beings, we know that having children brings labor pains and health problems, we really understand, so some men allow their wives to use pills" (tr. NS). While Shona culture, at least as interpreted to me, stresses men's authority over women and, in particular, the transfer of control over women's reproductive capacities to her husband and his family at the time of marriage, Shona marital norms also stress complementarity and mutual responsibility, so that a good husband takes care of his wife's ability to have children and does not abuse it. Many husbands did strive to live up to this charge, such as the husband of Mrs. Jongwe:

> My husband wanted children, because he said he was able to raise them. . . . I can say that at that time [during her childbearing years] I was a queen, because every time when I was pregnant I was not allowed to work [in the fields]. He paid money for a house maid, and when I was sick a private doctor would be called.[4] (tr. NS)

In this chapter, however, I focus on marriages in which men did not treat their wives like "queens" (or even, some women said, like "human beings") and in which male control of women's fertility was the source of stress for the wives. These accounts of marriages in which men did not treat their wives with the respect the women thought they deserved are also worthy of note because they show, in attenuated form, the gender conflict that marked many other marriages. Because the lines of male control and female resistance are so sharply drawn here, these cases are heuristically important for understanding the gender relations that shaped ideas and actions about family planning in most marriages.

The only surviving data on the extent of "private acceptance" is from a 1974 study of FPWs' job functions. As part of this study, 74 FPWs were asked about the major obstacles they faced in increasing the number of family planning clients in their area. In response to the statement "Women tend to be fairly ready to listen to education about family planning. What are they able to do if their menfolk are unwilling?" Ninety-six percent of FPWs responded that women in their area practiced privately, as compared with 63% who said that the women redoubled their efforts to persuade their husband, and 17% who reported that women asked the FPW for help in convincing their husbands (Geraty 1973:33).

More recent studies suggest that private acceptance is a live issue in the memories of Zimbabwean women. Gibney (1993:60) reports that, immediately after independence, discussions at women's clubs meetings in rural areas repeatedly raised the subject of women's desires for "safe, effective child-spacing methods which would not be visible to men." Gibney also found that many women reported that they had used birth control in secret without their husband's knowledge. She reported this result according to educational status, and found that among women with zero to four years of education 39% said they themselves had use contraception against their husband's wishes. Because of the extremely limited access to education that Zimbabwe women had before independence, and because of the massive expansion of primary and secondary education over the past 16 years, the women with the lowest level of education are also likely to be the oldest. Thus, this group is likely to contain the women whose experiences are the subject of this book—women who, in the 1970s, were already married with children.[5]

In my interviews, former FPWs estimated the percentage of contracepting women in their area who were private acceptors in the 1970s between 20% to 90%, depending on district. Most estimates were between one-third and one-half. I found no meaningful correlation between the economic structure of an area and the proportions of private acceptors claimed for it, except for a tendency for more private acceptors to be reported in rural areas as opposed to urban ones.[6] The number of private acceptors also did not appear to vary with the proportion of all women using contraception in an area, as FPWs reported both high and low levels of private acceptors for areas with high proportions of contraception users.

Although no one is sure just how many women were private acceptors, the issues of husbandly opposition to contraceptives and women's evasion are omnipresent in the work of the FPAR, from their beginnings in urban townships in the early 1960s onward. The organization developed strategies based on the assumption that many, if not most, women wanted to circumvent their husband's wishes and get contraception secretly. The very earliest FPWs who brought pessaries and foam to postpartum women in the townships in the late 1950s disguised themselves as antenatal nurses to get access to home. In the following decade and a half, as family planning became institutionalized in clinics, record-keeping forms had spaces for noting whether or not a client's husband was opposed to family planning, and in many clinics the records of private acceptors were stored separately from those who were contracepting with the consent of their husbands. The community-based distributor (CBD) system, was brought in, according to the FPW who claimed to have thought of the idea, to alleviate problems for rural women of travel time and cost, and also so that "nobody could know" that a woman was being given contraceptives in the privacy of her own home (interview with Mr. Alec Ndhlukula).

In discussing the logistics of getting contraceptives to women clients, FPWs were proud of the ways in which they could help women to hide their use of contraceptives. They praised the use of mobile well-baby clinics for distributing contraceptives under cover of providing basic pediatric care, and thoroughly approved of clinic bookkeeping systems that segregated the records of "private acceptors" from the records of those whose husbands were informed and approving.

> The women could easily understand but the men were very hard and difficult. Sometimes the women would just come without the husband's knowledge, they would just come to us. They would say, "We are bringing the children for a well-baby clinic." We would try to get the same dates as the well-baby clinics that were being done by Public Health. We would go together so that when they come we would meet them and talk to them. Everybody thinks they have just come for the well-baby clinic. (interview with Mrs. Eugenia Mashonga)

> We would go hand in hand with the baby clinics, the EPI [Extended Programme of Immunization] [nursing] sisters, so they [women] could just say "We are taking the child for immunization." At the same time we would motivate them to Depo, it was three monthly, they would also bring the child monthly so we could check on them . . . Since we were working hand in hand with the EPI sisters we would tell them [women who wanted to use Depo secretly] to go to the sisters, they would know when we are to come. . . . I remember one woman, she was very old, forty years, and she had nine children and she was nursing the ninth child, and she said, "Do you know what I have told my husband? I told him that the [ninth] child is very sick and must be weighed every month, and then I was told to bring the child for weighing and supplementary food supplies every three months," then every three months her Depo was renewed. She would bring the child to the baby clinic and we would see that the child is quite well from sickness. She went on like that for years. She said [to her husband], "I have taken the child to the clinic, and he was okay and he was weighed, but I have to come back in three months, the child still has some problems." (interview with Mrs. Eugenia Banga)

> At the time many of the mobiles [mobile clinics] were put in shopping areas, so they [women clients] could go for shopping. All the stations here in Zvishavane were shopping centers, so that if one was going, she could just say, "I am going to get bread or maybe soap," but she knows exactly what she will be after. She just runs into the mobile, then runs out. (interview with Mr. Richard Chidakwa)

So what we did for these women, we talked to them, explained the methods
to them, told them to choose what methods they want. But with the pill it
was difficult, they had to hide the pill, so most of them resorted to the injection. They had the injection, they leave their [record] cards in the clinic, we
give them a small piece of paper with the date to come in or the number of
their card, and when they come in we just pull out their card. So when somebody sees the date they won't suspect anything. But we never had any problems. (interview with Mrs. Shamiso Kudakwashe)

As Mrs. Kudakwashe suggests, private acceptance had major ramifications
for method choice; and the effects of private acceptance can be seen in the
skew of method preferences among Zimbabwean women. From the 1960s
onward, the contraceptive methods available through the FPAR and allied
clinics were the contraceptive pill, the IUD ("the loop"), and, after 1972, the
Depo-Provera injection.[7] Of these, the most popular by far was Depo.[8] When
I asked FPWs the reason why their clients preferred Depo, despite the fact that
it had more associated side effects than the other two methods and despite the
persistent strong rumors that Depo caused permanent sterility, FPWs gave two
main answers: (1) that Depo was convenient for "illiterate" or "drunken"
women who could not remember to take a pill every day; and (2) that Depo,
especially because it was dispensed through infant health and general clinics,
could be hidden from husbands (and in-laws, as discussed in chapter 5). After
1972, not even a telltale packet of pills could be found.

Oh, Depo was the most popular, Depo was compared to none! Because it had
a lot of advantages to the woman, the first is the privacy and the second is timing, it just gives someone to forget about it for three or six months . . . Depo
was compared to nothing! (interview with Mr. Timothy Nzuma)

With Depo the people came, they really came! (interview with Mrs. Tendai
Masvika)

Before Depo all women would like the pill . . . but when Depo came almost
ninety-nine percent were on Depo, they all liked Depo. (interview with Mrs.
Gloria Tekere)

FPWs linked the preference for Depo explicitly to private acceptance:

In those days the injection was favored, as I told you women were just hiding against their men because the men didn't want family planning . . . They
were telling me that the men were really angry about it, they could be beaten
because of it. (interview with Mrs. Gladys Chitsungo)

They were all in need of Depo-Provera just because they can do it privately
on Depo [rather] than on pills. In the evening [when the men are home],

men can see that she is taking pills, but with Depo you won't know it. (interview with Mrs. Promise Billo)

It was really popular and it really made the family planning go, the Depo, it was really very very popular with women for the fact that many men didn't actually permit their wives to be on family planning, so Depo was the best method for that. (interview with Mr. Timothy Nzuma)

Despite the side effects and the rumors of sterility that attended Depo, women quickly took up the new injection.

If you say your husband is opposed, women would come up with ways of how they are going to practice without their husband knowing. Some would actually opt for Depo because it would be their secret and the nurses. [AK: It was so popular] Yes, and the reason was that confidentiality was easy to maintain and replacement, unlike tablets that you finish a packet in a month, with Depo you could go for three months and then come back. You could just say, "I am going to the clinic for something," it as so easy to handle. So popular it could be seen as that women loved it, but it was for social reasons that they wanted it. (interview with Mrs. Salina Mumbengegwi)

With Depo, women could comply with their husbands' (and their own) desires for sex without risking pregnancy. They could also appear to comply with their husbands' wishes for more children without revealing that they were in fact taking steps to prevent those desires from being realized. In short, Depo let women take control of their childbearing without confrontation, or even discussion. The injection let women keep up a facade of being good or docile wives, to circumvent the operation of patriarchal authority in the home without confronting it directly.

Many women were using without telling their husbands. It doesn't mean that they don't tell them completely, no, they may tell them but they say, "If you use it I will divorce you, I don't want it," So women think about problems when giving birth, poverty in the house or the family, so they use it without telling their husbands. If he says, "I want a child," they say, "I don't know what is causing me from getting pregnant." (interview with Mrs. P. Marufu)

[AK: Did you have women clients who didn't tell their husbands?] Very much so. What we did normally was we asked the woman to go and talk to the man, so she would go and talk to him, and the man totally refuses. He doesn't want to hear anything about family planning, he doesn't want to see any pill, he doesn't want to see family planning card in the home. Some wanted more children, some might have one-sex children, girls only in the family, so he thought if she carries on he might get the other sex. Then the other lot, some said the woman could be running around because she knows she wouldn't get pregnant, she could be running around with others. And other men just didn't understand. So what we did for these women, we talked to them, explained the methods to them, told them to choose what methods they want. But with the pill it was difficult, they had to hide the pill, so most of them resorted to the injection. (interview with Mrs. Shamiso Kudakwashe)

Particularly men were not interested in family planning, only women because they were the sufferers, they could accept the methods. Some could just say, "I will do it while my husband doesn't know, if I tell him he will stop me, saying, 'what do you want to do, you are trying to look for other men, what do you want to do?'" So women were accepting the pill alone while the husband doesn't know and some could come for Depo-Provera and so on. (interview with Mr. T.J. Mugariri)

One FPW, Mrs. Hilda Bulle, used the injection herself because it allowed her to avoid a confrontation with her husband, as well as allowing her freedom from having another child while she decided whether or not she wanted to stay in the marriage:

The card [medical record] remained at the clinic and I did not take the card home. I remember my husband saying, "I want another child," and I said, "It's not my fault that I can't have a child, it is impossible," and yet I knew.

Non-FPWs in Wedza and Buhera also confirmed that the popularity of the injection was linked to its invisibility. Mrs. Jongwe's story about her marriage in the mid-1970s is typical:

My dear, giving birth is very painful. Men just want children, so it's up to us women to rest [create intervals between pregnancies]. I was injected privately . . . Men actually during that time, they didn't want to hear about family planning. My husband didn't want but I was stealing [using family planning without permission] . . . A doctor tried to explain to him after my second miscarriage that we should plan our family or he ought to give me a rest [abstain from sexual relations] but he refused point blank. I started stealing injections and the pill [using them without permission]. Pills were difficult to use because he was always looking for them everywhere. I used only two packets and I hid them in the toilet, then every time in the evening when I took one I swallowed them with saliva, not even water. (tr. NS)

As men became aware of Depo, they realized that their wives had a way to circumvent their wishes. As Mr. Bimha said resignedly, with the arrival of the injection, "a woman is a person who can have what she wants, no matter if you forbid her she will steal" (tr. NS).

## PRIVATE ACCEPTANCE AND THE VALUE OF CHILDREN

Why was private acceptance necessary? Why did men oppose the use of these new technologies by their wives? In nearly every interview that I conducted, when I asked, "What problems did you face when you were working for family planning?" the answer I was given was either "husbands" or the more general "men."[9] In the demographic and sociological literature on large-scale fertility changes, it is almost taken for granted that a sizable proportion of men[10] resist new means of fertility regulation and that, depending on the writer's perspective, either education and motivation or overall socioeconomic change are needed to neutralize this resistance. In this chapter, however, rather than asking, "What can be done about male opposition?" I ask instead "Why did some men oppose new means of fertility regulation?" and "What did women do about this?"

When I asked FPWs and non-FPWs why the men in their area did not like family planning, I received a variety of answers. Some interview respondents, FPWs and non-FPWs alike, gave answers related to the value of children to the family and the household economy. These reasons are consistent with mainstream thinking in demography, which stresses cost-benefit accounting of the value of the marginal child as the source of decisions about whether or not to have that child. Reasons related to this value-of-children calculation include the need for help in agricultural labor (particularly in decades past, when land was still relatively plentiful); the possibility that children might be economically successful and send money back for their parents; the bride-prices that fathers eventually receive for their daughters; and the assurance of support in the parents' old age. Less economically based aspects of the value of children include gaining status among men's fellows; wanting to have a "big name" as the father of many children; wanting to demonstrate affluence through their ability to support a large family; and the desire to leave many descendants to remember their father in religious ceremonies.[11] A subset of these reasons involved a sort of cultural reductionism, according to which men refused family planning because it was "part of our African culture" to want many children, and being a "true African" meant having a large family.

Non-FPWs claimed that men wanted both the material and symbolic advantages of having a large family, and thus either forbade their wives to use traditional or modern methods of family planning or married more women in order to have more children.[12] In recalling their own childhoods in the 1930s through 1960s, residents of Wedza recalled that

> Men wanted many children and some ended up having two or three wives for them to have more children. They want mostly boys for their [family] name to grow and to have their own village. Girls were for easy wealth by means of *lobola* [bride-price]. They want them also for easy work in their

fields. They didn't bother even if they didn't educate them. (interview with Mrs. Gudo)

Men wanted to have many children for easy work in the fields and support [in old age] and some they just wanted the big name. (interview with Mrs. Chapungu)

Men wanted many children then, even now we want them. We wanted them for the big name and to have my own village which I will be given by my chief and I will rule with my own sons. My children will help me in every-thing—work, [or] fighting when someone takes himself as superior to me. (interview with Mr. Rukodzi)

Men wanted children. . . . . They want children for them to boast around saying, "I am a man, see I have 17 children and many wives." (interview with Mrs. Hungubwe, tr. NS)

Men's desires for many children were legitimated by *lobola,* the bride-price paid by the family of the husband to the family of the wife. This payment transferred the wife's reproductive abilities to the lineage of the husband, and entitled the husband and his family to expect children. Some men interpreted the transfer of rights implicit in *lobola* quite literally, such as Mr. Rukodzi, who put matters rather crudely:

What can she do if I want children? If she won't have children, I divorce her and marry another wife who will obey my rules. A good wife will obey her husband in everything. Our custom has *lobola,* how can somebody I paid money for not obey my rules? When I want sex, even in the field, she must do so. (tr. NS)

All respondents concurred that men generally derived more benefit than pain from having a large number of children, especially during their youth, before families were firmly locked into the wage economy. However, both men and women were ambivalent about whether women derived more bene-fits from costs from having many children. Some older women mentioned the material support they expected to receive, like Mrs. Nyamera who said she was "looked after properly because of my daughter. I can go to Harare [where her daughter works] and have a comfortable life, I can go to Mutare [where another child lives], so having children is the best thing on earth" (tr. NS). Possible future support from children was also an incentive to have many, not only because of higher child mortality rates in past decades but also because "you don't know who will be good or bad [in moral character and respect shown to parents]" (interview with Mrs. Shirapopo, tr. NS).

However, most people spoke, without prompting, of women being forced to have children, whether because their husbands overrode their wishes, or because women feared sanctions in the form of divorce or being rejected in favor of another wife if they disobeyed their husband's wishes by not being sexually available or by not bearing another child.

> Men liked to have many children. As for women, some of the women wanted, but some were forced by their husbands and the conditions may force you to have [many children], let's say you don't want polygamy, that's when you have more children. (interview with Mrs. Hwiribidi).

> Men wanted to have many children for easy work in the fields and for support and some they just wanted the big name. Women were forced and there was nothing they could do because of *lobola* [the bride-price paid to their parents]. Some of the women were forced to be married to an elder man by their parents because they wanted *lobola*. (interview with Mrs. Chapungu)

> Women liked having children, but not all of them [liked having children] because pregnancy is very painful, so some they don't want to have children, that's why their husbands have many wives. *Lobola* makes a woman subject to everything. . . . You know my dear, the problems of childbearing are mostly for the woman. The men, no matter if you are pregnant, sex is sweet to them, but to a woman after the sweetness pain follow, and to care for the children that's mostly women's work. (interview with Mrs. Hungubwe)

> Some of the women wanted [to have many children] but some didn't. I think those who wanted just wanted to be thanked [appreciated] by their husbands and to avoid divorce and polygamy. Even the elders encouraged many children because when their daughter failed to have children or to reach the number her husband wanted, they gave the husband the sister of the wife. They did this because they were afraid that he will demand his *lobola* or marry another wife which means that the husband's wealth will be eaten by that other family. I can say that having children was encouraged by everyone at that time. (interview with Mrs. Ngururu, tr. NS)

Women had two strong motives for complying with their husbands' wishes for more children. The first was the fear of divorce, or polygamy if their husband was wealthy enough to afford two wives, and the second was the socially enforced sense of obligation brought about by the transfer of *lobola* payments from her family to his.

Even if a wife was not under pressure from her husband to have more children, if she withheld sexual activities from her husband to prevent pregnancy, she risked being supplanted. The specter of a rival wife, who might be more sexually or reproductively available to the husband, was often cited as a powerful reason for women in the years before family planning to expose themselves to the risk of pregnancy over and over again, even when they did not especially want additional children. The pill and Depo could not help the woman whose husband turned to polygamy because she would not have another child, but the new methods did help women to stave off rival wives by allowing them to be sexually available to their husbands without risking pregnancy.

## BAD WIVES AND "FREE WOMEN"

Non-FPWs in Wedza explained male resistance to new methods of contraception in men's desires for many children. However, FPWs pointed to other reasons for hating contraception, reasons that are not based on the goodness of having many children. These are reasons founded in fears about female sexuality, and the danger if it were to be unleashed or uncontrolled. Depo and the pill exacerbated these fears by opening up new opportunities for wives to go bad.

> Actually family planning was looked down upon as something . . . that would remove the control of men from sexuality especially the husbands from their wives so it was really frowned upon when it was introduced, because what do you want family planning for? You want to be promiscuous if you want family planning. So it wasn't taken as a very good thing if you bring it. . . . And we are seen as somebody promoting, how shall I call it, evil living in the society. Yes, immoral living. . . . And now talking about family planning for the woman who doesn't possess anything, who is just carrying the uterus and everything for the man would be a non-starter. 'How can you control my production machine?' my husband would say. 'How can you give it Depo so that it closes for good [referring to a very common rumor that the Depo-Provera injection induced permanent sterility]? Who are you to decide how many children I should have?' (interview with Mrs. Salina Mumbengegwi)

FPWs reported that the men they met during their rounds in the 1970s were strongly opposed to the new methods of contraception because of fears of promiscuity:

> [AK: The men talked about prostitution?] Yes, they were suspecting very much that if the woman is using contraceptives it's easy for her to do anything she wants. (interview with Mrs. Imelda Mudarikiri)

> A lot of them were private acceptors because the men didn't want. The men thought that if a woman went on family planning she now has a certificate to do whatever she wanted without the husband's consent. (interview with Mrs. Hilda Bulle)

> Another issue again, they were suspicious, they say that if a woman is taking a pill or whatever method of family planning she will be so free and independent, she will go about with other men because she is protected. (interview with Mr. Albert Katerere)

Some of us used to be chased with axes! Fieldworkers used to report, "I have arrived at such and such a house and I was chased by such and such a husband he said, 'you are bringing these contraceptives so that my wife can be a prostitute.'" (interview with Mrs. Stella Padoro)

The connection between prostitution and loss of control over women is strengthened by the fact that prostitution (understood as all types of unsanctioned sexual behavior, not merely sex for money) was also used by husbands to justify their objections to their wives engaging in other activities that gave them control over resources beyond the purview of the husband, such as earning their own income. Some FPWs experienced this husbandly objection in their own working lives. Mrs. Rita Masara was encouraged by a local white nurse attached to the mobile clinics to become a field educator in 1972, but her husband refused her permission on the grounds that she would have too many opportunities to be unfaithful if she had her own income: "He thought that if a woman in those days is engaged in [paid] work, she is going to be a prostitute. Then I went back to my husband, trying to educate him and motivate him until he agreed" (interview with Mrs. Rita Masara). Mrs. Phoebe Mpezeni and Mrs. Margaret Khumalo, two of the earliest FPWs who had worked as nurses in the 1950s, both said that they were called "bitches [promiscuous women]" and "*mahure* [whores]" by young men in the streets as they walked home from work, and they attributed these accusations of looseness to the fact that they earned their own incomes.

The intense worries about prostitute wives grew out of ideas about the nature of female sexuality. Both FPWs and non-FPWs spoke of female sexual drives as powerful forces, which can destroy men and families if not kept under check.[13] As noted in the last chapter, a woman's sexual activities were believed to have a direct impact on the health of her husband and her children, so that any sex outside sanctioned marriage could lead to sickness and death. Unsanctioned sex leads not only to embarrassment and humiliation for the man who cannot control his wife, but also to the spiritual and physical deterioration of the family.

Promiscuity (among women) was understood by my informants as an essential quality, something that was born into some women, who then needed the strong social controls of marriage and the extended family to control them.[14] Becoming promiscuous was not a choice that a woman made or a phase that she passed through, it was what she *was,* and was as far removed from human control as the vagaries of the weather. If a woman was born with this essential quality, she and her husband would be engaged in a constant battle to keep her promiscuous tendencies in check and thereby protect his family.

The pill and Depo could be weapons for the woman's side in this battle, as they would remove the sanction of illicit pregnancy from women's behavior. FPWs therefore had to persuade men that using contraceptives would not make

immorality any worse than it already was. They accomplished this by reinforcing prevalent beliefs about immorality in women, arguing that if a woman was
innately loose, her urge to promiscuity was so strong that contraceptives would
make no difference to such a woman—with or without protection, she would
be driven to seek out other men.[15] The only effect family planning could have
in this situation was to reduce the consequences for the husband, in the form of
ensuring that their wives did not bring home other men's children.

> [The men said] "You give her the injection or you loop her, which means
> that you have given her the freedom of having other men with her, she won't
> be afraid of becoming pregnant." I said, "You know, for a person to be
> promiscuous it means she is just naturally like that, whether you are married
> or not married, whether you are there or not there. For example, you go to
> the field, you are not at home. She goes to fetch water to the field, you are
> not there, she goes to the dip tank, you are not there. Having a man, a
> boyfriend or whatever, will that take two days or just an hour? She just finds
> an hour anywhere for that." (interview with Mrs. Elinor Dauya)

> There were some men who could say, "I don't want to see you at my house,
> teaching my wife to be a bitch [a promiscuous woman]." They said if a
> woman is protected she is free to go with any man. So we had to sit down
> with them and explain that prostitution is in somebody's heart. "Even if you
> don't allow your wife to be on family planning, if she gets pregnant with her
> boyfriend, would you detect that the pregnancy is not yours? We feel it is
> better if the woman is of immoral character, if you don't trust your wife, you
> have to decide if you want her to be pregnant. Then you will be sure that the
> pregnancy is yours." They thought about it and said, "I think you are right.
> It's better to be looking after my real child that I know is my real child."
> (interview with Mrs. Dorothy Dzuda)

> It [promiscuity] was really a big problem because each time you go deeper
> into a man discussing about family planning these are the issue that he
> would bring up. He would say, "now look, if my woman is on family plan-
> ning she knows she is protected and she is free to go around with these other
> men." That was simple, to try and help our men forget that. "Family plan-
> ning as we are talking of it today is a new thing, true. But before family
> planning, your chiefs here, did they not try the cases of adultery? There was
> no family planning, no pill, no one telling your wives to do this, but cases of
> adultery were tried by your chiefs, why? This is a matter of an individual.
> Be on family planning, or not be on family planning, if she is a loose woman
> there is nothing we can do. But what we do know is that the pill cannot
> change a woman." (interview with Mr. Alec Ndhlukula)

> In many areas they could say that the pill causes prostitution. We could say
> no, it doesn't encourage, even before we brought this pill prostitution was

Women chatting with a traveling FPW outside their hut. Source: FPAR 1978, a promotional brochure published by the FPAR.

there . . . There are people who are so eager in their projects [desires, i.e., to have sex] if they have the chance they will do it, we cannot prevent them. We just want their prostitution to be not having the child which will not be wanted. (interview with Mr. T.J. Mugariri)

Two aspects of the way the pill and Depo were delivered contributed to men's suspicion. The first problem was that the pill, the dominant method before Depo, was to be taken continuously by women, not just when they were sexually active with their husbands. The second problem was that many of the FPAR fieldworkers made their motivational pitches to women alone in their homes or gardens, or in groups in women's clubs and in women-only social space, far from the oversight of their men.

As a coitus-independent method, the pill had to be taken daily whether or not the husband was home and having sex with his wife. This led to suspicion that women were taking the pills so that they could meet other men, because they were continuously protected from pregnancy, not just on the nights they were with their husbands.

There were some women who thought you could take the tablet when you are having intercourse only, then they kept on having withdrawal bleeding. You take a pill tonight, then she goes home and for three or four days she is not taking the pill because the husband is away. Sometime she would do that because the husband would say, "Why are you taking the tablet when I am not together with you?" We used to tell them, "You take the tablets even at a funeral, even when your husband is away, because the pill works for 28 days to have a normal cycle." . . . Even the husbands will come and say, "Why does she take the tablet when I am out, not staying together?" We said this is the routine, in the package there are 28 tablets and she must take them all in order to have a normal cycle. (interview with Mrs. Annah Musarurwa)

The day she will meet her husband is the day she will take the pill. Then she will become pregnant and the blame is on the nurse now. "You gave me the pill to take, now I have missed my period!" "How did you take the pill?" "I took the pill when I met my husband, why should I take it when I don't do anything [i.e., have sex with other men]? When my husband is away you tell me to go on taking the pill, but that is impossible. What am I going to say to my husband?" (interview with Mrs. Elinor Dauya)

The husband will be working in the urban areas and she would be staying in the rural areas, and she would have to continue taking the pill, and he would worry about why she has to do that, she doesn't have to take the pill while I am not there, so there must be some prostitution associated with that. (interview with Mrs. Annah Mangwiro)

The second issue was the use of predominantly female FPWs visiting, exhorting, and preaching only to women during the 1970s. The educational work of the FPAR was begun by male FPWs, but they gradually came to occupy supervisory positions, so that by the early 1970s the great majority of the frontline field staff was composed of women. While this made it much easier to get the word out to through women's networks and house-to-house visiting, it also gave rise to suspicions that family planning was a conspiracy by and for disorderly women. Because FPWs were not seen talking to men, suspicions grew that they were actually trying to recruit fellow women into promiscuity. This problem was exacerbated in areas with high rates of male labor out-migration, where men were not around to watch over their wives' doings.

We went on and on, most time it was door to door, but the husbands, the men wouldn't be there. . . . [the men said] "For you tell us to space our children or to have few children, you are just talking nonsense, that must be some method [trick] of bitches [promiscuous women]. You are trying to educate our women to be bitches or to be promiscuous," that's what they were saying. "And who told you about this, and why are you coming to tell us? We know that you take this thing from Europeans, they want to kill us, because they are just testing their medicines to us," and it went on and on. When we went to the mothers to discuss, the first question was "How am I going to approach my husband about this? You tell me about these medicines, but what am I going to say, the thing is awkward. When my husband sees me with this packet I am going to be divorced." (interview with Mrs. Elinor Dauya)

The initial approach was wrong, it destroyed the whole concept. Had it been done properly [i.e., with the involvement of men] definitely I don't see any reason why men would have objected to family planning methods. Because this started with women the men became suspicious of it. (interview with Mrs. Annah Mangwiro)

With family planning the approach was wrong because they concentrated on women rather than men. It was concentrated on women, it was women [FPWs] who went to the clinics, women who went to the clubs, and that's where family planning was preached . . . The husbands were not happy, he will associate it with prostitution, [saying] "If you knew it was a straight-forward thing, why would you do it without telling me, behind my back?" (interview with Mrs. Hilda Bulle)

The history of the FPAR suggests that Mrs. Bulle's comment is not quite accurate—the FPAR did expend a large proportion of its resources, especially in the 1950s and early 1960s, on talking to male audiences. However, as the work of the FPAR expanded in later decades, more and more people had contact with female educators or educators/distributors than with the more senior men. This gave rise to the belief that family planning was directed to women by women, making an end-run around the husbands and depriving them of their place as gatekeepers of the home. Anything that was kept "hidden" from husbands had to be counter to their interests—had to be aimed at helping women subvert their men, whether through removing control over reproduction from the men or through encouraging women to look for sexual adventures with other men. The FPWs looked back on the sex-segregation of their work with regret. The idea of women FPWs talking only to women was premised on the false assumption that matters of pregnancy and childbirth were only of concern to women. However, the men of the communities disputed this assumption that the organization of childbearing was entirely a female sphere, and saw the femaleness of FPAR outreach efforts as a threat to men's rights in that sphere.

Sister Mary Aquina Weinrich's reports from the 1970s corroborate the memories of FPWs. Among Zimbabwean married couples in the mid-1970s, Weinrich found that "41% of the men against only 16% of the women expressed extreme opposition [to the new contraceptives]".[16] Male objection was stronger in the rural areas to the extent that, among the Tonga, an ethnic group that was almost entirely isolated from urban life, 90% of the men were opposed (Weinrich 1982:128).[17] In another survey of 263 pregnant and postpartum women, conducted for Alfreda Geraty by female FPAR fieldworkers in September 1973, 44% said that they favored the idea of using birth control. Presumably, the high approval rate was related to the recent or impending arrival of a new baby. However, 27%, or more than half the approvers, reported either that they had to get permission from their husbands or parents, or that their husbands were opposed to new methods of contraception (Geraty 1974:15).

Geraty's 1974 survey of FPAR fieldworkers also points to widespread male rejection of contraception, based on fears of unleashing promiscuity. For these studies, fieldworkers were brought to their provincial centers in small groups ranging for 5 to 14 people. When asked why people disapproved of the new methods of family planning, the reason that "it will cause immorality: wives will be unfaithful" easily came first in the number of rank order mentions, outdistancing objections related to health and objections related to nationalist politics (Geraty 1974:27). When fieldworkers were asked why, in light of the fact that women were generally more positive about using birth control than men, wives were unable to persuade their husbands to permit them to use it,

- 48% of the fieldworkers said this was because of "immorality fears [i.e., that the husband would think his wife was immoral for wanting to use family planning, or that she would become immoral if she did],"
- 26% said this was because it was against tradition for a man to listen to his wife, and
- 22% said it was because women were afraid to talk to their husbands (Geraty 1974:33).

The workers also described the attitudes of men in their districts:

Men who have wives in the Tribal Trust Lands live here in town with loose women. They see the women are not becoming pregnant because of our methods—therefore think our methods are encouraging all women to be loose. ("FU19," Geraty 1974:126)

Some say it's a way that promotes prostitution. ("MR23," ibid.)

Some say the new methods are making women to be prostitutes because they say a woman goes to buy pills or get injections while a man is away and that means she goes with other men. If there were no pills or injections she would not do that because she would be afraid to become pregnant. ("FR58," ibid.)

Depo and the pill were clearly viewed as things that pulled control over women's sexuality out of men's hands. However, for many men the burning issue was not only from whose hands the control was being removed, but also whose hands it was being put into. The colonial state, in alliance with disorderly and disobedient women, was undercutting men's rights to their control in the home, as discussed in chapter 6. Loss of control over women and sex was clearly perceived as the work of a hostile state, bent on dispossessing men of their rights to their women:

> What this government does is wicked. It gives these pills to our wives and even to our unmarried daughters, who now start love affairs with many young men and we have no more control over them. These pill pushers are seducing our children. (Weinrich 1982:130)

Men were primarily concerned about loss of sexual control over women and youth, but also had other objections to the FPAR and its cadres of FPWs coming into their villages. According to the FPWs, men perceived pills and injections as threats to more general male control over their families, to men's prerogative as the monitors of the interaction between their wives and the world outside the domestic sphere.[18] By handing out birth control, outside the optic of the extended family, the FPAR was insulting men's authority.

> Women were very responsive, they would take our advice and they wanted family planning. But . . . this woman would now take the packet of pills at home and her husband will say, "What is this?" And she will say, "These are the pills for me to plan my family," and we found that most of the husbands were not keen, because our African culture will say that the husband is the head of the house, so that the woman must have permission of the husband. This is why they are resisting, not that they actually don't want pills. This was proved when the male motivation campaign was done recently [in the early 1990s]. It was found that the men were actually very receptive, keen. It was our approach that was wrong, to go to the women. We should have approached men first, then the man will go to the wife and say, "Okay, you can go." And even if she brought this packet of pills he will say, "I know about that," not be taught by the woman. This woman maybe she is already taking the pills and the men will say, "Who gave you permission, who is telling you to do this thing?" . . . The men want to be the head of the house, they want to make decisions. They don't want a woman to make a decision for them even if it is a good decision. Perhaps he would talk to the other men and then tomorrow he would say, "Oh, I want this," as if it is coming from him. Men like to give decisions . . . you know even if you are at home the farm is not yours, it is the husband's, the house you are occupying your name never appears anywhere, it is the husband's. It is just the thought of seeing this woman as the one who has started this. And if this woman starts this thing, he should know, he is he head of the household. This is what they were resenting. They should know what the woman is doing. (interview with Mrs. Gloria Tekere)

> I was finding a very big resistance from men. Very much, maybe the way we approached people with family planning we did not target the men, we were targeting the women only. The men were furious because they were not con-

sulted first. According to their African culture men should be consulted whatever a woman wants to do the husband should be consulted first. (interview with Mrs. Ennet Mudzimwa)

This problem could be exacerbated in marriages where the husband already feared that his wife was usurping his authority from him, or was not adequately deferential. According to Mrs. Annah Musarurwa, in marriages where the wife had more formal education than the husband or was from a higher social class, family planning was a particularly sore subject:

> If the husband is not an understanding husband and the wife is better off than him [or] is having education, the husband will keep on saying, "You think you know too much, that is why you go for this family planning without my consent."

Similar accounts surface early on in FPAR reports on field educators' activities, as in the report by Mrs. Elizabeth Teubes, an early FPAR education officer who visited Epworth mission in November 1967 to investigate the concerns reported by Mrs. Ndhlovu, one of the educators under her supervision. Mrs. Ndhlovu "was afraid that men from Epworth might beat her if they were at variance with family planning aims, as one man had berated her when he found her at home giving pamphlets to his wife, 'because I am the head of the household and it is my place to tell her anything I want her to know'" (National Archives of Zimbabwe [NAZ] B/137/4—vol.1).

Men were also suspicious because these new innovations were entering their homes through women,[19] believing that women had been targeted to be Trojan horses, the bearers of a new and suspect technology because they were more credulous or naïve than their menfolk:

> Some even asked why did you go to our women without telling us? They didn't like that, they said you know we are the breadwinners and the heads of the families, why did you go and talk to our women without consulting us first? They were not very happy about that. They thought maybe there is something behind the whole thing, that we were going to the women. They thought that men were more intelligent than women, so we chose the women because they were weaker thinkers than the men, so it was an error that had to be rectified . . . they didn't understand why they were not involved to start with. (interview with Mrs. Shamiso Kudakwashe)

Men also objected to what they saw as implicit criticism of their abilities to provide for their family. Giving a woman birth control could be understood as an insult, implying that the husband was not a competent man and was unable to support his family. Mrs. Tendai Masvika recounted her meetings with one such man in Rugare township outside Salisbury. He shouted at Mrs. Masvika, telling her that he was a good husband and provider to his wife. When his wife was last pregnant, he carried her all the way to Harari Hospital on his bicycle—now how dare Mrs. Masvika imply that he could not take care of his family well and didn't deserve to be a father again. She reported that officers from a nearby police camp had to be called to calm the man down, and that she did not go back to Rugare for a long time thereafter. Other educators reported similar objections, mainly among low-wage earners such as farmworkers, who questioned, "Why is it considered that an African could not look after a big family?" (Report of Nora Warburton [educator], visit to Nyamandhlovu, August 1968, NAZ B/137/3—Family Planning Africans)

## FPWS AS ABETTORS OF SUBVERSION

Not only did the pill and Depo favor women who wanted to use contraception without their husbands' knowledge, but the FPWs themselves abetted women's subversive intentions.[20] Even FPWs who were themselves middle-aged married men from conservative rural backgrounds stated that they had no qualms about undermining other men's control of their wives:

Women definitely, young women they used not to have problems [objections] to family planning. They liked family planning . . . She is concerned of her health, repeating of pregnancies ruins her life, so she is afraid for herself. This is the reason why she goes to the clinic and she tells the clinic staff, "I have come here but my husband is against it, my mother-in-law is against it, so please keep my card [prescription] here in the clinic." So it was very confidential to the nursing staff because we wanted to help the people that needed help. [AK: So you thought that was all right?] Yes, it was all right. [AK: Even though the woman might be deceiving her husband?] Yes, it was all right. (interview with Mr. David Chibvongodze)

[AK: What about the issue where wives would be wanting family planning but their husbands would be objecting? Would you provide something for wives without their husbands knowing?] Yes, we would, we would. Even the clinic records would state that husband opposed, husband against. (interview with Mr. Alec Ndhlukula)

There were women who could accept but the husbands are against. So we must try to talk to them, saying, "Look here, you know you are the one with the burden, it is not the husband who will be pregnant. Since you are the one who will be pregnant and you are the one who is always with the children, the husband will be away, especially on the rural setup, he drinks beer and comes late, then you are the one who will be facing problems, because you will be having children all the time, you are the one who will be pregnant while the other child is not two years old, who will look after them?" So I told them to forget about the husband. [AK: So you would actually encourage them to deceive their husbands?] Yes, that was the way, so that they could understand. (interview with Mr. Richard Chidakwa)

Both Mr. Ndhlukula and Mr. Chibvongodze told me that women who became private acceptors did so out of the best maternal instincts—they wanted time to properly nurse and wean the last child before starting another pregnancy, and they wanted to be sure that they would have enough food and clothing for all the children in the home. However, when I talked to women who had actually been private acceptors, I found a wider range of reasons, many of which were less altruistic. Some feared they would lose their attractiveness, and their husband's attention, if they had too many pregnancies; some did not want another baby when they were uncertain whether or not the marriage was going to endure; and some who were employed either in high-status jobs in town or as underpaid commercial farmworkers believed that they would lose their jobs if they got pregnant. Several female FPWs said that they themselves had been private acceptors and did not see why other women should not follow suit. Mrs. Hilda Bulle said,

A lot of the ladies did it privately and I am one of the ones who did it privately, even myself. He [her husband] would not have approved, and I wasn't sure if I wanted to keep in the marriage for the rest of my life [taps hip to show the site of the Depo-Provera injection, laughs].

FPWs enthusiastically described the ways they helped women to be private acceptors, encouraged them to go ahead against the wishes of their husbands, and even provided them with suggestions about how to escape detection. FPWs from all parts of the country described how they suggested to their clients that they bury their contraceptive pills in buckets of mealie-meal, the ground maize used to make the staple sadza, on the assumption that no husband would ever be involved in making sadza, the most common strategy. Other plans included deception and subterfuge:

If it is that you have met them [clients] in the garden or plowing the field, whilst you are talking to them you also take the hoe and start plowing and leaving the contraceptive pills [in the furrows] whilst others are not watching. You will be talking and putting the contraceptives where people are busy plowing. The client is aware that you have come for this reason, she leaves the contraceptives there in the dirt [and collects them later]. Some used to send their friends to collect contraceptives for them. They tell their friends, "You know my husband is very against, can you do me a favor and collect my contraceptives?" And the CBD is made aware that whenever you are coming you leave the contraceptives with Mrs. So-and-So. (interview with Mrs. Rita Masara)

We had to face difficulties in welcomes when we were visiting homes. Because the husbands were the people who could give consent, yet they said they could not like family planning. It was the husbands, they were really cruel. We had to find tactics to reach the home, praise their children, a good rapport, so they would accept you. Then we would ask about baby clinics and the children, do they go for baby clinics, we advise the women to go for [women's homecraft] clubs. We were just introducing something to be welcome, to be welcome in the home. I could ask the husband if the woman goes for clubs, for sewing and what what, I could come there and teach them how to use their [sewing] machines, then I become popular to that home. (interview with Mrs. Elizabeth Mlambo)

FPWs used tactics such as "bush injections" (giving women Depo shots in secluded areas such as graveyards or rubbish dumps) and code phrases such as "my cousin from Bulawayo is here" to announce the arrival of a CBD (these examples from Mrs. Elizabeth Utete).

Not only the FPWs but also the medical and paramedical professionals with whom they worked were involved in deception, particularly when a husband suspected that his wife was "stealing" and tried to confirm these suspicions. To keep the women's secrets, the collusion of doctors and clerks, often white, was essential.[21] The encounters between suspicious husbands and clinic doctors and administrators summed up, in microcosm, the gender subversion and racial challenges to male power that many men feared. The clinic, and all that it embodied, represented a power greater than the power of the husband in the family, intruding into the most intimate domains of male power:

There were cases where husbands wondered why their wives weren't getting pregnant . . . Then the men went to the clinics to say, "Oh, my wife, Mrs. So-and-So, I believe she is on family planning and I would like to buy a packet of pills for her." Then the sister would go through the cards and she would see the card had husband against, and so she would say, "She is not on family planning." (interview with Mr. Alec Ndhlukula)

The husband sometimes they could go to the clinic and say, "My wife is pregnant and I don't know why because she is on family planning, so I want to see if she is taking every month." "What is her name? Let's see in the [record] book—no, Baba, she is not taking any pills," Once they [clinic staff] could see a husband they knew not to risk it so the secret was just kept. (interview with Mrs. Winnie Pasipanodya)

Depo was popular because people will say, "If I am given Depo where can he [her husband] trace it?" But sometimes they go amenorrheic and he says, "Let's go and see a doctor." Sometimes they don't have any bleeding, then he will start saying, "Why are you not having periods?" "I think I am pregnant." Then it will go on and on, "How come you are pregnant but it is not showing? Let's go to a doctor." But the doctors were all motivated. They knew what to say in a case when such problems come up, they would just say there is nothing. The husband says, "Maybe she is going for some things I don't know about [i.e., secretly using contraception]," and the doctor would say, "There is no evidence of Depo." The doctors were all informed. (interview with Mrs. Margaret Khumalo)

Some men would actually come to the clinic at Spilhaus here to say, "my wife is not at home, I have heard she has come here for family planning, can I see her card?" Some would try some tactics and say, "I would like to see my wife's card." What we would do is we would try to look for the card and we would find the card and we would not show the husband and we would hide it away and we would say to each other, "If you see such a man, just say the wife didn't come here, we don't know her. How is he going to prove it?" He was coming as a spy, saying, "I would like to see my wife's card," and then we would suspect. "Let us just say we don't know, we didn't see it, we didn't see the woman." (interview with Mrs. Gloria Tekere)

As the 1970s went on and the pill and Depo became more widely known, men, especially those who worked in urban areas, became more aware of the signs that a wife was using the methods. FPWs believed that information was circulated through male-only informal social networks about the signs that a wife was secretly using contraception and the best ways to catch a disobedient wife in flagrante delicto (a mirror image of the informal networks of women who told each other about the existence of the new methods and helped each other hide pills from husbands).

Some would put them [pills] under the mattress, some would put them in the mealie-meal. But then these other ones [husbands] would fish it out. Some would hide them in a pot, when there are many pots in the house, but this man would sometimes just get the pills when his wife is not there, he would just search and when she comes he would say, "I have found this, so you are using this!" Maybe the men would be talking to each other at the beer halls, to give each other ideas where these women could be keeping their things. (interview with Mrs. Gloria Tekere)

Men also became attuned to the side effects of Depo and the pill, especially menstrual irregularity.

Some of the men they know information through other men. So they know that if the woman bleeds like what, like what, they know that woman is taking a Depo without my [the husband's] authority. So the side effects they had known about it, the grapevine and so on . . . some [women] were beaten to hell and went back to the educators crying, and they [husbands] still want to beat the educators, so it was really troublesome . . . If there is a side effect, the educator is also in trouble, the nurse is in trouble because men were knowing about these side effects. (interview with Mrs. Marjorie Mugwagwa)

They [clients] had problems [with Depo] because the husband would be wanting to know why she is not having a period. [AK: How did the husbands know about this?] Talking with other people, yes, because it was a group of people working in one place, it was just like a family staying in one house, so each one has to discuss about what is happening in his house, either at a beer hall or either at workplaces they were discussing. Since the family planning was there they wanted to know how it operated. They tell each other. So they [their wives] had problems. "Why are you not having your period, are you pregnant?" "No." "But why, where is the period?" So what we used to do after giving a woman Depo-Provera, we used to give a packet of COC [combined estrogen and progesterone pills] and we used to instruct the woman that she has to take those tablets at the end of every month, she has to take seven tablets to bring on the period. Then the following month she has to remain with another seven tablets, she takes them, then she has breakthrough bleeding, until the time she comes for the next shot . . . So some had a problem of having continuous period with Depo, she starts a period, it goes on for 10 days. The husband wants to know, why is she having this period for so many days. Women used to come back and we give COC, we advised them to take a packet of pills to make the period stop. Then after that she can have breakthrough bleeding like a period at the end of the packet. (interview with Mrs. Stella Padoro)

Some of the woman, as you know with Depo sometimes you have your menses and sometimes you won't, some could just say, "I have pretended to have my periods, after three days I have finished and then we start meeting again, because he is going to ask me why are you not having your menses," because you know they were talking sometimes in the bars, and the educators like Mr. Chibvongodze was explaining also to them, then the man if he sees that the wife is not having periods he might be suspicious: "I think my wife is using this Depo," because he might have heard from his friends in the bar or in lectures. (interview with Mrs. Phoebe Mpezeni)

FPWs were harassed because of the threat they posed to men as well as because of their association with the white minority regime during the late 1970s, as the war heated up. They report being chased away from home by irate husbands wielding axes, being called *muroyi* (evil witch, with connotations of being one who brings discord into the community) and being given nicknames that contain images of theft and destabilization, such as "the one who takes the uteruses of women" (interview with Mr. David Chibvongodze).

FPWs who were traveling educators reported active "de-motivation" campaigns by local men aimed at convincing prospective users that pills and injections were threats to their marriages. "Some even had personal hatred to me, thinking my work is very bad. They were going around influencing mothers 'Don't join that, it's rubbish. If you go on family planning your husband is going to chase you away and you won't be respected in the community'" (interview with Mrs. Rita Masara). FPWs based in clinics encountered angry men, suspicious that their wives had sought contraception there.

> I remember one day I inserted a Lippes loop [a type of IUD] at the clinic, the lady was from a place called Mabvuku. The following morning I am coming, I was a bit late, and there is this big man, and I saw the wife pointing at me and then the man said, "Are you Sister [nursing sister] Chikara?" I said, "Yes." He said, "Are you the one who has inserted a loop into my wife?" I said, "Yes." He said, "Why did you do this?" I said, "Because she asked for it." He said, "Why didn't you get my permission?" I said, "She came here asking for the method and I gave her the method, I don't know about your background, the marital [situation]. And she had been beaten and she said, "Don't worry sister, as long as it doesn't kill me I will not stop." So those are some of the situations. He had actually pulled the thing out of her. (interview with Mrs. Florence Chikara)

Other reported threats and attacks from husbands (which may have been embellished to emphasize the courage and persistence of the FPWs):

> Some said, "We want to take you and throw you in the river, because you have come to destroy our families." And these husbands would beat their wives once they were seen visiting that mobile clinic. (interview with Mr. Richard Chidakwa)

> Most of the husbands were so very much against. They were accusing the family planning methods that "You want to stop our wives from having children!" . . . They would see you there in the road and start shouting at you, "You killer!" (interview with Mrs. Imelda Mudarikiri)

> They said, "If I see a family planning [worker] here [in the house], I will chop off his head, I don't want a family planning worker here!"(interview with Mr. David Chibvongodze)

Mrs. Margaret Khumalo, one of the earliest FPWs, reported that in the townships of Harare, in the early 1960s, groups of men stopped and searched nurses whom they suspected of bringing contraceptives to their wives:[22]

> It was really difficult because men had heard that there were nurses who were telling women to go on family planning, so whenever they met you they want to know what are you doing in the townships, they had heard

about it. So I used to travel with a tray, cotton wool, ligatures, methylated spirits, I said, "I am just going to clean the [umbilical] cords of the children who are from maternity, I am just doing maternity work." "Okay, fine, go ahead." They would stop me and search, they would search what I have got. So I would have a packet of those Volpar pills that were inserted, then I will put them in my bra so they will search my bag and find nothing. This was happening in all townships, it was very tense in those days. Mufakose, Highfields, these were the popular places where this would happen.

Some husbands feared that female FPWs were colluding with their wives, in a sort of subversive female solidarity. They insisted on proof that there were indeed other men who worked for family planning, that it was not just a movement by and for disorderly women:

They [local men] started talking about it: "Are there any men who also do this job, because we have seen only women?"

I said, "Yes, in Harare [then Salisbury], we have got them."

"We want to see one of them!"

"With pleasure, I can write them or phone."

. . . I wrote him [a senior male educator] a letter. I said, "Please I have got a problem in Midlands, if you come here yourself I think it will be easier. Village 7 and 6 are now becoming very hot for me because men are hostile about this family planning . . . They said, 'we want to see a man not a woman, now!' . . . There are men who want to see you, especially you because you are a man and they want to know how you feel about this family planning". . . . He came to my house in Mkoba and we talked about it. He said, "Are they very hostile?"

I said, "Some of them are very hostile. . . . "

Then we went there and they were surely waiting for us. I said, "This is [Mr. X] I told you about so if you have some questions you can ask him" . . . He was a very good man, he had so many tactics. They said, "[Mr. X], tell us about family planning, and why are you sending women so that they meet women when the men are not there?"

He said, "No we don't do that, only that men are always at work. If you say to your wife, 'When this family planning educator comes tell her to come when I am here,' and then give the date to your wife, then we will come. We would also like to have men but no one has come forward to work for the family planning"

. . . Then they said, "Where do you come from, do you practice family planning at your place?"

He said, "I do, even myself, if you want some of you I can drive you to my place and you can see my children". . . .

They asked questions, questions, questions. Then they said, "All right, we would like to call you again, not today, because we have not finished, these two are going to work."

He said, "All right, you can tell to this lady and she will call me."

When he went away they are quite sure that this man he will come back again, because as I had called him he came. All that surrounding area, part of Village 7 and part of Village 6, they were now getting to understand that planning is not like that. (interview with Mrs. Winnie Pasipanodya)

## CONCLUSION

The complex interactions between men, their wives, and the FPWs demonstrates the powerful effect that patriarchal relations had on the diffusion of contraception. Men rejected these new methods not just because they might constrain women's highly-prized fertility, but also because they were perceived as a threat to male control of female sexuality and over the interactions between the domestic sphere and the outside world. The story of the reception of new fertility control methods is as much about the social construction of masculinity as it is about fertility per se. However, the story of conflict over family planning in the home is not merely the story of male attempts to repress women's activities. The creativity and agency of the women, in coming up with strategies of subversion, is also part of this story.

The introduction of new technologies of fertility regulation, and a new set of gatekeepers for these technologies, had the power to at least partially endow women with control over their fertility, beyond the vision or the power of their husbands. The desire of women to gain control over the means of controlling their fertility—to seize control of the means of reproduction—and the need for this seizure of control to be invisible to the eyes of the husband had strong ramifications for method choice, leading to the dominance of the Depo-Provera injection, the most private of all available methods, over the pill and the IUD. These technologies and the FPWs who distributed and promoted them were demonized as pernicious, destructive elements in both the family and the wider society.

## NOTES

1. In Zimbabwe and in other southern African contexts, women did retain normative claims to certain fields, and to the revenue generated by these fields, and used nagging, complaining, public shaming, and appeals to kin and neighbors to shame their men into honoring these claims. See Schmidt (1992) and Thompson (2000a) for examples of these strategies whereby Zimbabwean women protected their claim to agricultural resources.

2. The examples Mrs. Masvika gave to support this statement all concerned sexual and reproductive functioning, such as the use of certain infusions of roots to tighten the vaginal muscles after giving birth, or the knowledge of herbs and charms to keep husbands from straying to other women. This selection of examples suggests that the realm of sexual and reproductive matters is especially marked by female secrecy and evasion.

3. This phenomenon—women killing themselves out of anger at their husbands' squandering of the crops they had grown—is well-known and much discussed in Zimbabwe,

although I do not how frequently this actually happens. In Shona communities, suicide is the most extreme and public way of shaming one's husband by drawing attention to the ways in which he has failed to uphold his part of the patriarchal bargain by providing for his wife's sustenance. In addition, a person who commits suicide can return as a *ngozi,* an avenging spirit, and punish the person who drove him or her to suicide.

4. Nonetheless, even Mrs. Jongwe, who had 12 children, used the Depo injection secretly during the 1980s, because, she said, her husband did not agree with her wishes to wait longer between pregnancies.

5. My own work with middle-aged and elderly women who were not FPWs corroborates Gibney's findings, as all of them report that they knew women in their neighborhood who were using contraception against their husband's will.

6. The high rates of male labor migration, leading to prolonged male absence from their rural homes, may account for the fact that rural women found it easier to be private acceptors than women in towns or living with their husbands on commercial farm estates.

> In the rural areas the advantage we got is that the father will be in town working while the mother is at home, then she had an advantage that she could use family planning and when the father comes she can just hide the pills, she can just come for her injections without his interference, which is really different from the situation on the commercial farms because they were together, the husband wouldn't like to see his wife having pills, so it was more difficult to be a private acceptor. (interview with Mrs. Eugenia Mashonga)

7. FPAR records show drastic increases in the number of acceptors and in couple-years of protection in 1972 and 1973, as Depo was introduced. While I am reluctant to conclude that all of this increase can be attributed to Depo (and while I am generally suspicious of the accuracy of FPAR pre-independence quantitative data), this does support the FPWs' contention that Depo-Provera appealed to many women who believed themselves unable to use other contraceptive methods.

8. See Kaler (1998) for a discussion of the Depo saga in Zimbabwe after independence.

9. In the few cases where this was not the answer, I was told that the biggest challenge was "politics," specifically, the opposition by African nationalists and their sympathizers to new methods of family planning on the grounds that these were intended by the white regime to sterilize African women and reduce the African population. However, even nationalist opposition to the new methods relied strongly on notions of proper gender norms and their subversion by these new technologies, as I argue in chapter 6.

10. Readers should remember that the private acceptors discussed here actually represent a sizable underestimate of the number of men who did not want their wives to use contraception. The women discussed here represent only those marriages in which the wife successfully subverted the husband's wishes in this respect. In an unknown number of other marriages, the wives complied with their husband's rejection of the pill and the injection.

11. Sensitive to these considerations, all the FPWs stressed that they promoted child spacing *(kusiyanisa vana)* rather than child limiting *(kusaita/kusabereka vana)*. The mid-1970s FPWs' training manual stated explicitly that "NO advice should be given by fieldworkers concerning the number of children desirable. This is frequently asked for but the fieldworker MUST NOT give advice on this matter" (FPAR [date unknown]:3).

12. People stressed that the male calculus of the benefits of children has changed drastically since the 1960s and 1970s, with the rapidly rising cost of living. The need for money

to raise children, especially to pay school fees, was given as the main reason why a sensible man in the 1990s would not emulate his fathers.

> A fool will have 10 children, I mean nowadays, and they are uneducated which means the number adds to 12 fools, including father and mother. When I say now, I mean life is expensive on all bases, so if you see someone unemployed having 10 children, you can say they are a fool. (interview with Mr. Tsinza, tr. NS)

13. The descriptions of women's sexual nature given here are from people who ascribed these qualities to other people, mainly men talking about women, women talking about what they think men think about women. However, I do not know much about how women themselves thought about their own sexuality. Some of the older women in Wedza were quite earthy in their descriptions of their own marital lives, and gave my research assistant and me gratuitous advice on what makes for a good sex life, which suggests that women did not think of themselves as asexual or of sex as exclusively for men's pleasure. A colleague, Allison Goebel, who was doing research on divorce patterns in the area reported that women ascribed many divorces to sexual problems, specifically to men's inability to be good lovers, a theme that also appears in a few places in this book (Goebel, personal communication).

14. Male promiscuity was understood quite differently. Although an adulterous husband was not necessarily a good thing, the danger of a man straying was of an entirely different order from the danger of a bad woman. None of my interviewees mentioned any crises for the community posed by the presence of immoral men, only by immoral women. Interestingly, where men did come in for blame for sexual immorality among the elders of Wedza and Buhera, it was in their inability to satisfy their wives sexually, so that sexually hungry women would turn to other men. This was linked to processes of cultural change and to the degeneration of Shona ways under the onslaught of *chirungu,* as young men were chastised (in absentia) for rejecting the traditional herbs that had made their forefathers able to satisfy even the most voracious woman.

> I think the problem [of widespread promiscuity] is caused by men, they have sex out [i.e., outside the marriage] then they can't fulfill the desires of their wives. To solve everything the wives will find another partner. These men are now ignoring the traditional methods of eating herbs to make them strong [i.e., sexually virile], they are now useless in the bedroom. That is the cause of immorality. (interview with Mrs. Mbizi, tr. NS)

15. The fact that they could present this rather unflattering portrayal to men as a description of their wives, without the man reacting with indignation, suggests how deeply the idea of the innately promiscuous woman had permeated ideas about female sexuality.

16. Weinrich also reported that, based on her observations outside a Bulawayo family planning clinic:

> As to the married women who attend the clinics, most of them do so in the mornings when their husbands are away at work. To avoid discovery by their husbands, these women prefer injections to pills. . . . husbands have good reason to suspect wives who attend family planning clinics. (Weinrich 1982:135)

17. The data on the Tonga, however, may be biased because of exceptionally high rates of male labor out-migration in the area, which would presumably leave only the older men at home to answer the survey.

18. Which is not to imply that Shona women were exclusively, or even primarily, concerned only with domestic life. The historiography of Zimbabwe is filled with accounts of Shona women engaging with the market, the state (in its many forms), and other institutions, and the resulting conflicts with men over their engagement.

19. See Mrs. Pasipanodya's account of being asked to produce a man who worked for family planning below.

20. The FPWs I interviewed had no qualms about telling me how they helped women to circumvent their husbands' proscriptions of family planning. However, Dr. Esther Sapire, the former medical director of the FPAR, said that she remembered that some of the early FPWs were afraid to challenge male authority by assisting disobedient wives. She portrayed the approval of gender subversion within the FPAR as emanating from the top down:

> I remember it was a problem that they [husbands] didn't want their wives to use it and then you'd have to stop what you were giving them or tell them where there was another clinic where they could get the injection. Say the husband found a packet of pills, the nurses would quietly tell them "Don't come here again, he may be watching, go to the other clinic there and get the injection." I always felt that if an adult woman came I didn't need her husband's permission [to give her a Depo injection]. The culture required that you did, so there was a problem. Once they were sufficiently emancipated and recognized they weren't going to be baby machines constantly they had the right to make that decision. If you put your head back to 30 years ago when that was really quite revolutionary to say that, I personally had to feel very strongly about that to carry that through and to convince the staff that it was okay to do that, to give them courage to do that, particularly the black women, it wasn't their culture and they knew that the husband was supposed to have a say, and they had to be made to feel comfortable. (interview with Dr. Esther Sapire)

21. While the FPWs described collusion between clinic personnel and women who wanted to hide their contraceptive use from their objecting husbands, contemporary records suggest that the picture was somewhat more complex. FPAR records from the late 1960s and early 1970s, once family planning had expanded dramatically in scale following 1965, contain complaints from educators and FPWs about noncooperation from Department of Health staff, as well as the staff from the Native Affairs Department (later Internal Affairs), who were reluctant to cooperate with the FPWs. However, I found no indications of clinical staff or others actively working against women who were private acceptors, by telling their husbands or otherwise revealing their secrets. It does seem, though, that some clinic staff were more enthusiastic than others about colluding with private acceptors.

22. This was also a time of rising antigovernment political activity in the townships, and Mrs. Khumalo believed these young men were members of the youth wings of some of the nationalist parties.

# 5

# CONTRACEPTION AS DISRESPECT: FERTILITY AND POWER IN THE EXTENDED FAMILY IN THE TWENTIETH CENTURY

## INTRODUCTION

Husbands were loudly and vocally perturbed by the pill and the Depo injection. However, they were not the only family members to raise suspicions about young wives who wanted to use contraception. Other members of the extended family, particularly mothers-in-law, watched the wives zealously, and attempted to police the younger women's fertility, in the interests (or so they believed) of the extended family as a whole. Thus, while tensions between genders were the most visible form of family upheaval, struggles between the generations over controlling women's fertility were no less important.

The power to reproduce, a power that was biologically the property of the young and the female, yet necessary to the social power of men and elders, was inevitably the center of struggles in Shona communities, even before pills and injections appeared on the scene. The arrival of these new methods, with the new set of gatekeepers who handed them out to young women, and their availability to women without the knowledge of men or elders, simply sharpened pre-existing conflicts over the nature of marriage and what the young owed to the old.

These generational tensions within extended families did not suddenly burst out as a result of pills and injections. They evolved out of the patterns of Shona women's life course, and were sharpened by the particular historic setting of the 1960s and 1970s, in which elders felt themselves losing control over the youth on many fronts. By "running after pills," young women were perceived as breaking the tacit cultural compact that gave elders the right to supervise the reproductive acts of their juniors, part of a wave of disobedience among youth that provoked consternation among their elders.

Elders, particularly elder women, expected to gain power as they moved through the lifecycle in Shona communities. The promise of having power as a mother, grandmother, or mother-in-law could leaven the relatively power-less position that young women, especially young wives, found themselves in vis-à-vis their husband's family. Kandiyoti (1991) describes this accrual of power with age as part of the "patriarchal bargain" that women make:

> The cyclical nature of women's power in the household and their anticipation of inheriting the authority of senior women encourages an internalization of patriarchy by the women themselves . . . subordination to men is offset by the control older women attain over younger women. (108–9)

This patriarchal bargain has been well documented by African social historians. For many women, their power (defined both as autonomy—their control over themselves—and as their control over the activities of others), varied as they passed through different stages of their lives. For example, Geiger (1997) asserts that young Moslem women in Dar es Salaam experienced a drastic increase in their personal autonomy once they entered "middle age," which was marked by the dissolution of a first marriage and the end of their period of seclusion as young wives. Women who entered this postdivorce period were free to remarry the husband of their choice, and were in most respects "less subservient" to men and elders than when they were younger (33). Similarly, Schmidt (1992:23) describes how Shona women attained positions of ritual power and respect after entering menopause (see also Maxwell 1993:374). In their movement through the life course women gained not only autonomy and respect from others but also the ability to control the lives and actions of younger women, just like men did. When young women entered into marriage in patriarchal, patrilocal Shona communities, they were marrying not only a husband but also a set of in-laws, and their "patriarchal bargains" were made not only with men but with elders of both sexes.[1]

Fertility regulation was a particularly contentious area within marriage. Older women had two main reasons for objecting to their daughters- and sisters-in-law using pills and injections: first, these technologies violated both the spirit and the letter of *lobola,* according to which a wife's potential for bearing many children to her husband's family was the bedrock of the marriage agreement. Second, the family planning workers (FPWs) and medical personnel who brought pills and injections threatened to displace elders from their niche as gatekeepers of older, "traditional" ways of regulating fertility. Elders were thus threatened with the possibility of losing control over reproduction not just to young men and (especially) young women, but also to the unfamiliar institutions and personnel of colonial biomedicine, in the form of nurses and traveling distributors.

## SHONA MARRIAGE: THE IDEAL

Among Shona marriages, as everywhere, the ideals that were held up as normative often differed substantially from actual lived experiences. Nonetheless, the very existence of these ideals was a potent symbolic resource that elders could draw on to legitimize their claims on their sons and daughters-in-law. In their idealized version, Shona marriages were patriarchal, patrilocal, potentially polygamous, and established by contract between lineages rather than between individuals. While the details of how marriages were arranged vary from regions to regions, certain principles are common to the ideal Shona marriage (Bourdillon 1982, Chizengeni 1979, Gelfand 1973, Holleman 1952, Schmidt 1992, Weinrich 1982).

The young man to be married should seek the assistance of his father and paternal relatives in order to pay cattle, or in later times, money, to the father of his prospective wife. While the two young people involved might choose each other, all other details of their marriage were handled by their families as corporate units. Marriage between the two families was solidified in stages marked by rituals of gifts and exchanges between the families, mainly from the husband's family to the wife's, beginning with gifts presented by the prospective husband's intermediary to open negotiations through a sequence of exchanges marking the phases of the marriages, culminating in gifts (usually a cow) presented by the husband's family to the wife's mother on the birth of the first child. Along the way, the marriage might be solemnized in a court or celebrated in a Christian church, but these were not required for a marriage to be generally recognized as legitimate. Above and beyond the formal exchanges, the relationship of reciprocal obligation for mutual aid between the families carried on as long as the marriage endured, although the relationship might be weaker for second or junior wives.

This form of marriages not only solidified the relationship between the two families, but also bound the younger generation to the elder. In the ideal Shona marriage, young men who needed cattle or money to pay *lobola* to acquire a wife became indebted to their fathers and uncles, who controlled the family's accumulation of wealth, and who were in a position to permit the young man to marry or refuse him permission by refusing to release any of the family's assets for *lobola*. Similarly, the new wife should be acutely aware that her status as wife depended on the willingness of her husband's family to spend their resources to bring her to their home and that she owed them respect and obedience in turn.

All ethnographic accounts concur that, according to the idealized version of Shona marriage, women are married so that children may be born.[2] The transfer of *lobola* payments, which indicates that a legitimate marriage is under way, is intended to secure the man's family's rights to the woman's reproductive capacities and to claim any children resulting from that union. Sexual relations may occur between betrothed couples before *lobola* is paid (usually after the exchange of preliminary payment called *rutsambo*), but ownership of any children born before *lobola* is paid could be disputed between the two families, especially in case of divorce or repudiation of the wife. A man was expected to seek out marriage and a woman to have children not only so that he could achieve full social adulthood, but also so that he could fulfill his obligations to his family and his ancestors by perpetuating the lineage. Thus, a husband's family was expected to express deference and respect to the wife's family for providing the husband's family with the means of increasing their family through the provision of a childbearing woman. If a woman did not bear children, she could be returned to her family and the *lobola* repaid, or her sister could be sent to the husband's family as a second wife at no extra cost.

Throughout this process, women as the medium of exchange remained perpetual minors. Even though many women might be able to resist unwanted marriages, by drastic means such as threatening suicide or running away (e.g., Schmidt 1992), my interviewees endorsed the general principle that wives were meant to function as a medium of exchange between families and a means of perpetuating the husband's family. Mrs. Salina Mumbengegwi described this predicament of married women, and its implications for using contraceptives:

[Before the 1980s] there was no legal age of majority. There was me being handed over to my husband by my father, my husband to take control of me, and should my husband die my son has to take over. So the context has to be explained that this was an era when Zimbabwean women were minors from the cradle to the grave. And therefore talking about controlling of anything by women was something you couldn't talk about because it was out of existence for most women. . . . Most of them, with strong rural ties, with strong beliefs in respecting the authority that was there, they respected that they didn't belong to themselves. First and foremost they belong to their fathers. And secondary they would belong to their husbands and maybe then to their children. So when you talked of family planning to this woman I think the legal age of majority should have come first. Because when you talk about controlling your fertility when you don't control anything, what are you talking about? More so, fertility was the core of a woman and this is why when you didn't have fertility in the case of infertility you were worthless as a woman. And not worthy to be passed from your husband to the next man because you don't have that thing that the next man would want to control. And now talking about family planning and everything to the woman who doesn't possess anything, who was just carrying the uterus for the man, would be a non-starter. . . . You are committing a crime against the man who owns the reproductive rights in this woman.

With marriage, a wife became a perpetual outsider in her in-laws' family.[3] Because Shona marriages are exogamous and Shona law and religion reckon descent through the male line, the new wife did not share the same ancestors, totem, or spiritual protection as her husband, in-laws, or children. She was expected to undertake the least desirable tasks in the homestead and to defer to her sisters-in-law in the grounds that it was their *lobola* that enabled their brother, her husband, to marry her. A common term for husband's sisters, *vamwene,* translates literally as "owners." Because the children she bears will be of the same lineage as her husband and his sisters and brothers, they all have a vested interest in overseeing her reproductive life. The idea of a wife as a means of increase for the lineage as a whole, and not just for the one man she marries is evident in the practice of widow inheritance, whereby upon a man's death his brothers were able, and in many cases expected, to marry his widow, so that her reproductive abilities would be kept in the family. (All accounts of this practice stress that a widow should not be forced to marry her late husband's brother, if she did not want to, and that she had the option of refusing and returning to her own parents, or of living alone, although she might not be able to take her children with her if she did so.)

But if wives were disempowered with respect to their husband's family, they could be powerful, albeit at a distance, with respect to the women who married their brothers, sons, and nephews. Women could also achieve positions of influence outside the family, as leaders of ritual or religious practice, and women from some elite families could attain political power, although these means of exercising power are outside the scope of this chapter.[4]

## SHONA MARRIAGES: THE REALITY OF CONFLICT AND CHANGE

However, this idealized vision of Shona marriage was not what existed in the 1960s and 1970s, if it ever had existed in its pure form. Though patriarchal and gerontocratic norms were still invoked by men and elders to justify their control over the lives of women and juniors, the material bases for this control were increasingly unstable. Younger men and women were struggling with their elders on various fronts to control their own future.

Social and economic trends were gradually but decisively severing the younger generation from the control of the older. While Shona society, like all cultures, had always encompassed contradictory dynamics, the pressures of late colonialism helped to create a social world in which the control of the extended family over both production and reproduction could be weakened. Weinrich's 1979 survey of urban and rural Zimbabweans suggests that the lives of the younger generation, spent partially in the social spaces governed by white capital, led both younger men and women to resist the authority and guidance of the older generation.

> As soon as some sons have grown up and become able to support themselves, they tend to drift away to live their own lives. This is a possibility open to the young people which they never had under the communal mode of production, and this growing independence of children undermines the father-son dyad. Some are assisted in this endeavour by their employers, because employers very much encourage individualism for their own sakes. Parents, on the other hand, try hard to prevent their children's independence but seldom succeed in this for more than a few years. . . . a father's economic control over his children's income decreases within a very short period of time and that as his sons may earn more than he does, his economic power-base is undermined. A father may have worked hard to give his sons an education, but once his sons earn, he depends on their goodwill to reward him for his efforts. He can plead, but he can no longer command as he did in the past. (71)

This economic dissociation between sons and fathers had implications for the ability of a family to control the marriage and subsequent family life of its sons. The possibility of employment in the towns, circumscribed though it was by racial segregation, meant that young men could amass the wealth needed for *lobola* without the assistance or approval of their elders. Weinrich found that the proportion of *lobola* transactions anchored in the exchange of cattle (which the elders controlled) relative to the proportion anchored in monetary exchanges (which was more easily obtained by the young) had declined during the mid-twentieth century, indicating that elders were less able to impose their will on their juniors:

> Elders no longer control the allocation of bridewealth. The young have become financially more powerful than their fathers and senior kinsmen. Financial independence, moreover, gives them greater freedom to choose their marriage partners than in the past.[5] (97)

Weinrich saw this development as a mixed blessing for wives. On the one hand, it meant that their sisters- and mother-in-law might no longer have legitimate grounds to dominate them, because the family as an entity had not paid the *lobola* and therefore no *vamwene* relationship existed between the women of the lineage and the ones who married into it. On the other hand, it could also mean that wives would not have recourse to those same women in the event of a conflict with their husband and would not be able to appeal to them as intermediaries.

The memories of men and women in a rural area of north central Zimbabwe who came of age in the 1950s confirm Weinrich's observations (Thompson 2000a). Among the men, a prominent theme in memory was of the new opportunities for independence from their fathers afforded by work in the white-owned mines and commercial farms. This new independence enabled the men to pay their own bridewealth and to acquire the necessities for setting up a productive household, such as a plough and harrow. Although not all men could take advantage of waged labor to make themselves autonomous at a relatively young age, they perceived the possibility of this autonomy as a radical break with the lives of their own fathers and grandfathers.

The men and women in Wedza, who I interviewed, had mixed feelings about this change in young people's financial and marital independence. Middle-aged people, born in the 1940s and after, saw their growing independence from their parents in terms of their new identity as being a "person of today," subject to new opportunities and constraints that their parents knew nothing about, while members of the oldest generation regretted their loss of influence over their sons and daughters-in-law. They linked this loss of influence explicitly to the growth of conflict over reproduction and marriage:

[Long ago] we paid *lobola* for them [sons], but not now, they are paying for themselves. That's why we don't have any word if he wants to divorce. (interview with Mrs. Mvuu)

According to me I don't want [family planning], but there is nothing I can do because he [her son] paid his *lobola* alone and he supports [his family] alone. So there is nothing I can do. Even my daughter, she just does what her husband likes. (interview with Mrs. Haka)

We [old] men, we want children, but our families are now very small. One child, maybe it will be a girl, and then they [sons and daughters-in-law] decide to stop, so no Nyenze in the next generation. We don't want, but there is nothing we can do. He pays *lobola* alone, and he will rule his wife alone. There is nothing we can do. (interview with Mr. Nyenze, tr. NS)

Mrs. Hwayana, at 93 years old, said that young women in the latter part of the century had become emboldened not only by the availability of new methods of contraception but also by frequent recourse to "love potions," which could befuddle a son's judgment so that he would not divorce his wife even if she was refusing to bear children. Love potions and contraceptives combined to allow daughters-in-law to contest the wishes of their mothers-in-law for the continuation of the son's family:

No matter if men don't want [their wives to use family planning], what can they do? Women just steal [use it privately]. I don't know what is happening to our children, too much love potions. I told him [her son] to divorce her [his wife], but he just loves her, so [it must be] love potions. There is nothing I can do, but I don't want it. (tr. NS)

Along with the growing financial independence of young people relative to their elders, labor out-migration by young men in the mid-twentieth century also contributed to growing friction within extended families. The absence of men, to a degree, enabled women to act autonomously of their husbands in making decisions about the family plot or family matters while their husband was away.[6] This de facto autonomy could bring them into conflict with their husband's de jure authority, when the husband wanted to impose his wishes on the family. Weinrich's demographic investigation of the population distribution in the rural and urban areas demonstrated that everyday life in most rural areas was determined by women who made up far more than half of the population.

[H]ardly any men in their twenties and thirties stay in the villages and even those who were at home at the time of the 1969 census . . . were often only on home leave and ready to return to the towns and the mines. This means that most women, who in the past because of their junior status, had relatively little say in community affairs, had to assume the main responsibility for the economic welfare of their families. Legally they had no right to make important decisions but had to wait until their husbands returned home or consult their in-laws, but in reality such restrictions broke down. (27)

Weinrich's observations were corroborated by the researchers for *We Carry a Heavy Load,* the first survey to investigate women's perceptions of their lives in the rural areas, which was conducted at independence in 1980. When asked whether a woman could control land in the rural areas, respondents were split, with some of them arguing that women did control land because they were the ones to oversee it when their husbands were away, and other arguing that women should not forget that the land remained the possession of the husband's family and that they had no right to it (Zimbabwe Women's Bureau 1981). Clearly, there was no consensus as to who did or should control important family assets in the rural areas.

In addition to the economic changes that introduced distance between the older and younger generations, the different life experiences of the younger generation contributed to the opening of a generation gap between the aspirations of the younger men and women and their parents' aspirations for them. In particular, the spread of European schooling in the 1960s and 1970s forced open this gap. Barbara Tredgold, the white director of the Federation of

African Women's Clubs, which enrolled approximately 10% of the women in Rhodesia, spoke to this concern in a speech at the 1968 annual conference:

Many parents, particularly African parents, are worried because they cannot enter new knowledge with their children and therefore they feel that their children have a power they will never have. We all know a hundred stories of children pretending to bring messages from the church or from the teacher and getting permission to do the most extraordinary things because of these 'messages.'

But more than education, labor migration or town employment, the liberation war in the mid-1970s wrenched apart the relations between young people and their elders, and, to a lesser extent, between women and men. When the guerrillas arrived in the villages and rural areas, they made alliances with women and youth in order to get food, shelter, and tactical information. The youth and women who fed the guerrillas thus found themselves with unexpected power vis-à-vis their elders (Kriger 1992, Maxwell 1993). The very existence of the guerrilla armies also provided an alternate model of social organization as compared to the village and the extended family. In some liberated areas, the comrades imposed new organizational structures that short-circuited existing power relations. These structures included the creation of women's affairs committees and the organization of *vanamujiba* and *zvimbwido,* youth auxiliaries to the comrades, whose behavior ranged from disciplined and circumspect to anarchic and threatening vis-à-vis community elders (Kriger 1992, Maxwell 1993).

Many young people also left their homes without permission to join the liberation armies, to the great consternation of their parents who found that they had lost control over the labor and whereabouts of their sons and daughters (Kaler 1997, Staunton 1991). The outflow of young people was substantial:

More and more young people were crossing the borders to join the liberation forces. This crossing the borders had reached a new intensity in March 1975 when 40 boys and 3 girls from forms 4, 5, and 6 of a mission school in eastern Rhodesia crossed into Mozambique. By March 1977 it was reported that 25,000 African children were missing from the school rolls (*Rhodesia Herald,* March 12, 1977). By April their number had risen to 36,000 (*Daily News,* April 2, 1977). Towards the end of September 1977, the Rhodesian Ministry of Education reported that 378 African primary and 14 secondary schools had been closed and 90,000 children were "without education" (*Sunday Times,* February 19, 1978), most of whom had crossed the borders. (Weinrich 1979:43)

In the camps, many young people had left as much to escape the domination of their parents as to create a new socialist Zimbabwe. In her survey of women

guerrillas in the guerrilla camps in Mozambique, Weinrich found that one striking characteristic of these women is their youth:

> 72% are between 15 and 19 years of age, 26% between 20 and 24 years, and
> only 2% between 25 and 29 years. . . . only 30% had consulted their parents
> before leaving, 70% left quietly, fearing opposition. It is a very important
> step for young women to do anything, which might lead to a break with their
> families, for their whole upbringing binds them strongly to their families,
> especially their mothers. (44)

One of the main reasons why women joined the liberation armies was their
rejection of marriages arranged by their elders (115). Even for the majority
who did not leave their home to join the war, the very existence of the liberation armies with their unorthodox models of gender and generational relations
challenged existing social orders, and contributed to the atmosphere of a
social world in flux.

Taken together, the possibility of relative financial independence from their
fathers for young men; the increase in female-headed families; and the youth
orientation of the liberation war armies meant that the bonds of obligation
between the generations and the genders were already straining and fraying
when the pill and Depo arrived on the scene. No sudden drastic reversal of
power relations between men and women or between old and young occurred
in the 1960s and 1970s, rather a series of dramas were played out in individual families and communities. Fertility, at the center of the literal as well as
symbolic perpetuation of family life, was implicated in many of these struggles, and pills and Depo often took center stage in these dramas.

## THE DAUGHTER-IN-LAW'S FERTILITY AND THE EXTENDED FAMILY

As young men and women evaded their elders' authority, childbearing
became a battleground between the young and the old. Elders and in-laws
tried to impose their wishes as to the number and timing of their sons' and
daughters-in-laws' children, and legitimized their efforts by reference to
ideals of "our Shona culture," which dictated that control over childbearing
should be vested in men, in elders, and in the family that a woman married
into. Younger people, and especially younger women, resisted these claims of
authority, and used the pill and the injection to do so.

The early days of family planning were as marked by conflict within genders
as between genders, particularly in rural areas. Living in the village, a young wife
often had daily, or even hourly, contact with her husband's female relatives, who
often had very definite feelings about how many children she should have and
when she should have them. Women in towns and peri-urban areas might con-

nive with their neighbors to hide their contraceptives, according to FPWs, but in the rural areas a wife would have more difficulty escaping the eye of her mother- and sisters-in-law, especially if her husband worked elsewhere. While a friend might be trusted to help out of female solidarity, an in-law could not be so trusted. FPWs told of women whose efforts to use contraception secretly without the knowledge of their husbands were thwarted by his female relatives:

I remember my sister-in-law, the mother-in-law threw away the tablets so that she fell pregnant, because she had two girls and they wanted a son, and they were having squabbles with the husband, and she was a lawyer working at the magistrates, she was an educated woman, and when she was at work the mother in law took all the tablets and flushed them in the toilet. So when she came back wanting to take the tablets the domestic worker said, "Mama took the pills and flushed them in the toilet." So she didn't have pills for three days and then she became pregnant, even though she was having squabbles with the husband. She had a boy. (interview with Mrs. Hilda Bulle)

Mothers-in-law would not have it. They would say, "Why, why must these young people do this?" I remember once an old woman said, "I hope you are not teaching these girls to stop having babies." She would ask, "How many children have you got?" and "I hope you are not telling her to stop having children because I had 10 children and I am still alive. So don't give them that education." All of the old people were very much opposed, they said, "I want my grandchildren, I want them whether they are 10 or 12." That's when they tell that young woman, "If you have got one child the man will just go and take another wife, so that she will have more children for him." Mothers-in-law were instructing their sons that if a woman has got one child and the child is 12 or 13, you must have another wife and children, you must have more children. (interview with Mrs. Margaret Khumalo)

Mothers-in-law, that was a bit tricky because their sons were in town working and then the daughters-in-law were at home, and the daughters- in-law didn't want the mothers-in-law to know about their private matters, family planning is one of them. . . . We could always tell, if we got to a village and spoke to the women and one or two of the younger ones they didn't participate, they didn't ask any questions, nothing, we could always tell that they were the daughter-in-law and the only way they could have responded is when they were spoken to. (interview with Mr. Alec Ndhlukula)

Dealing with these tensions between the generations over young women's fertility was part of the daily work of the FPWs. They used deception to evade not only suspicious husbands but also mothers- and sisters-in-law, in order to get access to the young wife who needed family planning:

Some women don't talk about it [family planning] when their mother-in-law is there. I say, "Oh Grandmother, I have to come to see you, how are you feeling, what of the back? [old women are thought to be prone to complaining about lower back pains]." Then she will be relaxed. I will then say, "I am going now, why can't she accompany me [to the gate of the homestead], the young one, the daughter-in-law?" Then that's where we could make our conversation. (interview with Mrs. Imelda Mudarikiri)

Mrs. Annah Mangwiro's brother, who was present for part of my interview with her, described how his sister took it on herself to police his wife's child-bearing:

I experienced it, in my case my wife and my sister had a fight over that one, they actually fought over family planning. She [his sister] didn't accept it at all. She was so protective of her brother, she didn't allow anything of that sort. I remember my mother used to moan and moan over it, why do you stay so long without another, you haven't had another kid in so many years, she would moan and moan over it. The pressure that comes from the family, it's too much.

Mothers- and sisters-in-law perceived themselves to be looking out for their sons' and brothers' interests, protecting the interests of the family from the doings of a potentially disobedient wife:

Relatives, female relatives, they would say, "You know your wife is on family planning" and they [the wives] would be told, "I want a pregnancy in three months time." Some women had to fall pregnant to appease the husband. [AK: What if they didn't get pregnant? You can't always get pregnant just when you want.] Then you will be divorced. There was a lot of pressure really. (interview with Mrs. Florence Chikara)

Some could even say that this family planning is used by those who want to go about with other men, so that is why the mother in law is so concerned. If the daughter-in-law takes this she will go about with other men, not my son, maybe she will kill my son with [sexually transmitted] diseases. Those were all sorts of problems that the in-laws would not want the daughters [in law] to use family planning. (interview with Mrs. Gladys Chitsungo)

Mothers- and sisters-in-law claimed that a young wife who used family planning was breaking both the letter and the spirit of *lobola*. Even though sisters-in-law were not directly involved in providing the cattle or money for *lobola* payments, the cattle that their husbands had given for them often provided the *lobola* for their brother to marry in his turn. In addition, the number of children that their brother had directly affected the fortunes of their shared lineage.

They [young women clients] wouldn't go for family planning in front of the mother-in-law or sister-in-law. I don't know where we got this battle of female in-laws sort of guarding each other. They would want many grandchildren so limiting the number of children would mean probably less grandchildren for her and cheating her son or brother [AK: who paid *lobola* and now you have gone off to the clinic . . . ] Exactly. They don't get what is due for what they paid for. The job that you are married for, to bear children, you won't do if you are controlling your fertility. (interview with Mrs. Salina Mumbengegwi)

Some [mothers- and sisters-in-law] used to say, "*Takakuroora*" [it is us who have married you] to the *muroora*.[7] Some used to say, "You can't have three or four children while me, I had 12 or 13, why do you want to stop having children while you are very young?" (interview with Mrs. Janet Ngadya)

They could complain that "we want more children from the *muroora,* we just pay *lobola* for children, if she doesn't have children it's no good." And some would even go to the extent that they would have gatherings of talking about the sister-in-law that delayed to get a child. So we were encouraging them to use family planning for only two years and then get a child, so they don't cause problems in the family. (interview with Mrs. Gladys Chitsungo)[8]

The question of *lobola* and of who had paid *lobola* for whom shaped attitudes to family planning. Women's attitudes to the use of family planning depended not only on their gender, their beliefs about fertility or contraception, or their political attitudes, but also on their relationship to the particular person who was contemplating using family planning. Many of the women who wanted their sisters-in-law to get pregnant might also be using family planning for themselves, either secretly or openly. FPWs remembered mothers-in-law who refused to sanction the *muroora*'s use of the pill or the injection, but simultaneously encouraged their own daughters to use it. As Mrs. Phoebe Mpezeni put it, women were thought of *as mothers-in-law* or *as sisters-in-law* rather than as fellow women, when evaluating the use of family planning by a daughter-in-law:

Mothers- and sisters-in-law would say, "We don't want this family planning because our brother is not going to have more children." She will decide as a mother- or sister-in-law. There were some who were very cruel, there were some who wanted their *muroora* to have more children instead of her own daughter. They would prefer that the *muroora* has more children. If their own daughter uses it [family planning] they don't mind. . . . to say the truth, women used to like it very much with the exception of those in-laws.

They [older women] don't want [family planning] but . . . they encourage their unmarried daughters to have pills because if they have unwanted children it will be a problem to them [the older women] too. She will leave all the kids with them, and go to find work in another town, and bring another baby again. They don't want their *muroora* to use because they want their families to be big. (interview with Mr. Tsimba, tr. NS)

Older women were undoubtedly aware of the difficulties younger women faced with spacing pregnancies or with having more children than they could manage, but were constrained by family politics from broaching the subject with their daughters-in-law. Mrs. Dorothy Dzuda suggested that some sympathetic older women were reluctant to suggest family planning to daughters-in-law because it might distress their sons, and cause the sons to become angry with their mothers. Because mothers-in-law generally lived with their sons and were supported by them, the costs of potentially offending a son were much higher than the costs of offending one's daughter's husband, who lived far away with his own paternal kin. Thus, sympathetic older women had less to risk by suggesting family planning to their own daughter than to their daughters-in-law.

They [older women] were the people who were very influential to their daughters, especially the daughters. They were afraid to talk to their daughters-in-law because some felt that the daughter-in-law will tell the husband that, "It's your mum who has told me to join family planning," and that will cause problems in the family. So at that time I found that the old women were more free to their own daughters than to the daughters-in-law to advise them to go for family planning.

While young women would be warned overtly against using the new methods by their mother-in-law, they might be covertly encouraged by their own mothers to seek out contraception for the sake of their health.

Not all in-laws and elders were obdurately opposed to the use of family planning. FPWs stressed that they took care to approach older women, even though they might be past childbearing themselves, because of their influence within the female world of the family and homestead.

[AK: Would you educate even the old people who are past childbearing years?] Yes, we would do that just because we wanted them to help us, because when you come to a home you will find that there is those young women and there is an old woman. If you educate and motivate and win that old woman, she will support you and say, "You young ladies who don't want to space your children, why? Long ago we used to space our children with these one, two, three methods. So you see what this man here is saying is very correct." So that's why we wanted to talk to those old women, because we know they are going to help us by talking to these young ladies. (interview with Mr. Albert Katerere)

To persuade the mothers-in-law to support the daughter-in-law's use of family planning, FPWs relied on rhetorical strategies, which did not challenge the division of power in the household, but that acknowledged the mother-in-law as an integral part of the marriage. FPWs asserted that mothers-in-law had rightful influence in their son's lives and described the ways in which it was in a mother-in-law's self-interest to limit or space her son's children.

When I went to those old aged women, I had to start with praising them "Oh, you are looking after your children very well," and so on. Then I have to introduce the subject: "This is very nice, if a daughter-in-law can bring the child up to three years without having another pregnancy, and you won't have the problem of washing the nappies [diapers] while the mother is away." Because if the child is weaned too early the mother-in-law has the problem of washing the nappies, feeding the child, doing everything with the baby at her back because the mother is having another child. And I would encourage them: "Now it is your time to rest, because you have finished our work when you brought your children up. You should be having grandchildren who can assist you by giving you some water to drink, or whom you can send to do something or tell to do something, not the kids to carry at your back." And they found it was a very sensible thing. Because the daughter-in-law can't be carrying two babies at a time, and you are supposed to be carrying that other one, and they don't want that when they are old. (interview with Mrs. Dorothy Dzuda)

Some mothers-in-law will sympathize with the daughter-in-law, if the husband says, "I don't want." She finds out that when this child is six the daughter-in-law will already have two more, then it's a burden to the mother-in-law also, she will have to take care of those children. Sometimes they just said, "Take the family planning and give to me to hide the package, I will do this for you." (interview with Mrs. Elinor Dauya)

Disagreements about childbearing between *varoora* and their mothers-in-law did not begin with the pill, of course. Many older women still remember ongoing family tensions throughout the twentieth century, between an older generation who wanted to see plenty of descendants, and a young *muroora* who worried that the children were coming too often and too fast. However, the pill and Depo brought along a new set of social relations governing access to fertility control, relations that made it easier for young women to use contraception without the agreement of their elders.

Getting hold of pills and injections was a radically different experience from getting hold of traditional child-spacing methods before the 1960s. Access to the older methods was granted mainly through networks of elder women, especially mothers-in-law, but also including some blood kin such as grandmothers and through some elder women who were known as traditional healers. This layer of gatekeepers might or might not agree with a young woman's desire to prevent or delay a pregnancy. This gatekeeping was major reason why young women turned away from the traditional methods that had served their mothers and toward the new, dubious, and potentially dangerous technologies.

## "DOING TRADITIONAL": THE FAMILY AND COMMUNITY AS GATEKEEPERS OF FERTILITY

Regulating fertility is nothing new for the Shona. The FPWs provided new ways to regulate fertility, rather than introducing drastic new ideas about it. Indeed, FPWs emphasized the continuity between new and old means of birth control, stressing that the injection and the pill were just new ways of achieving the same results as the old herbal preparations, charms, and periods of abstinence or prolonged breastfeeding.

However, FPWs elided one important distinction between old and new: The new methods, to a much greater extent than the old ones, could be accessed and controlled by individual women acting on their own. The gatekeepers of the old methods—husbands, mothers-in-law, and traditional healers[9]—were replaced by a new set of gatekeepers for the new methods[10]—clinic staff, community-based distributors, and nurses. These people often had very different ideas about who should control childbearing within a family and were markedly more likely to favor a woman's professed interests against those of her husband.

In all my interviews, I asked why people chose to use the new methods, specifically the hormonal ones, such as the pill and the injection, instead of relying on the older traditional ones. The answers I got were not always what I expected. Very few people spoke in favor of the innate superiority or effectiveness of the new methods. Indeed, the majority of non-FPWs, and at least half the FPWs, told me that when used correctly the old methods were very effective, and presented their own experiences or the experiences of older women in their family as evidence. The old methods were described as being healthier and better able to "go with" an African body without troublesome side effects, such as bleeding and headaches, or impotence in male partners. Nonetheless, Zimbabwean women did turn away from the old methods and toward the new ones. I believe that the social relations governing access to the two types of methods lay behind this switch.

The traditional methods were all female-dependent—things that must be done by a woman rather than a man (except for withdrawal). My interviewees were quite adamant that traditional methods were taken by women, not men, and that there was no method that a man could use to protect his wife from impregnation. They told me that contracepting was only done by women, while men were responsible for finding herbs to make them "strong husbands" or to "strengthen their backbone" (i.e., to increase their potency). However, while these methods were female-dependent, they were not female

FPW talking with a passerby (who may be a satisfied client, as suggested by her smile and the presence of her one young child. Source: FPAR 1978, a promotional brochure published by the FPAR.

controlled—at least not controlled by the woman who was seeking to avoid conception. Each method was embedded in a web of social relations and was dependent on someone—usually a female elder—to provide the secrets that made the method work. Access to traditional methods was controlled by men (usually *n'angas*), female elders (usually in-laws), or by both.

You know the African method of family planning, it was actually discussed between the husband and the mother-in-law. The whole family [of the husband] was involved, it was looked at as the family unit. [AK: It all went through the husband's family?] Right, it was his family. (interview with Mrs. Annah Mangwiro)

[AK: Were men opposed to their wives using traditional methods?] No, because the elders would have talked to both of them [young married couples]: "If you don't want to spoil your child the woman has got to do this or you have got to do this." So they would agree, the two of them. So there was no problem. The parents of the husband, his aunties, they would go to his aunties. [AK: So it was not something that the wife could just go and do?] No, it comes from the elders, they do believe in that. (interview with Mrs. Imelda Mudarikiri)

When a woman was using traditional they would go together with the husband and it's the mother of the husband who had that type of *muti* [medicine]. Sometimes if she fell pregnant when the baby was small she [the mother-in-law] would say, "Why did your people not teach you to do something, why didn't your own mother teach you?" (interview with Mrs. Eugenia Mashonga)

Men's cooperation was needed not only for abstinence and withdrawal, but also for fertility-suppressing herbs or charms:

Some had herbs . . . to tie around the waist. They make knots, if they want to plan [to remain without pregnancy] for four years they put four knots around the waist, two knots here, two knots here. It mustn't be broken, it mustn't be taken off, it must stay there for four years. Now when they want to have a baby this string mustn't break by itself, they must untie it nicely and put it somewhere safe. [AK: Who unties it? Can the woman undo the knots herself?] No, the husband has to be the one. [AK: Is he the one that puts it on?] Yes. (interview with Mrs. Regina Chokwenda)

They used the herbs to drink. The husband will give the wife while they are standing on the doorstep [of the home], husband outside, woman sitting on the doorstep, then the husband will give the wife some herbs to drink. But the husbands, although they were giving those herbs, they were using again withdrawal. Both were family planning, husband to withdraw and also to give the herbs to drink. (interview with Mrs. Janet Ngadya)

Even when a man's assistance was not needed to implement the method, their support was needed because the traditional methods were highly visible to men.

To use that [a contraceptive belt] needs agreement with your husband, because a string around your waist is not a private [secret] thing to your husband. (interview with Mrs. Chapungu)

They had to agree with their husbands because a string is a public thing to your husband, the waistline is his to see any time. (interview with Mrs. Ingwe, tr. NS)

Beyond the husband, relatives and family members were also involved in the reproductive decisions of young women, and nearly all the women I spoke to complained of pressures from their in-laws to have more children. One woman described traditional family planning as "planning *by* the whole family" rather than planning of one's family. However, in some cases the interference of in-laws could actually help young women whose babies were coming too fast, as the husband's relatives ordained that the couple should wait longer between births, to protect the mother's and children's health. These birth intervals were created through a series of prohibitions and permissions on sexual intercourse between husband and wife.

These prohibitions and permissions embody two of the most important features of the social regulation of reproduction in Shona communities: (1) the inscription of sexual activity within a system of power and authority in which sexual behavior was subject to public approval and was not the private affair of the individual[s] concerned; and (2) the collective nature of the repercussions of illegitimate sexual or reproductive activity. These inscriptions may have changed their form over the past few generations, but have never entirely disappeared.

The interdictions against intercourse carried the possibility of fatal harm coming to members of the extended family if the married couple indulged in illicit sexual activity in having intercourse before the time of prohibition was over.

They [wives] used not to have sex with their husbands soon after the birth, it was a way of spacing births. When they want to have sex with their husband they used to go to the old *ambuya* [in this context, mother-in-law] and say, "My son or daughter is old now, so what can I do before I meet [have sex with] my husband?" Now she could be instructed by the *ambuya*, "The child is old now so *kuvhurisa nzeve*, [literally "open the ears," resume sexual relations with official blessing from the family]." They were told by the *ambuya*, "If you meet your husband before you come to me I am going to go blind. I need to give you some instructions." I used to ask one, "Why do you do this?" and she said it was a way of spacing, to frighten these women so they cannot meet their husbands as early as six weeks. [AK: So if a woman comes to her *ambuya* after only two months, the *ambuya* can say, "Don't meet your husband now, if you do it now I will go blind."] Yes, so she was afraid to meet her husband and that was family planning. (interview with Mr. David Chibvongodze)

After birth the man was not allowed to have sex with his wife. The man had to go to the midwife and say, "I want to re-enter my bedroom." After he says so the wife will go to the midwife to perform the ritualistic process like to take 50 cents and cook mealie-meal, just a small dish. When she [the midwife] arrives, the midwife will take all her things as payment and then the midwife will let the wife put a few drops of milk in the baby's eyes . . . If the wife has sex before these rituals the baby will become blind and the midwife will suffer from backache [an ailment often associated with sexual activities]. To cover all this will take some months, and the baby will be growing [i.e., the baby will be old before a sibling comes along]. (interview with Mr. Shorechena, tr. NS)

When a woman wants to have another child, she goes to ask permission from her mother-in-law, saying that the present child has grown, please tell me that another child can come now. When a child is born, both parents go to the elder female relatives of the husband with a pot of beer [as an offering of respect] to report, "We have a new child, congratulations to the whole family!" When the child opens his or her eyes, they go again to report to the elder female relatives. They go again when the child has begun to walk. Then when they want another child they say, "The child has grown and we want another child, please advise us what to do [i.e., tell us to resume sexual relations]. He or she is now able to walk and to herd goats. Could you make it possible that we become pregnant?" (interview with Mrs. Ivy Mhlanga, tr. AK)

Some of them had rules which they were told by their grandmothers. They could meet a man after the child was six or eight months [old]. They were not allowed to touch their husbands or even to be touched until the child is six months, seven months. They could not do it before the granny gave permission. This was a belief that the child could die. They were told that the child could die. So to protect your child keep this rule. (interview with Mrs. Elizabeth Mlambo)

One FPW recounted how in her own marriage, abstinence for the purposes of child-spacing was facilitated and maintained by a chain of social pressure involving both her in-laws and men from her natal family:

I had my first child in 1973, another one in 1974 then 1975. My own father came using the right channel to the people who were supposed to speak to my husband [her husband's father and paternal uncles] to say, "We think childbearing is being overdone, you can [might] kill my child [i.e., the wife]. Why don't you talk to them that they slow down? Probably they don't know what to do." And this was a concern for many men, this was a men's point of view. [AK: That it was too fast?] That it was too fast, the children need to be spaced. . . . [T]his was my father, because he was seeing that I was having babies too close, he was sort of saying why don't they . . . space the children? She can't have a child every year. She will die from childbearing. (interview with Mrs. Salina Mumbengegwi).

Some women tried to use traditional methods secretly, sidestepping the gate-keepers. My interviewees were divided as to whether it had ever been possible to be a private acceptor of indigenous methods, or whether access to these methods was too tightly controlled by elders and traditional healers for a woman to use them without first having obtained approval from her husband and his family. Using traditional methods secretly was difficult for two reasons.

First, traditional methods were public and visible compared with the discreet packet of pills, or the invisible injection. Other women would keep careful track of who among the younger women were "doing traditional." Even if a husband and wife had agreed together to delay the birth of their next child, it could be difficult to keep this secret from the women of the family if the wife was using traditional methods.

> They [women using traditional methods] were told by the healers to take these herbs and put them on your waist, and we were telling them, "Look here, even if someone is wearing a dress it can be seen, it will be seen." They didn't want it to be seen. We were telling them, "When you take the pill there is nothing to be seen. In the communal lands people go to wash in the river and all the other people go, maybe four or five women together, they will see you with all the beads and the like [around the waist], are you not ashamed?" Some would say, "Ah no, I must surely be ashamed." We told them that if you use family planning, our methods, no one will know what you are doing. (interview with Mr. Richard Chidakwa)

Second and more important, the gatekeepers of traditional methods were very selective as to who they would help. According to Mrs. Tendai Masvika, old women were often secretive and jealous about traditional methods that they knew and would refuse to tell young women, other than the few whom they approved of, saying, "*Imi muzukuru wacho chete* [this is only for you, my granddaughter]" and telling them not to share the knowledge with other young women. By contrast, said Mrs. Masvika, "we [FPWs] are not jealous, we want this to be free for everyone to practice . . . the family planning *ambuya*s are open to everybody, telling everyone. We don't select you my sister, you my cousin, I will tell only you." For older women, the ability to direct the fertility of their sons and daughters-in-law was a source of power that they were reluctant to give up by making the sources of their herbs and medicines public knowledge. Mrs. Judith Rasika, a FPW, "did traditional" even while she was working as a health worker, but the death of her mother-in-law left her without her ways of regulating fertility:

> They [traditional healers] were the ones who could help you, but access to that healer was very difficult. They didn't want to be pointed out in public as people who knew these things. . . . So a mother who wanted to not become pregnant had to find a healer, but finding a healer was very difficult. Their medicines used to work but the problem was to find those people. Like myself, my mother-in-law, the mother of my husband, but she died, so she died with her medicine. She died and I don't know the medicine, I don't

know where she used to get it. She didn't tell me, she would only give you the medicine to drink but she didn't want us to know about it. (tr. AK)

According to Mrs. Njiva,

As a young woman you couldn't consult a *n'anga* or a traditional healer, so your elder aunt or grandmother will do that for you. If you agree with your husband, it's easy to go to a healer together. (tr. NS)

Mrs. Njiva and others did concur that in their youth some young women would try to gain access to the traditional methods by themselves, but that such independence was fiercely resented by the corps of older women and healers who sought to monopolize sexual and reproductive knowledge.

Even women who were lucky enough to find someone to help them with traditional methods would not talk about what they had found or how they had acquire this method. According to Mrs. Tendai Masvika, in her youth "it was difficult to find people who practice traditional, they won't admit that they do so. Women just say they don't menstruate, and they don't know the reason why they don't menstruate" (tr. AK). This was confirmed by members of the oldest generation in Wedza, who were born before the 1940s. They emphasized that they did not want their knowledge of contraception to become public knowledge and were determined to control access to traditional methods.[11]

It [traditional methods] is private because I can't shout it to anyone. No! No! It can't be given to unmarried people, why? They want to prevent what? No, we don't allow that! We give to married people who have a problem like having pregnancy while still breastfeeding. (interview with Mrs. Nyamera, tr. NS)

Elders know, but they give only those whom they love, because in our custom everything is private. That's why our kids run after modern methods. We know but we will die with our secrets. (interview with Mrs. Mbira, senior, tr. NS)

I can't say that all people know. The elders of the family know, but in our culture everything is a secret. Even now, we know a lot of medicine but we keep it to ourselves. (interview with Mrs. Tseve)

In our tradition we give medicine to those who have problems, not these new methods which they give to anyone who wants it. It's not good. (interview with Mr. Bimha, tr. NS)

Mr. Kondo, 94 years old, said bitterly that Western medicine had stripped his generation of their authority:

I know a lot of traditional herbs, but now no one wants these things, because young boys and girls call our traditional herbs as dirty, they want white pills. I am going to die with my knowledge. I don't tell anyone because they are now following Western culture. They are now running after pills, even unmarried girls. . . . We are hanging between half black and half white, we shall suffer for this. (tr. NS)

The traditional methods of fertility control were surrounded by secrecy and exclusivity, which concentrated power in the hands of elders who knew the roots, herbs, charms, and rituals. Many interviewees, who are now middle-aged, remembered how their seniors guarded this knowledge and often would not even admit that they knew of such methods, let alone disclose the secrets of the methods.

Some used [traditional methods] and I heard about them, but you know our culture is full of secrecy. Those who know will just do it for themselves and their relatives. (interview with Mrs. Shirapopo, tr. NS)

Elders and relatives taught this [traditional methods]. As I told you, our elders do everything privately, some they know but they pretend as if they don't know. (interview with Mrs. Ingwe, tr. NS)

Some elders kept their knowledge and medicines secret to maintain a commercial monopoly on contraception. According to Mr. Nhuka, who described himself as a traditional healer,

Me as a traditional healer, I don't tell you the names [of the herbs he used] because my ancestors don't allow me to show people their plants. . . . Our culture is full of privacy because to be a healer is like a business so we make money and wealth out of it, that's why we give roots [rather than leaves or easily-identifiable parts of the plants] and crush everything so the patient can't identify it. He or she will come tomorrow if that problem comes again [rather than seeking out the curative herbs on their own]. (tr. NS)

Among the non-FPWs I spoke to, all those who knew of traditional methods stressed that they would not give their knowledge away except to the young women they approved of, and that they would only allow these methods to be used in those cases that they considered to be of genuine hardship or necessity for limiting the number of children.[12] The older contraceptives were thus handed out according to the priorities of the elders, sometime in consultation with husbands, which did not always accord with what young women saw as their best interests. Elders often had very definite ideas about the tempo of childbearing and the number of children that should be born, and control over contraceptive methods helped them to actualize their agendas.

My grandmother refused to tell me about it. She said I cannot use [traditional methods] because there was no war [at that time]. She said she used traditional methods long back because of the tribal wars[13] [which created insecurity and made many families into refugees], so our generation was supposed to have many children to make up [for the losses in the wars]. (interview with Mrs. Mbira, junior)

They [older women] are the ones who just watch some of the women suffering by having baby after baby, they know how to prevent it but they don't want [to tell the younger women]. They just said, "let her have her children while she is still young." (interview with Mrs. Shirapopo, tr. NS)

Although elders were in general pronatal and wanted to see their lineage grow, they were not bent on reproduction at all costs. Interviewees stressed that elders would give contraceptives or allow fertility regulating measures to be taken when they deemed that the health of a mother or a child might be at risk—by a pregnancy begun too soon after the last one—and that health considerations could override the importance of bearing children for the lineage.

Not all of them [women who wanted to contracept] are helped, but those who have problems like getting pregnant while breastfeeding are those who are helped, but they have children after a certain time. Elders, aunts, and those who know will give. (interview with Mr. Jenya)

The elders know, they help if you need it, but if you don't they don't bother. (interview with Mrs. Mbira, junior, tr. NS)

Mrs. Hwiribidi claimed that she had the power to bless ordinary water and give it contraceptive properties, but she said that she did not give anyone her water unless they met her standards of having a genuine hardship in taking care of their children. Merely not wanting to have children did not count as a hardship, because "to God having children is not a problem. I give to couples who are having problems. We just want the baby to reach the stage of walking; that's fine, then you can have another baby" (tr. NS). My interviewees were divided as to whether it had ever been possible for women to use traditional methods without the knowledge of their husbands or members of the extended family, with about half claiming that women could and did do this, and the other half claiming that access was so tightly controlled that it would have been impossible. However, they agreed that any woman who wanted to use these methods privately would need a great deal of luck and persistence.

Women who wanted to use indigenous methods privately faced two major problems. One was reversibility. Most indigenous Shona contraceptive methods rely on two active agents or processes: one that stops fertility and one that later restores it. Even if a woman is able to obtain the first agent, if she is unable to later counteract the effects of the contraceptive, she is doomed to infertility or subfecundity. All of my interviewees knew stories about women who had been in that position—perhaps the person who had given them the fertility-stopping herbs had left the district and taken the antidote or had died, or perhaps the bush that the woman had jumped over to stop her fertility had been cut down or had grown too high to be jumped in the opposite direction. Both the physical world—the trees, bushes, or anthills that had figured in the traditional methods—and the social world—the network of people who provided the methods and their antidotes—were subject to change, so that any method could suddenly become irreversible. Using traditional methods outside the network of elders and traditional healers was a risky business, with the possibility of permanent sterilization. For example,

I know one who went to a certain witch doctor and she was given this medicine. She was supposed to go back when she wanted a child but unfortunately this person died. I said, "Now what are you going to say to your husband?" She said, "I can never say anything, because when I went there first I didn't tell him." (interview with Mrs. Imelda Mudarikiri)

Mrs. Nyati reported that her unmarried sister had fallen victim to a similar problem after making use without supervision of contraceptive herbs to abort a pregnancy in progress:

What happened is that the dosage she was given to take was more than [necessary] and all her ovaries came out and she is sterile even now. The boyfriend dumped her like a rotten thing. He is married to someone who is fertile. (tr. NS)

Even educated elite women with resources of money and time could find themselves trapped into sterility through unsanctioned use of a traditional method. I was told of a rich doctor's wife who had traveled across the country in order to secretly "jump a bush" so that she would not become pregnant. However, when she went back to undo the contraception by jumping over the bush backward, she found that it had been cut down for firewood. The woman then had to live with the fear that her husband would divorce her in favor of a new, more fertile, wife (interview with Mrs. Moyana . . . I never learned whether she was actually divorced or not!).

The second problem was the issue of access to genuine contraceptives. Women who sought out herbal preparations or charms by themselves, without the assistance of a knowledgeable *ambuya* or other wise person could not be sure that what they obtained was really what it purported to be. Such women could be easy prey for quacks or unscrupulous *n'angas*. In addition, women did not always trust their mothers-in-law or local healers to give them the genuine article. Mrs. Dzoma reported that the older female relatives whom she

approached for help deceived her by promising her a contraceptive and then
giving her a placebo, because of those relatives' desire to see more children.

> I don't trust those traditional methods, some of them will give fake things,
> because they did that to me. I was given a string to tie around my waist but I
> became pregnant with that string around my waist, so I don't believe that they
> [elders] will give people true things. These old women first asked, "How many
> children do you have? Don't you know that our life is based on children?" So
> I told them that I had two [children]. At first they refused, but I kept on trying.
> That's when she gave me that string, but that same month I became pregnant.
> I think they had [functional contraceptives] but they refused to give. (tr. NS)

Mr. Nyamudzwa said that while most people who used traditional methods
went to their relatives, "those who were afraid of being given wrong things
consulted *n'angas.*"

Traditional healers might also refuse to help not because they believed that
the woman concerned should have more children, but because they feared the
consequences from other members of the family if the contraceptive method
went wrong and rendered the woman unable to conceive again:

> I found that with these old methods people would think, "If I advise my
> *muzukuru* [granddaughter] about this she will end up without children and
> she will hate me, that *ambuya* has done something to me, that's why I don't
> have children, because she gave me some *muti* after my last child and there
> are no more, I have stopped taking that *muti* and I am no longer having chil-
> dren." So it will cause anger in that family, the old people, everybody now
> will come across saying, "You are no good, *makaroya muzukuru wedu* [you
> have cursed our grandchild]." They were afraid. These methods could work
> but the dosage and the size, weight and whatever, it was technical. (inter-
> view with Mr. T.J. Mugariri)

> They don't give herbs to prevent, because if they [the women who took the
> herbs] become sterile, they will blame them, I mean the people who gave.
> (interview with Mr. Bhiza, tr. NS)

Like the mothers-in-law mentioned earlier, some healers were also reluctant
to give traditional assistance to young women because of their fears of anger-
ing the young woman's husband, if he did not agree with his wife's plans:

> Elders knew, and traditional healers . . . They give only when there is an
> agreement between couples, because they were afraid of divorces. A string
> is a public method to your husband because the waistline is his to see every
> time. (interview with Mrs. Gudo, tr. NS)

While men and women might not trust the nurses and FPWs with their alien devices surrounded by rumors of sterility and other problems, they also did not entirely trust their own traditional healers or elders. Mrs. Pfunye reported that some women who used traditional methods without success were quick to jump to the conclusion that the healer they had consulted for the methods was a quack, even when it was their own use of the method that was at fault:

> We had problems even long ago [Mrs. Pfunye was born in 1918] because not all of the methods will be good for you. You might tie something around your waist, but you become pregnant, but someone else will tie that same medicine and it will work perfectly. That's why some said the healers were liars, but no, that's not it. I tied a string with beads and herbs around my waist and it worked perfectly. (tr. NS)

Even those women who used traditional methods with the full permission of their relatives could feel a need to also secretly use the new methods. The prevalence of "false *n'angas*" and the deterioration of knowledge and supplies from what they had been "in our great-grandmothers' days" meant that older methods might not be reliable. Use of the new methods could provide double protection, even though these methods might have to be kept secret from the husband or mother-in-law.

> They used to [use traditional methods] but to say the truth they could come and say, "Look, I have been using this African method but I am pregnant, I have been using this *muti* but I didn't have my period," so so many became pregnant, so everyone knew that traditional method is not hundred percent so that is why people stopped using and come for this Depo and new methods. [AK: Did people ever use traditional and modern methods at the same time?] Yes they did that, it was their way to pretend, to pretend to their husband that "I am using that [the traditional method given by the elders]," it is quite true. She used to say, "*Ndakasungirirwa,* [literally "I have been tied," I have protected myself against conception] I have tied this African method, *muti,* so I won't become pregnant," while she is taking the pills. She hides them somewhere . . . at five o'clock she takes the pill before the husband comes. (interview with Mrs. Phoebe Mpezeni)

> It was an advantage to women, to the young women, because they could say, "I want to go to the granny and be given some *muti* so that we can nurse our child [wait until the child is older before having another]," only if the husband would allow them. If the husband was opposed it was easier for her to take the new methods. She could say, "If you want I can stop this traditional medicine and I can conceive." If she wanted to take more time before she was pregnant, she could say, "I don't know what is happening, but the old

lady [who supplied indigenous methods] promised that I will be all right."
Then she could stop from taking the pill. Some men liked their women to
practice with the old method, the traditional one, but it was to the advantage
of the young mothers to take this from the old women and then go to the
clinic. The husband could just think she is taking the *muti* from my mother
or my granny, but she is actually taking medicine from the clinic. Some did-
n't even use the old medicine, because some who had tried it and it failed
them, so they had no faith in it. They would say to the husbands, "I am using
that from the granny," but in actual fact she is taking the pill, which she did-
n't tell their husband. Most of them were not telling the husband that they
were taking the pill. (interview with Mrs. Winnie Pasipanodya)

For other women, the failure of traditional healers to make good on their
promises led them to switch completely to the new methods:

[T]here were these women at Rugare who went to the African doctor, the
*n'anga.* They were given two bottles and they were given medicine. The
*n'anga* said, "Now you are not going to have pregnancies." But after two
months they had both gotten pregnant. They went to that *n'anga* and
scolded him. On the way back we meet together, they said, "Mrs. Raradza,
from the day I get my baby [give birth], I want to be *kusungwa* [literally
"tied," here, protected from conceiving], this *n'anga akati nhingi* [says non-
sensical things]." *Saka* [therefore] this is a nice story to say that modern
family planning methods are best. (interview with Mrs. Blandina Raradza)

To the FPWs, encroaching on the territory of *n'angas* and *ambuyas,* the
tight controls on traditional methods were an incentive for young women to
try the new methods.

You sit down with the [potential family planning client], you talk and discuss, how did she start off, where did she get it from, and when she wants to
have a baby what happens. People were very free, it depends on how you
approach them. Give them the time, and don't say you are discouraging
them from taking this [traditional methods] "because I want you to take this
new thing now, so you must stop this now." First of all talk, do they understand how it works, if this happens what happens. Then you talk and talk
and talk until you come to a stage where you are saying, "If you are using
this method and this happens, that happens," and they normally get stuck.
"If that happens I don't know what to do." That's how you convince them.
Some said, "I have just had this method given to me by my grandmother,
but how it works I don't know and the grandmother might die or something," then you convince them and they go around and say, "*Ambuya,* let
me take this now, this is better and I understand it more." (interview with
Mrs. Shamiso Kudakwashe)

FPWs also pointed to the existence of clandestine abortions throughout the 1950s and 1960s as evidence for their prospective clients that access to indigenous methods was too tightly controlled. If the women who aborted had been able to get family planning "privately," they would not have exposed themselves to the hardship and shame of abortion.

The invisibility of the new methods also enabled women to claim innocently that they truly wanted another child and couldn't imagine what was keeping them from conceiving, putting up a façade of agreement with the pronatal desires of their husband and his family. The pill and Depo enabled women to get their own way in matters of reproduction, while maintaining an appearance of being dutiful, would-be-fruitful wives:

> Some men didn't like [long birth intervals]. Most of them [wives] . . . could say, "I want to go to the granny and be given some *muti* [medicine] so that we can nurse our child [wait until the child is older before having another]," only if the husband would allow them. If the husband was opposed it was easier for her to take the new methods. She could say, "If you want I can stop this traditional medicine and I can conceive." If she wanted to take more time before she was pregnant, she could say, "I don't know what is happening, but the old lady [who supplied indigenous methods] promised that I will be all right." Then she could stop from taking the pill. Some men liked their women to practice with the old method, the traditional one, but it was to the advantage of the young mothers to take this from the old women and then go to the clinic. The husband could just think she is taking the *muti* from my mother or my granny, but she is actually taking medicine from the clinic. Some didn't even use the old medicine, because some who had tried it and it failed them, so they had no faith in it. They would say to the husbands, "I am using that [medicine] from granny," but in actual fact she is taking the pill, which she didn't tell her husband. Most of them were not telling the husband that they were taking the pill. (interview with Mrs. Stella Padoro)

Pills and injections brought with them a whole new set of gatekeepers, in the form of FPWs and nurses, who stood outside of the dramas and politics of the extended family. In addition, far from being secretive, FPWs had a professional interest in enlisting as many women as possible as clients and in many cases a missionary zeal for the creation of smaller, better, more "modern" families. While women had reservations about the methods, they still sought out the pills and injections, and hid them from husbands and in-laws.

> They were happy, especially women, because they liked the injection. You can have it privately like what I did. Traditional methods you will be given by aunt or grandmother and they will say it out some day, but injection is for me and that's all. (interview with Mrs. Mbizi, tr. NS)

I can say that some of the women were happy, because men want children but they were not able to look after them properly. . . . Our traditional [methods] are perfect, but some have rules to follow, some [the user must] drink every day. You can't hide a cup of medicine every day, so an injection is better. (interview with Mrs. Hwata, tr. NS)

They liked modern methods, especially women, because it was easy to hide and secret from men. Traditional methods you have to consult someone and so there was a lot of gossip. (interview with Mrs. Mhene, tr. NS)

The previous set of gatekeepers felt themselves being gradually excluded from reproductive life in their communities. Mr. Kondo, a 94-year-old traditional healer, was strongly opposed to the use of pills or injections, on the grounds that they were an insult to African culture and that they produced dangerous side effects in women, unlike his traditional medicine. However, he said that after the introduction of the pill and the injection, women no longer sought his help with his traditional methods.

I myself, I don't want to hear about pills, especially family planning pills. I give traditional medicines to those who want . . . but women like it [pills] very much. Because they don't want to have more children, again they are happy because they don't even come for traditional methods, they just like the injections and pills. (tr. NS)

## CONCLUSION

The arrival of new ways to control fertility was inevitably tangled up with pre-existing relations of power, which allotted birth control to some individuals and not others. The clash between FPWs, on the one hand, and *n'angas* and *ambuyas,* on the other, as opposing gatekeepers of fertility control was exploited by young women, who saw in the new contraceptives a way to partially extricate themselves from family politics around fertility. The introduction of new technologies of fertility regulation, and a new set of gatekeepers for these technologies, had the power to at least partially shift the locus of control of fertility from the husband and his family to the individual wife. Compared with the older means of fertility regulation, the pill, the injection, and the intrauterine device (IUD) were easier for a determined woman to get access to and thus made it easier for women to make their own decisions about the tempo of childbearing.

When acknowledging the importance of conflict-laden social relations throughout the history of contraception, however, one must be careful not to oversimplify the identities of the parties to the conflict: to assume that men, as a category, opposed the advent of the pill, the injection, and the IUD, while women as a category welcomed them; or that elders monolithically opposed the new methods, while young people did not. Instead, the line separating those who approved of the new contraceptives and those who did not is much more subtle.

I suggest that those who had a vested interest in upholding the idea that a particular woman's reproductive abilities existed for the benefit of the family, which paid *lobola,* were likely to vent their spleen on the encroaching FPWs during the 1960s and 1970s. Mothers-in-law and sisters-in-law often fell into this category, both because they had their own material and symbolic interests in seeing that their brother or son had many children for the lineage, and also because they were usually in proximity to their daughter-in-law. However, mothers-in-law were also mothers to their own daughters, for whom they might urge the pill, and sisters-in law-were also wives who might be facing too many of their own babies coming too fast.

Opposition to, or support for, contraception was thus fluid and highly situation-specific. What was acceptable for oneself might not be acceptable for one's sister-in-law. A whole range of social identities—mother-in-law, sister-in-law, *mwene, muroora, ambuya,* wife, mother—overlay women's identity as women, producing a very differentiated response to contraception, which depended not only on who one was but on where one stood in relation to the person doing the contracepting.

## NOTES

1. My Zimbabwean women friends speak of the time of their marriage not as "when I married Mr. So-and-So" or "when So-and-So and I got married" but as "when I joined the Murengwas" or "when I became one of the Shayanewakos," suggesting to me that they see marriage as joining a whole groups of individuals of different ages, sexes, and positions, rather than as a relationship strictly between their chosen husband and themselves.

2. A woman is married not only so that her husband's family can have children, but, indirectly, so that her own family can also increase. The cattle or money acquired through a woman's marriage were ideally supposed to be used by her brother to pay *lobola* for his own wife, so that his sister's marriage enabled his own to take place. A sister thus made the births of her brother's children possible. This relationship gave women a position of authority and influence vis-à-vis the sons and daughters of the brother who used their *lobola* to pay for his own wife, and she was thought to have special interest in the health of that family and in ensuring that they had children for the approval of her ancestral spirits.

3. I am focusing here on legal rights, positions, and obligations of women in their husbands' families, not on the subjective experience of being a daughter-in-law or sister-in-law. As I noted at the beginning of chapter 4 with respect to the husband-wife relationship, the existence of asymmetrical power relations does not necessarily mean that wives were never treated with respect and consideration by their in-laws. Among women, the lived experience of being a *muroora* (one for whom *lobola* or *roora* has been paid) varied greatly depending on the personalities involved, just as the experience of being a wife did. However, the formal relations of obligation and responsibility between a young wife and the family into which she had married existed as a symbolic resource that could be drawn upon by mothers- and sisters-in-law to justify their involvement in the reproductive affairs of the *muroora.*

4. Schmidt (1992) and Courville (1993) stress that colonialism and capitalism eroded the bases of women's religious, political, and economic power, adversely affecting women's influence and control over their lives.

5. "Greater freedom" did not imply complete freedom. In the Tribal Trust Lands, where the majority of Africans were forced to live, older men still controlled the allocation of land and thus constrained the ability of young men to set up their own homestead once they married. Well into the 1970s, as land pressures intensified, young men remained partially tied to their elders by the need to secure title to some land, if they wished to have a home appropriate to a married man in the family neighborhood. Without such a home, young men would remain perpetually *majaya* (youths), not yet mature adult men (Thompson 2000a).

6. However, while the husband might not be there in patrilocal Shona communities his relatives were very likely to be nearby keeping either a supportive or a suspicious eye on the doings of his wife, so that her autonomy from his family was not complete. As discussed below, mothers- and sisters-in-law often took themselves as proxies for their absent son or brother, especially when issues arose concerning the sexual or reproductive behavior of his wife. This meant that wives could easily come into conflicts with their female in-laws regarding contraception.

7. The young wife, literally "the one for whom *lobola* has been paid."

8. Mothers- and sisters-in-law may also have felt that their own reputations were at stake in the behavior of the new *muroora*, although none of my interviewees talked about this directly. In most Shona families, the women of the lineage were responsible for socializing the new arrival into the correct behavior for a wife and for ensuring that she fit smoothly into the rhythms of family life. A new wife who did not have children, just like a new wife who did not work well in the fields or who refused to cook well, was a reproach to the ones who were supposed to teach her (as well as to her own mother). For sisters-in-law of the *muroora* who wanted to get married themselves, a family of well-socialized and productive women was a good advertisement to a prospective husband, so that having an industrious, fertile *muroora* was a way of enhancing their own marriageability.

9. There is no exclusive or exhaustive definition of what constitutes a "traditional healer" in most Shona communities (although in the 1990s, the Zimbabwe National Traditional Healers' Association was attempting to do so and to register all traditional healers). Most people draw a distinction between a *n'anga* (sometimes translated as "witch doctor." or a person who is skilled in magical arts, such as placing and removing curses, foretelling the future, or bringing about desired outcomes in business, family life, and romance), and herbalists who correspond more closely to North American ideas of primary health care workers, with knowledge of medicinal plants and herbs as well as some charms for health. The latter are more likely to be female than the former. Neither a *n'anga* nor an herbalists should be confused with a witch (*muroyi*) who is always malevolent, or a spirit medium (*svikiro*) who is capable of divination and who plays a major role in many religious rituals. Generally speaking, both *n'anga*s and herbalists acquire their knowledge through their parents of the same sex, whether through genetic transmission of a predisposition toward magic or healing or through education and study, although it is possible to acquire this knowledge through apprenticeship. Most healers do not devote much of their time to their healing work until they are quite old, usually after menopause for women. As with most sources of symbolic prestige in Shona society, achieving status through healing is mainly for the old rather than the young. Most healers, especially herbalists, operate mainly through extended-family networks, although some become locally famous.

10. I do not mean to imply that in moving from indigenous to exogenous methods of fertility regulation, women moved from a situation of restricted access to fertility control to one of complete freedom and autonomy. FPWs still acted as gatekeepers of this technology and controlled its dissemination according to their own notions of when and to whom it was appropriate to provide information. According to one educator who worked in a particularly hostile community,

> They [local people] didn't like their children to have family planning methods. Even if she is above 20 years of age [i.e., a mature adult] as long as she is under the control of the parents they didn't like their children to have family planning. As a result to communicate with them and be friendly I was not supplying family planning to any child even though she is over twenty. (interview with Mrs. Stella Padoro)

11. However, these same people often went on to tell me or my research assistant about the very methods that they claimed were "secret." They justified this disclosure by saying that they believed that Mrs. Shayanewako and I would keep the secret and would not tell anyone else in the village. This suggests to me that the concern with secrecy surrounding the methods was not because the methods were somehow taboo or sacred in the Durkheimian sense, but because knowledge of the methods was part of their power base and they would lose power in their communities if the methods were widely known. Revealing the methods to me (an outsider) or to Mrs. Shayanewako (my agent, and someone who was widely known to be sociable yet discreet) did not threaten their power as gatekeepers.

12. However, women from Wedza recalled the buying and selling of traditional methods. Even those who were not supposed to have fertility control, such as young unmarried women or their lovers, could, if they paid a premium price, obtain contraceptives or abortifacients from healers. The possibility of bribing a healer, however, was not open to most women, who did not have control over sufficient wealth in their own right. All of the accounts I heard of healers being bribed to turn over their secrets to unmarried people involved women with boyfriends or lovers who had access to their own earnings. These transactions predated the introduction of money into their communities, as Mrs. Pfunye, born in 1918, recalled that her paternal aunt gave a goat to a local healer in exchange for contraceptive roots, which she passed on to Mrs. Pfunye. While contraceptives were clearly a source of wealth for some healers, most elders claimed that they granted access to their secrets not on the basis of who could pay them but on the basis of whose character and lifestyle they approved of.

13. It is not clear what events in Zimbabwean history Mrs. Mbira's grandmother was referring to Given Mrs. Mbira's age (born in 1946), it is possible that her grandmother was referring to the upheaval that followed the advance of white settlers from South Africa at the end of the nineteenth century, pushing Ndebele people out of their land in the west of the country and forcing them to compete with the Shona for land and resources.

# 6

# CUTTING DOWN THE NATION: AFRICAN FERTILITY AND AFRICAN NATIONALISM, 1950s TO 1980

## INTRODUCTION

From the very beginning of family planning in Zimbabwe, the rights and wrongs of contraception were debated as heatedly among politicians as they were among family members. Unlike the tensions over family planning that permeated families, however, political debates over family planning used idealized abstractions, such as "the nation" or "our African culture," rather than specific individuals and families, as the terms of debate. While a mother-in-law or a husband might be concerned about the consequences if Muroora so-and-so got the injection or if a wife was using the pill while her husband was away at work, in political debate, the entity at risk was an imagined community, the entire political entity called Zimbabwe. In this chapter, I focus on these more abstract but no less consequential struggles over who should control women's fertility and how it should be controlled.

What emerges from this chapter is the indestructible link between fertility and nation-building. The widespread nationalist hostility to family planning, with its implications for disrupting "traditional" patterns of gender and generational power, can be seen as a gendered expression of nationalism, even

though Zimbabwean nationalism is itself not a masculine gendered phenomenon. The liberation movement, like all mass movements, was itself a site of
contestation between genders and generations, as different groups strove,
sometimes in harmony and sometimes at cross-purposes, to position their concerns on the agenda of national liberation.

However, even though nationalism as a whole was not gendered masculine,
many of the nationalists were, as were many of the audiences to which they
appealed. Thus, nationalists combined appeals to defend the Zimbabwean
nation with appeals to shore up the gendered and generational interests of the
participants in the discussion. In political rhetoric, Africans were not only
constructed as political subjects denied the right to govern themselves, but as
farmers denied their land, as workers denied just wages, and, in the case of
family planning, as fathers denied their children and as husbands denied the
exclusive possession of their wives (for examples of the diverse social identities claimed by participants in the liberation struggle and the grievances that
flowed from them, see Frederikse 1984:52–56).[1]

Contraception, with its promise of new ways to control women's bodies,
new players and stakeholders in fertility, and a potentially drastic shift in the
locus of control over reproduction, was almost fated to be a major bone of
contention during the nationalist period. Women and their rights, their powers, and their symbolic significance are always symbolically present in the
cross-cultural vocabulary of nationalism, which in all languages speaks of
motherlands, the rape of the nation, or the sons of the soil (or *vana vevhu*, as
the Shona-speaking freedom fighters termed themselves) (McClintock
1995:354). Beyond their semiotic importance, Yuval-Davis and Anthias
(1989:7) identify five ways in which embodied women are implicated in the
construction of nationalism, whether or not their voices are recorded as part of
nationalist debates: (1) as biological reproducers of the members of the
nation; (2) as the ones who reproduce the boundaries of the national groups
(through rules governing sexual access); (3) as creators and transmitters of
national culture; (4) as the bearers of national difference and distinctiveness;
and (5) as active participants in the struggles leading to national liberation.

Just as the idea of "African woman," and the construction of femininity was
a touchstone for nationalist rhetoric and practice, so too was the construction of
masculinity and the idea of "African man." During the first three-quarters of
the twentieth century, masculinity was threatened and degraded by the white
colonial regime. While historians still argue about the extent to which African
men gained power at the expense of African women as a result of colonialism,
it is clear that African men were humiliated and disempowered relative to their
European counterparts. White colonists appropriated the material bases of
masculine—identity, cattle, land, and labor—and intervened in African men's
rights to control their women and children, directly through laws governing
marriage practices and family residences, and indirectly through the provision

of alternatives to patriarchal control for young men and women. In this context of degradation, the promotion of birth control was read as another attack on masculinity, this time on men's rights to form and head their own families.

For men, then, the nationalist movements were social spaces in which they could reassert themselves as men. Within these spaces, men could not only fight to reclaim the land and their political sovereignty, but could also name and denounce the threats to their manhood. These assertions coexisted uneasily with ideological orientations toward sexual equality within the liberation armies, and with the interests of the many women among the guerrillas, resulting in a complex and often ambivalent relationship between the guerrillas and the family planning workers (FPWs) whom they encountered.

Even outside the formal organizations of nationalism, ordinary Zimbabweans recognized the connections between Zimbabwean women's bodies and the Zimbabwean national struggle for liberation. The idea of family planning as an anti-African political measure was already in the air of the townships and rural areas when nationalists adopted it as one of their tenets in the 1950s. Among people at the grassroots, fears that family planning, an instrument of the white regime, might affect a partial transfer of power over fertility between genders and between generations were strong. Thus, family planning was easily translated into an issue of nation-building and a useful rallying point for potential supporters, especially male supporters.

## THE BEGINNING OF THE "THREAT TO THE NATION": THE LATE 1950S

Anxieties about "white" birth control had been part of Zimbabwean political culture for decades before the liberation war and, even before such birth control was available in the country, part of a set of persistent and pervasive rumors that the white government wanted to annihilate Africans or, failing that, to annihilate future generations of Africans. Rumors that medicine, technology, or even foodstuffs deriving from the whites could cause sterility among Africans have been circulating since at least the 1940s and persist into the present day.

The first attack on white-sponsored birth control for Africans came in 1957. Edith Gates, of the American Pathfinder Fund, addressed audiences in the Harari township in November, and Dr. Gibson, a Bulawayo gynecologist and member of the tiny Bulawayo Family Planning Association, addressed the Bulawayo (Municipal) African Advisory Board and the Bulawayo Social and Cultural Club, a discussion group for African elites. Both addresses raised a storm of opposition and condemnation within African nationalist circles, which disseminated to street-level gossip and speculation in the townships.

The strength of this opposition is remarkable, because at this time the organization that was to become the Family Planning Association of Rhodesia

(FPAR) consisted only of two six-month-old committees of a few liberal white amateurs in Bulawayo and Salisbury and had no finances, no institutional sup-port from the white government, and most importantly no plan of action (Spilhaus 1981:1–7). No one in Rhodesia, outside of a few elite urban white women, had ever actually used the new methods of birth control, and none of the key medical technologies—the pill and Depo—existed. The governments of the day, both national and municipal, were lukewarm at best to the idea of set-ting up family planning clinics for either Europeans or Africans, if not down-right hostile. Given that contraception was so weakly positioned in Rhodesia, the vehemence with which the first hint of white interest in contraception for Africans was received suggests that the very idea of white involvement in African reproduction and sexuality struck a powerful chord with black men.

This vehemence had roots in the widespread opposition to the white gov-ernment's efforts to control other forms of African productivity. In particular, African life in the late 1950s was colored by opposition to the Native Land Husbandry Act (NLHA), through which the white regime tried to force Africans to change their methods of farming and land tenure and, thus, their relationship to their ancestral lands.[2] The chief offense of the NLHA was that it forced African farmers to reduce their holdings of cattle on the grounds that the Native Reserves were overpopulated and overgrazed, selling them off, often to white commercial buyers, at prices far below the animals' true value. In addition to depriving farmers of valuable property, this destocking of cattle also cut deeply into the social relations on which community life rested. Without the use of cattle to offer as bride-price, to seal marriage agreements, or to settle disputes between family members or aggrieved parties outside the family—in short, to act as a medium of exchange in many important domes-tic relationships—rural family life as well as economic prosperity was threat-ened by the rapacious white regime. The bitterness of forced destocking and the symbolic importance of both cattle and children as signs and means of successful family life was extreme. Even in the late 1970s, more than 25 years after the NLHA was introduced and 15 years after it was abandoned in the face of noncompliance and violent opposition, FPWs recall that they were called "human destockers" and accused of being sent to finish the genocidal job that the government had begun by cutting down the numbers of cattle.

Like cattle, children were crucial to weaving the fabric of social life in Zim-babwean families. The connection between cattle and the family, and between cattle and children, was clearly made by nationalist leaders. "They have come for our cattle—next they will come for our children," warned the political lead-ers in the reserves. For example, Sadzamari Abraham Kurima was detained in 1959 under the Preventive Detention Act in part for the following action:

> On 11 January 1959, Kurima addressed a meeting of the Mtoko Branch of
> the Southern Rhodesia African National Congress and told the gathering

that when the government said there were too many cattle in the reserves, they were not to argue. When the time came for destocking, they should take their surplus cattle and their wives and children to the sale pens and when a man's cattle passed over the weighbridge [to be measured for prospective buyers] the wife should take the child from her back and put it with the cattle, saying to the government official, "The cattle are too many—so are the people. You must sell this child as well." (*Southern Rhodesia Cabinet Conclusions,* May 1959: Statements of Cases under the Preventive Detention Act)

When Edith Gates arrived in Bulawayo and started talking up contraception, it seemed that human destocking was now to follow cattle destocking. According to the Statement of Case for another political detainee of the time,

At Harari on the 1st of May 1958 to a meeting of the African Commercial Workers' Union, attended by some 400 person, he [Raymond Kufakunesu Mhizha] said, "Rhodesia is the African's country and not for settlers, people must not be afraid to fight for a good living. Europeans first destocked cattle to make Africans poor, then Africans were confined to poor small areas thus causing them to reduce their population to make room for Europeans from overseas. A European girl [Edith Gates] was called from America to preach birth control while at the same time the city council [of Salisbury] erected [workers'] hostels for single Africans only, thus preventing further any family life. There is not one country under the British government that has freedom." (*Southern Rhodesia Cabinet Conclusions,* May 1959: Statements of Cases under the Preventive Detention Act)

Rumors that sterilization was taking place under cover of medical efforts, such as vaccination campaigns, existed in scattered pockets throughout Rhodesia for at least 10 years prior, but had been largely restricted to remote areas and marginal religious groups.[3] However, with the visit of Gates and the formation of small family planning committees, the issue moved into the focus of the nationalist political groups. The Southern Rhodesia African National Congress (SRANC) in particular took up the cause of opposition to birth control, passing resolutions against it in public meetings throughout December 1957 and challenging white doctors who they held to be stooges for the government's desire to destock Africans.

Some leaders of African opinion, Mr. J.M.N. Nkomo (president of SRANC) in particular, do not like the idea of planning African families as is being suggested by a team of gynecologists headed by Dr. Gibson in Bulawayo. . . . At a meeting organized by the Bulawayo Social and Cultural Club recently, Dr. Gibson tried to explain the aims and objects of family planning. Dr. Gibson said some people had a mistaken view of the motives of the family planning movement. They hold the view that it is government inspired for the purposes of stopping Africans from multiplying while Europeans increased their numbers by immigration. He said the family planning movement had nothing whatsoever to do with the government. It was a voluntary movement designed to help those who did not want to have children and in certain cases those who could not get children. The basis of its approach was economics, he said. Mr. Nkomo attacked the view very strongly. He said that he himself was convinced that the object of this movement was a political one, whatever the doctor had said. . . . He said that he did not see any point in introducing to Africans something which the Africans themselves neither liked nor asked for. ("Bulawayo Opinion Varied on Family Planning Scheme," *African Daily News,* November 19, 1957)

At Harari on December 1, 1957, to a meeting of the Harari branch of the SRANC attended by some 100 persons he [detainee Raymond Mzhizha] said,

I attended a lecture on birth control by Mrs. Gates an American in Harari. I asked her who had given her money to travel here and if there were any clinics in the federation for whites. She did not answer my question but went on talking to the women about the scheme. It then appeared that the government of the country is behind her mission with a political motive behind her plan. The whole idea is to make plenty of room for overseas whites in this rich country, as the country does not grow bigger the government plans to reduce the African population to make room for their youngsters to come. There is no doubt that the British people have forgotten that this country is the country for the Africans and they take it for their own country. I tell you brothers that this was our country and is ours and shall be our country forever, let us fight for freedom in this good rich country of ours. (*Southern Rhodesia Cabinet Conclusions,* May 1959: Statement of Cases Under the Preventive Detention Act)

In an appeal to the educated and Christianized African elite, the SRANC denounced family planning as being contrary to the spiritual as well as political health of Africans:

A system of birth control among the African people of southern Rhodesia came under severe criticism at a meeting of the Southern Rhodesia African National Congress held in the recreation hall yesterday. . . . A resolution which will be sent to the mother body for action was passed. It stated, "that this meeting of the Southern Rhodesia African National Congress condemns the proposed birth control among the African people as ungodly and un-Christian fighting against the laws of nature and therefore unacceptable to the African people. The congress views this move with great suspicion in that there is a political motive behind the scheme of birth control." Speakers at the congress severely criticized the church for failing to make a vigorous attack on the government on the idea of birth control. . . . One of the most fiery speakers at the meeting, Mr. M. Mhizha, said that the gift of birth belonged to the almighty God alone and that no other person had the right to interfere with the laws of God and nature. Other speakers felt that Africans spent a lot of time on talking without taking real serious action on matters vital to their security. Speakers proposed that the African people should seriously consider the idea of boycotting the Christian church unless the church proved to the contrary that it was against the whole idea of birth control. The government was accused of trying to destock human beings as they were doing with African cattle. ("Congress Says Birth Control is Ungodly," *African Daily News,* December 2, 1957)

In Salisbury, rumors took the form of beliefs that the government was building medical clinics in the reserves in order to secretly sterilize women en masse. According to the Statement of Case justifying the detention of Raymond Mzhizha, cited above, he attempted to stir up emotions by telling a meeting of the Harari branch of the SRANC that

The government built hospitals long ago and I believe that the government is destocking there. They do not want the Africans to increase beyond the two and a half million that we are today; the government now plans a direct destocking and this plan must be fought away, straight away.

In the rural reserves, rumors circulated that the government was going to build clinics there to sterilize women. On the front page of the *Bantu Mirror* for December 1, 1957, the Chief Native Commissioner issued a statement reaffirming the government's commitment to building clinics in the rural areas, and condemned "mischief makers" for spreading rumors that these clinics were part of the program of human destocking:

The mischief makers he meant were those people who were alleged to have told people in the Chiota and Sipolilo reserves that the government was going to destock the native population and was embarking on a programme of building clinics for the purpose of teaching Africans birth control. "This allegation can only be regarded as an attempt to mislead the masses in the reserves," said Mr. Morris. ("Government Will Continue Building More Clinics")[4]

Even the government-controlled, antinationalist *African Daily News* referred to rumors that doctors were preparing to sterilize women and destock children:

Feelings are running high in African political circles these days because of the suggestion that there be birth control in the African community . . . There is no question of a mass vaccination of women thereby making them sterile, as one speaker mischievously suggested in Salisbury over last weekend. No family would be forced to curtail the number of children it has if it does not want to do so. . . . It is difficult, in fact impossible to believe that the motives behind this charitable work are political, directed at culling people like stock. If that was the attitude of the scientific community towards the African people why has so much work been done to combat malaria and mosquitoes which killed Africans by the hundreds in the last few decades? Deadly diseases have been brought completely under control and so many lives saved in the existing hospitals that we cannot believe political motives are now at work in the field of medical science. ("Birth Control Again," editorial, December 4, 1957)

In all these denunciations of the white government, the voices of African women were conspicuously silent. The *African Daily News* published a short feature on African women's views of birth control, in which various "women in the street" were interviewed as to their feelings about whether birth control was un-Christian or un-African. No woman would go so far as to say that she liked birth control or would used it herself, but, unlike the men, many women expressed a guarded neutrality on the subject, claiming to have no definite opinion on the subject but saying that birth control was a purely private matter, which "should not be a subject of public discussion and speculation" ("Women Not Opposed to Birth Control," December 9, 1957). A male columnist for the African weekly went further, attributing male hostility to birth control to gendered fears as much as to political suspicion:

Each time the question of birth control has appeared for discussion on the public agenda it has caused much sweating under the collars of African men who have not been slow to bring it under fire. It is the view of the African women on this question which I have been unable to find out. They have not come out in the open either to support or to oppose birth control. Because of their silence I may be excused to think that they do support the idea but they cannot say so in public for fear they will be in for all sorts of accusations from their husbands. But the African men have come against birth control. When last year [*sic*] an American woman gave a lecture to Hararians on birth control [during Gates' first lecture tour in 1955] she met quite a large amount of opposition from men who said that they did not like the idea. . . . It seems that the real reasons why on the whole African men are hostile to the idea of birth control has often been purposely left out by the opponents of birth control because it is not so palatable to mention in public but it is commonly discussed in private: the reason is that birth control would leave the African woman open to the temptations of infidelity because she lacks the protection usually given her by possession of a child and by the fear of having a child. That is the real reason behind the solid wall of opposition by Africans. ("Birth Control and the African People" [column by *Rolling Stone*], August 28, 1957)

## LEADING THE ATTACK ON FAMILY PLANNING: THE MEN OF THE NATIONALIST ORGANIZATIONS

After 1957, the issue of birth control faded temporarily from national prominence, until the 1970s, when the national liberation struggle gradually intensified into a shooting war against Ian Smith's Rhodesian Front.[5] At the same time, the family planning programs sponsored by the FPAR with help from the Rhodesian Front also gathered steam. The question of population control, genocide, and cultural degradation through family planning re-emerged as a nationalist concern, appearing in the *Zimbabwe News,* the *Zimbabwe Review,* and other organs published in exile.

These liberation movement publications[6] were produced in exile—in Zambia, Tanzania, and eastern Europe—and circulated among the exile community and, clandestinely, within Rhodesia itself. The journals were both chronicles of the development of the war and sources of inspiration for those who were supporters of the nationalist cause, although not actively involved as guerrillas. In the exhortations to rise up that filled their pages, the writers relied on information flowing back and forth between the underground political networks in Zimbabwe and the movement's leadership in exile. Consequently, domestic economic and social issues were assessed in terms of their implications for the liberation struggle. Particularly in the early 1970s, before the exigencies of the shooting war consumed most of the editorial space in the journals, the writers and editorialists talked up such domestic issues as the introduction of an unpopular soy-based meat substitute in Salisbury shops aimed at the "African market," rumors that "coloured" women were being recruited into prostitution to service foreign mercenaries, and the shortage of school supplies in township schools. Thus, the appearance of family planning in these pages suggest that the editors and writers perceived this as a subject that had already struck a chord with their highly politicized, mainly male[7] readership, and which could be turned to the end of garnering further support for the liberation movements.

References to family planning peaked in the years surrounding 1974, as a result of an unfortunate coincidence. This year was International Population Year, which the FPAR commemorated through intensified educational campaigns and frequent press articles and editorials concerning the problems of overpopulation. It was also the beginning of the Rhodesian Front's ill-fated "Settlers '74" campaign, intended to attract one million white immigrants to a Rhodesia being depleted by an exodus of white capital and skills as the war intensified.

Within the organs of the liberation movement, family planning and population control were framed in several different ways. The spread of family planning was held up as another example of white settler malevolence, spreading sterility and reproductive diseases through a "subtle war of annihilation" directed against the Zimbabwean people ("The True Terrorists," *Zimbabwe News,* November 1972). At the same time, family planning was also used as an indicator of the white government's desperation, and a measure of how much they feared the emergent black nation, that they would go to such measures to cut the nation down. Family planning programs were frequently juxtaposed with accounts of the Rhodesian government's efforts to attract more white immigrants and retard white emigration, so that family planning for Africans became constructed as a desperate but futile white attempt to rebalance racial population ratios and stave off the inevitable demographic and political victory of the blacks. Finally, although less frequently, family planning could be juxtaposed with other examples of the white regime's disregard for sexual morality or the "decency" of African mothers, as the regime coaxed then into prostitution and sexual decay.

The dominant frame for family planning was mass murder and genocide, a demographic attack on the African population. Family planning was woven into a portrait of the white regime bent on killing Africans. One prong was through killing Africans who were already alive:

> The settler regime in racist Rhodesia is currently engaged in a vicious campaign to reduce the African population. The present campaign is a two pronged program. Firstly the regime is trying to use natural methods in its evil intentions. Among natural measures is the clique's deliberate denial of medical treatment to the African population.[8] For example, despite the fact that the regime has confirmed information to the effect that there is a cholera outbreak among the African population[9] in the eastern districts of the country, no anti-cholera vaccines have been sent to these areas to control the outbreak. In this the regime wishes to see as many Africans as its devilish intentions wish die of the cholera outbreak. If this does happen on a very large scale the regime will blame the cholera outbreak but never reveal that this is in fact official policy. ("Campaign: Population Reduction," *Zimbabwe Review,* December 29, 1973)

The second prong was the prevention of African births. The editorialist for the *Zimbabwe Review* continued:

> Committed as it is to this fascist policy, the regime has also resorted to artificial methods in its quest to reduce the African population. . . . The settler clique has recently adopted a new policy to reinforce its notorious so-called family planning program. This recent measures stipulates a prerequisite for the employment of African women. It states that no African woman is permanently employed unless she agrees to the government demand that she start using contraception as a direct method of curbing the growth of the African population.[10] Whenever the would-be employee refuses to concede to this blackmail . . . she is subjected to further intimidation and harassment. (ibid.)

Family planning was described as a pollution that was spreading insidiously throughout Zimbabwean society, even into the rural heartland where wives and elders were being pulled into cooperating in the destruction of the African race in the name of "development" and "health":

> On the population front the settler regime is carrying out campaigns among Zimbabweans, scaring them with tales of fatal diseases and poverty for planning large families. The capitalist and racist system squeezes every Zimbabwean within an impossible economic orbit of survival and it is within this orbit that the Zimbabwean is being forced to develop his [*sic*] concept of family planning. Chiefs in the rural areas are being ordered by the regime to bring forward co-operating agents to be used to circulate in their areas preaching the doom of large families [a reference to field educators and community-based distributors]. Almost every day in all languages over Radio Rhodesia programmes are being put out to advise Zimbabweans on family planning. Every clinic has an office to advise every mother on family planning and offering sterilizing injections to be applied without the knowledge of the husband. ("Other Fronts of the Struggle," *Zimbabwe Review,* November 17, 1973)

> According to the racists the panacea for [under]development is the pill— birth control for the African population. The instrument for administering this inhuman exercise is the Rhodesian wing of International Planned Parenthood—the Rhodesian Family Planning Association. Since 1972 several maternity clinics have been opened in both urban and rural areas. From these centers the sterilization of Africans is carried out, the pill is freely distributed and the tube [possibly a reference to the IUD, known as the loop?] is popularized. Needless to say this is why the Africans have become apathetic [suspicious] about the treatment in hospitals and clinics. ("The TTLs," *Zimbabwe Review,* July 26, 1975)

In addition to being a form of demographic destruction, family planning was also constructed as a form of spiritual degradation, part of white efforts to turn Africans away from African values, rooted in family and respect for life, and toward shallow and spiritually barren materialism. The materialist emphasis of the FPAR's public relations campaigns, stressing how smaller families had higher standards of living than large ones, was cited as evidence that the settler regime wanted to make Africans crass and greedy and rob them of their family values:

> The issue here . . . is the basic philosophies of life involved. Why all this missionary zeal to save the Africans from the "dangers" of big families as though it is something bordering on a sin or a disease? Africans regard humans and their association as their priority value, therefore the greater the number of humans with a closer association, the greater is the life content-

ment derived. The concept being fostered behind the Rhodesian birth control campaign . . . is said to be "improvement" of African economic welfare. It is an attempt to treat Africans to an accumulation or capitalistic concept. "Prefer more money [rather] than more children" is the idea. "Find pleasure on material care and accumulation [rather] than in human care and association" is another way of putting the idea fostered. (*Zimbabwe Review,* January/February 1970, reprinted in de Braganca and Wallerstein 1982:156)

Family planning campaigns were also constructed by the nationalist movement in a third way: as a sign of the regime's increasing desperation and their fear of the demographic power of the Zimbabwean population, especially when coupled with the political and military power of the liberation movements. Just like the gun, the birthrate was a weapon, which the regime sought to disarm through family planning. As the article cited above continued,

Next to the insecurity the enemy fears from the red-hot barrels of the guns is the preponderantly engulfing population increase of the Zimbabwean population . . . population proportions have never favoured the racists. There are eighteen Zimbabweans to one settler racist. For some time the settler consoled himself by the fact that he held the gun against the disarmed African. With the upsurge of the liberation movement that consolation no longer exists . . . They [the white population] see the power of the Zimbabwean population and the armed struggle ending their dreams of a permanent paradise of economic monopoly and fictitious class of a privileged race. It is as though a rock is about to fall on them—indeed it is—and hence their frantic abuse of the idea of family planning among Africans. (ibid.)

The futility of Rhodesia's family planning campaign was frequently compared with the futility of the Rhodesian Front's "Settlers '74" campaign to encourage white immigration. In the liberation movement journals, the two campaigns were juxtaposed to demonstrate the hypocrisy of the white regime's claim that family planning was purely a nonpolitical humanitarian endeavor. This rhetorical strategy was also used to good effect by local politicians and grassroots opponents of family planning to discredit the FPAR by accusing it of complicity in the regime's population control strategies. According to the *Zimbabwe Review,*

While the settler dictatorship is busy in the Western world campaigning for an unlimited inflow of white settlers into Rhodesia, with an astronomical target of a new million by the end of the year, at home it cries of high birth rate. . . . If settler Rhodesia has so much land and so many job opportunities as to warrant new immigrants, as many as one million by the end of this year, why then is there a problem about the natural growth rate of the African population? ("What an Absurdity!" *Zimbabwe Review,* May 4, 1974)

One particular *Zimbabwe Review* article drew together all the themes through which the liberation movements approached the issue of family planning in their journals—white disregard for African lives as shown through using family planning as a weapon of war, white fear of African demographic superiority as measured by the promotion of family planning, and white hypocrisy by calling for white immigrants at the same time as cutting down blacks:

> Welfare facilities are non-existent for the rural Africans who form over 94% of the total population. Where they exist they are just not enough to cope with the demand. Whites received free medical attention. Everything is free for the white man, but Africans are expected to pay for the treatment they get and the fees for treatment are continuously being raised every year. The official explanation for this constant increase is that Africans are being made to see the need for birth control under the transparent pretext that Rhodesia is overpopulated. But ironically the government is spending large amounts of money recruiting white immigrants from all over the world. If Rhodesia is overpopulated, why then recruit immigrants? This subtle war of annihilation is what we are fighting in Zimbabwe. Despite their attempt to force Africans into using birth control, despite their attempts to eradicate Africans from the face of Zimbabwe, despite their efforts to counteract the growing African population by importing people from the slums of every Western country, the fact that twice as many African children are born every year as the total white population remains. With the present population growth of 3.55% per annum, the settlers are fighting a losing battle and they know very well what this means to the hot seat they are now sitting on. This subtle terrorism is what we are fighting. ("The True Terrorists," November 1972)

## THE COMRADES AND THE PEOPLE

How did this anti–family planning rhetoric play out at the grassroots, when the comrades were actually in the field, interacting with ordinary villagers and farmers? The relationship between the comrades and the ordinary people of Zimbabwe has been a subject of intense academic debate for more than 10 years. No clear consensus has yet emerged: Ranger (1985) asserts that the comrades' message of national liberation through war complemented the revolutionary consciousness that Zimbabweans had developed after decades of white oppression; Lan (1985) claims that the guerrillas integrated themselves into pre-existing spiritual and symbolic frameworks; while Kriger (1992) argues that coercion and the threat of violence accounted for more peasant cooperation with the comrades than did peasant sympathy. The contradictions among these accounts, each based on different local studies, points to the impossibility of making generalizations about the whole of Zimbabwe and the whole of the liberation war. Maxwell (1993) is closest to the mark when he says that relations between the comrades and the civilians depended more on locally specific factors, such as power structures and patterns of socioeconomic differentiation, than on any ideologies or strategies of the guerrillas that pervaded the entire war effort. My own interviews with FPWs from across the country confirm Maxwell's conclusions, as the FPWs reported great local variations in their encounters with the comrades.

However, some general themes did emerge from my interviews, which support the contentions of Ranger, Lan, Kriger, and Maxwell. These themes affected the ways the comrades dealt with family planning. First, the comrades professed what Kriger (1992) calls "cultural nationalism," aligning themselves with the virtues and values of an idealized African culture. This cultural nationalism included repudiating the trappings of white culture, especially those that were perceived to be weakening the nation spiritually. Even before the organized liberation movements supplied an economic and political explanation of colonialism, "youth groups directed their anger at Africans who used perfume, wore short skirts, straightened their hair, and in other ways participated in the symbols of African cultural domination"(Kriger 1992:97). While the Zimbabwe African Patriotic Union (ZAPU) might state, as matter of policy, that "the masses of Zimbabwe . . . have adopted the Marxist-Leninist principles as the weapon to destroy colonialism, imperialism, racism, and fascism," the masses themselves were more likely to be won over by the movement's commitment to asserting traditional African values, in tandem with its commitment to ending racial discrimination in land, education, and politics (*Zimbabwe People's Voice,* March 17, 1979:11). Despite the ambiguity of the term "traditional," I use it because it fits most closely with the way the guerrillas described themselves in the literature of the time, and because the people I interviewed used it when describing the comrades.

In tactical terms, the guerrillas' insistence on valorizing (and when necessary, defining) traditional practices served them well. When small guerrilla units had to find their way through unknown terrain, their claim to be bearers of African authenticity was a potent way to make connections with the local inhabitants. The invocation of tradition and African culture in the struggle, often effected with the aid of mediums of the ancestral spirits, was "a remarkable act of cooperation between ancestors and their descendants, the dead and the living, the present and the past" (Lan 1985:xviii). There were many pragmatic reasons for the guerrillas to seek the approbation of the mediums, such as the mediums' ability to mobilize lineages and families, and the mediums' traditional guardianship over the fruits of the land in some areas. This alliance with spiritual leaders also solidified the objections to imported practices for many of the guerrillas. Mediums were known for objecting to many aspects of European life, including new agricultural techniques and methods, and the damming of rivers. Mediums also generally refused to have daily contact with European food, clothes, clinics, and transport (Lan 1985:42–43).

In turn, the guerrillas reinforced the traditional proscriptions and commandments of elders in particular localities, which had been in danger of collapsing during the settler rule. In northeastern Zimbabwe, for example, "it was widely believed that if you defied the *mhondoro* [local guardian spirit] and worked on your field on *chisi* [rest days proclaimed by the *mhondoro*], you would be fined and beaten, perhaps killed, by the guerrillas" (Lan 1985:166). The comrades themselves observed many of the warnings, prohibitions, and proscriptions sent by the ancestors, and these observances were credited with saving many lives:

> There were rules which the comrades were following in the war. They were not allowed to sleep with a girl, to shake hands with girls and not to be cruel to people . . . The comrades were not eating okra or vegetables or the intestines of any animals. (interview cited in Lan 1985:134)[11]

Even guerrillas who had not had traditional upbringings found themselves upholding traditions and values, which might not have formed part of their lives prior to their involvement in the struggle, for psychological as well as pragmatic reasons. Looking back on the war, one young guerrilla from an urban background said, "I didn't believe all the things my father used to tell me until I was in the bush myself. Then—well, you just had to believe" (Lan 1985:xv, see also Nhongo-Simbanegavi 1997:147, 158 for sexual and menstrual taboos among the comrades).

The comrades prohibited or severely limited contact with European structures in the territories they controlled. The most commonly reported prohibitions were on schooling children and dipping cattle. Schools and dips were often the most obvious signs of European presence in the Tribal Trust Lands (the African rural reserves) and also epitomized colonial interference with children and cattle—the two resources of greatest spiritual and practical value under the traditional economy:

> Our ancestors had beasts and they never needed dips. You're being cheated. Fees [paid for the mandatory cattle dipping] are being used by the government to buy ammunition. (Lan 1985)

Similar arguments were made concerning school fees. Thus, as was the case for limiting family size, cooperation with white schemes could be construed not just as abandonment of culture, but also as complicity in the destruction of Africans.[12]

In their encounters with the more traditional rural people, the guerrillas had to counter fears that they were communists who did not believe in the value of marriage or childrearing (Martin and Johnson: 1981:89). Rumors about the breakdown of family life in China and the Soviet Union, part of the anti-Communist campaign of the white regime, had reached even remote parts of Zimbabwe (Frederikse 1984). The fear of the guerrillas as a potential cultural threat can only have been increased by the rumors of unorthodox gender and generational relations in the armies, ZANU and Zimbabwe People's Revolutionary Army (ZIPRA)—women wore trousers and bore arms as well as men, the young might be placed in positions of command over the old, and the armies lured many young people away from home and authority. Indeed, says Nhongo-Simbanegavi, "one of the most noticeable changes of the war was the inversion of the status" of old and young, across both genders (1998:20).

The guerrillas compensated for this fear, and solidified their alliance with elder and local traditional authorities, by upholding customary practices concerning domestic stability in the areas they controlled. " 'There were no divorces during the war,' according to a woman teacher. 'It was not allowed. What would happen to the children?' " (Kriger 1992:100). There were even reports, cited both by Kriger and by the women of *Mothers of the Revolution,* of the guerrillas intervening in domestic disputes and chastising and punishing men who beat their wives or drank excessively, which was very popular with the women (who also formed the backbone of the guerrillas' in-country supply and information networks). Reports from operational commanders in the field to their superiors outside the country stress the importance of riding herd on new recruits, ensuring that they do not disturb local marriages (Nhongo-Simbanegavi 1998:196–98). In the southern sector of the country, guerrillas pressed their local supporters to ensure that all young women dressed and behaved appropriately: "young women [must be] well-dressed culturally and not act lumpenwise" (cited in Nhongo-Simbanegavi 1998:217).

People of Wedza district confirm Kriger's observations about the freedom fighters' support for cultural norms that reinforced women's rights to good treatment from their husbands. They said that the comrades made strong appeals on the grounds of "tradition" to restore morality and harmony to family lives that had been corrupted by colonialism and the influence of an alien culture. The comrades were described as being in favor of traditionally large families and opposed to divorce, especially when a man wanted to divorce his first wife to take a younger second wife. This met with the approval of the married women in the area, who bore the bulk of the responsibility of feeding and caring for the guerrillas:

They encouraged us to have children, and they didn't want divorces. (interview with Mrs. Mbizi, tr. NS)

They opposed family planning, they wanted us to have children who will fight in the war. (interview with Mrs. Ngavira, tr. NS)

They wanted people to live peacefully [with their spouse], no divorce, and they wanted many children. (interview with Mr. Mbiti)

They encouraged us to have many children, they say [the children will be] tomorrow's warriors and ministers [in government]. They didn't like divorces. (interview with Mrs. Mhene, tr. NS)

Many said the guerrillas chastised men who were known for divorcing, encouraging them to stay with their first wife and not to abandon older women in favor of younger ones (interviews with Mrs. Mbudzi, Mr. and Mrs. Mharapara, Mrs. Gwee, and Mr. and Mrs. Horiori).[13]

Family planning did not emerge as a major theme of the guerrillas' political education, at least not in comparison with burning issues such as getting more land for displaced peasants. However, when people were asked about it specifically, some memories of anti–family planning speeches emerged.

During the war sometimes the comrades told the people that they should not use family planning from white people because during the time of war we are losing children . . . they told us that the children you bear will be fighters who will fight for the country until they win, some will become doctors and nurses. (correspondence with Mrs. Banga, tr. AK)

Yes, we heard this because the freedom fighters did not want us to listen to what was said by the whites. If the children are too few, we will all be lost fighting in the war. (correspondence with Mrs. Maita, tr. AK)

One woman told me of extreme opposition to family planning from the comrades, which I was unable to corroborate:

Yes, we heard this [that family planning was bad] being produced from the mouths of the freedom fighter during the liberation struggle. Even many people were killed for the sake of family planning. Some people were told to be pregnant and give birth [after] three months. If they came and found you without a baby, you would be killed. (correspondence with Mrs. Chingono)

## RUMORS OF DEATH AND STERILITY

Africans' concerns about family planning were mainly expressed in the form of widespread rumors. These rumors drew on strong and growing suspicion of white medicines on the grounds that they were Trojan horses, seemingly benevolent things that, in fact, would kill and mutilate the Africans who used them. From the 1940s, rumors circulated about the effects of both preventive and curative medicines. Most of these rumors focused on the effect of white medicine on the sexual and reproductive systems of Africans, in particular that they would sterilize Africans and make them physiologically as well as politically impotent.

These rumors tell of the tensions of colonialism and of African fears about white intentions, rather than being literal accounts of actual events. Many different types of fears can be seen through these rumors: fears that the war might go on forever, so that Rhodesians wanted to decimate the next generation of potential Zimbabwean soldiers; fears that the regime wanted to take over more African land; fears that the products of *chirungu,* such as vaccinations, were fundamentally alien and even toxic to Africans; and fears of an international cabal, including the United States, arranged against the Africans of Zimbabwe. The truth in these rumors lies in the way in which they expressed shared beliefs about the world before and during the liberation war. Real events underlay the rumors: Ian Smith *did* declare that the state of Rhodesia would last a thousand years; Africans *were* being systematically dispossessed of their land throughout the 1970s; unsafe pharmaceutical products, including Depo-Provera, *were* being used on Africans; and foreign governments, including the United States, *did* align themselves with the Rhodesian Front. Rumors about family planning were a way of articulating these truths, as well as a way to talk about family planning itself. The contraceptives themselves served as a lightning rod drawing together different political issues and concerns, just as they crystallized concerns about gender and generational authority, as shown in earlier chapters.

The first reported rumors of sterility associated with acceptance of the white benefactors' goods came in 1948, a drought year during which rumors spread in eastern Zimbabwe that the drought-relief maize offered by the government was imbued with sterilizing compounds (Roger Howman [former Chief Native Commissioner of Rhodesia], personal communication). During the 1950s, Ministry of Health annual reports make frequent reference to sporadic resistance to measles and smallpox inoculations, although it is difficult to say how much of this resistance is due to political objections to these things as coming from the white government, and how much was the result of sectarian religious beliefs that prohibited medical treatment not based in prayer.[14] However, by the 1970s it had become clear that the rumors about the sterilizing and other debilitating effects of white medicine had gone beyond small religious groups. Reports from provincial medical officers of health indicate that their efforts to promote preventive medicine were being read as efforts to sterilize or poison the African population.

Rumors of sterilization and toxicity dogged the Ministry of Health's efforts to disseminate any kinds of pills and injections. In 1966, an African member of Parliament informed his colleagues that the existence of a government-funded family planning program spelled trouble for smallpox vaccination and other preventive health measures. He attributed this to widespread suspicion that the government was bent on reducing the number of Africans and would go as far as to trick people into being sterilized under the guise of vaccinating them against smallpox:

For the information of the house, this [voting to fund the FPAR] is something we are going to be sorry for because so many Africans, after having
heard of this, they will not go to hospital, they will not turn up at the clinics
to be vaccinated. I am living with Africans and I am telling you what the
Africans are thinking. They say the Europeans are trying to get rid of the
African population. This is what they are telling me, this is the information
I am collecting. We are getting into difficulties when there is an outbreak of
smallpox in the country and the vaccinators are sent into the Tribal Trust
Land because we will hardly get any people to be vaccinated. They will say
there is a certain medicine which has the property to destroy all means of
this and that, and their arguments will be hard to correct.[15] (M.P. Makaya,
*Parliamentary Debates,* March 9, 1966:1497)

The fact that pills and injections were available free to those who could not
pay, at a time when most medical care was not free to Africans, also aroused
suspicion among potential family planning clients.

People were suspicious because the first time as they were being given for free
they wanted to know why they were being given free, and I went to the extent
of saying that it was a way of helping those who could not [afford to pay], but
those who could afford they went to their doctors and they could pay but those
who could not afford they could go to family planning and be given, only as a
way of helping. . . . Definitely they were suspicious, saying, "Why are they
coming as just a free thing?" (interview with urban-based supervisor[16])

One of the most persistent rumors was that the pills and injections were
medicines for animals, either to sterilize them or to make them tame and
docile, which were being given to African women, or had been found to be
dangerous in the United States and were now being dumped into African
countries by a regime that was either uncaring or actively malevolent.

We know when you take this thing from Europeans they want to kill us,
because they are testing their medicine to us," so it went on and on and
on . . . they say, "this injection, we read from the papers." What did you
read about this injection? "We read that these things are being tested in
overseas countries. They are given to dogs and animals, now how can you
give this to our people while it is for animals? Or these are just medicines
that are being thrown away which you are coming to give us? (interview
with female FPW active in the townships)

There was time when people said they heard Depo was being for horses,
they said once you were injected you would not have children forever. . . . The Depo they were scared that once you are injected you won't
have children any more. With the horses, I don't know who brought that

idea but I understand some horses like the horses at Borrowdale [race track] they say they use the Depo for them not to have any young ones. That's how they were thinking about that. (interview with male urban-based supervisor)

Some of the people, they say that the Depo was used in other countries to tame donkeys and that message spread to the people, this was the rumor, so now they are using this for our wives, so we had got a very difficult situation.... Some people became afraid, that was the reason, that Depo-Provera is not good to be used for human beings, it was just meant for animals. Because they want to oppress us down they are bringing this to Africans. (interview with long-serving male rural field educator)

Other rumors concerned the effects of the pills. The most common version was that the pills and injections caused permanent sterilization; however, rumors that they caused impotence in men also circulated. The white regime was suspected of attempting to chemically castrate African men, to make them like tame and placid donkeys.

Some of them were saying, "We have once heard that [a prominent white politician] said in Parliament, 'We want to castrate the blacks,'" so because of that people were saying, "Ah, now here is the person who is now coming to castrate us." (interview with urban-based supervisor)

I remember one time that one of the nursing sisters went to the city council brewery, she had a lapel pin, FPAR, she went to try to arrange for a meeting with the men [who worked in the brewery], and somebody saw her go in there and noticed the family planning pin. They rumors then went out that something had been put in the beer. That message went out and I believe sales for that week [makes a gesture of plummeting] [beer from the city council was a drink largely for working men, as opposed to the home-made beer brewed by women]. (interview with long-serving male Harare educator)

## WORKING AT THE GRASSROOTS: FPWS' ENCOUNTERS WITH THE NATIONALIST SUPPORTERS

Beyond hearing rumors, every FPW experienced more serious harassment from the people in the communities where they worked, which escalated through the 1970s as the political situation heated up. FPWs were accused of being agents of the white regime, preventing the birth of future soldiers for the liberation war, collaborating with whites in Rhodesia and abroad to use Africans as experimental animals for new drugs, or willfully damaging the bodies of African men and women. At least two and possibly as many as five FPWs were killed in the course of their work.

However, the relations between FPWs and the freedom fighters themselves were not as uniformly bad as those between FPWs and the freedom fighters' local supporters. The liberation movements might threaten that "if women agents who are being trained . . . for such suicidal campaigns [as family planning] do not take advice and stop being used against their people, they will suffer the consequences," but many FPWs reported amicable or at least tolerant relations with the comrades at the grassroots (*Zimbabwe Review*, January/February 1970, reprinted in de Braganca and Wallerstein 1982:157). Many groups of guerrillas arrived at a modus vivendi with the FPWs in their areas, and others reportedly were neutral toward family planning, or even approved of it in private, while they condemned it publicly to bolster their support among local men and elders. It was the local supporters of the nationalists—the ones whose communities were being directly affected by the FPWs' work, the ones whose wives and daughters were the users of these new methods—who voiced their political opposition most consistently.

FPWs and nationalists encountered one another on many different terrains. Not only in the FPWs' daily work but also in their homes, at weddings and funerals, at church meetings, and at social gatherings they encountered accusations that family planning was a political weapon, a tool to reduce or destroy the African nation through the wombs of their women. FPWs were often asked to prove, not just their political allegiances, but their very identity as Africans and Rhodesians.

> [People said] "Why do you want us to be few? You want us to be few because you want the Rhodesian forces to come and kill us when all our children will be dead. Because the government doesn't want us to have many children, because if the children are many they will go out of the country and then come back and fight. Why are you interested in working for such people? It is not a job for an African woman because the Europeans are trying to make us few, why are you helping?" So we had to explain to them, no, that is not the reason. . . . It's not a matter of having few children so the Europeans will come and kill all of us. It's a matter of spacing your children, not limiting . . . we are not doing this to have few Africans and many Europeans. (interview with female FPW who worked in a clinic)

FPWs were asked to prove that they really lived in the country, that they were not spies sent from another country:

> [In a discussion with a male neighbor] He called the next man, he said, "hey, Baba Nhingi, this woman comes from family planning." The other man said, "Ahh, I know from Zambia that they are doing that because they don't want people to be many, and then from there the whites will come and destroy our country." Whether he had visited there, I don't know what he knew about Zambia. He was furious. . . . I went [later] that afternoon with these six men outside, two of them were drinking beer. He [her neighbor] said, "This is the lady who talks about family planning." They said, "Are you a Rhodesian woman?" I said. "Yes, I was born here in Chivhu, that's

where my home is" . . . They thought I was just working for the *varungu* [white people]. (interview with female FPW who worked in Midlands)

Male family members of FPWs also received political criticisms from fellow men for allowing their wives or daughters to work against the African nation, as well as for allowing their wives and daughters to corrupt other women and take them away from their husbands.[17]

Like the accounts that circulated in the liberation movement journals, the opposition that FPWs faced in the field had two main themes. The first was the argument that family planning was a logistical threat to the war effort—if women were refusing to have babies, there would be no more soldiers to fight. The second argument was that the pills and injections were racist tools, part of an ill-defined program by whites to bring the black nation to its knees. A medicine emanating from the white colonialists was not to be trusted, as whites had always treated blacks as animals to be tamed or as fodder for their own plans, including medical experimentation. The contraceptives were even more threatening because they worked on sexual and reproductive organs, important symbolic sites of African identity.

These arguments varied significantly by gender. Women were much less likely to make an issue out of the political connotation of the pill and Depo than were men. While some of the FPWs recall changing their work routes to avoid the homes of women whose husbands were known to be active in nationalist politics,[18] all of the "politicians" who confronted FPWs openly were male. Geraty, in the early 1970s, came to the same conclusion, observing that "there is less opposition from women, especially on political grounds" (Geraty 1973: 30). This is not to say that women embraced the pill and Depo unreservedly— as we have seen, women had serious concerns that these new methods would cause health problems or problems with their affinal kin, or would contribute to a loosening of morals by the younger generation. These objections were grounded in the immediate personal consequences of contraceptive use for themselves or for family members, rather than the more abstract idea of threats to the African nation as a political entity. Although women were vibrantly active in the liberation struggle, as both leaders and supporters,[19] their gendered political consciousness did not incline toward seeing contraceptives as a political problem or their own bodies as vectors of corruption and impurity for the nation. Their fathers, sons, and husbands thought otherwise:

Among the men I would say that the majority showed no interest [enthusiasm for family planning] because they thought that, one, it was a means to reduce black African numbers and, second, they thought that once their wives went on family planning that gave them the freedom to run around with other men. . . . The men in towns, they would always say, "You are being sent by white people to reduce our numbers," that there are political motives for this.

They would state their case and then we would state ours. They would say what their fears are, their suspicions, political suspicions and that the women would have the freedom to run around with other men. . . . [AK: Did women bring up this issue of destocking?] Very rarely, it was mainly men that came up with that. (interview with one of the first male FPWs)

The most common political objection voiced by men was that family planning would "cut down the nation," reducing the supply of soldiers (or votes) for a military (or electoral) victory over the whites. Given that it would have taken more than a decade for any children born during this time to grow up to an age at which they could either fight or vote, this expressed concern about a demographic threat to the African nation should not be taken entirely at face value. Rather than referring to actual concerns about the eventual military strength of the liberation armies,[20] I believe that these concerns should be read, both literally and symbolically, as fears about the spiritual as well as physical annihilation of the nation, effected through the closing-down of women's wombs.

During that time it was very sensitive but I managed. It was political, it was before independence and Chitungwiza [the huge African "bedroom community" outside Salisbury, sometimes referred to as "Rhodesia's Soweto"] is a place where politicians and I would say the whole township was full of people who were politically minded. They would dash in the clinic and say, "What is going on here, are you doing family planning? You are making the nation low, you are cutting down the nation by giving pills." Into my clinic, they came right into it. (interview with an FPW who worked as a township nurse)

To start with, it was during the war and people thought maybe the mission was to reduce the African population. So that was a question that each and everyone asked every time. It was really in people's minds. Isn't this a mission of reducing the African population so that the war goes on and then the other side wins? They were conscious of that. (interview with female FPW who worked in Mashonaland East)

They were saying they are against family planning, they think you are killing people, stopping the population. How do you think we will operate if you reduce the population? . . . Even the nurses were against it. They didn't understand about family planning. They were saying, "you want our people to stop having children," even the nurses. (interview with female FPW from Midlands)

During that time it was difficult because we were now in the war, so people could interpret in the wrong way. It was just using tactics because some they could misinterpret that it's the white regime wants to reduce African population and the like, and then you have got to explain that no, we are doing this for the health of the mother and the child, the father and even the coun-

try, giving them the advantages for each person, and some could understand
a little bit. But it was a difficult time, especially from 1976 up to 1979 it was
really bad. . . . [people said] it was part of the regime wanting to reduce us.
(interview with senior male FPW from Manicaland)

Some men attempted to trick FPWs into revealing the true intent of family
planning by asking them what the white government said was the ideal number
of children in a family. Training materials for FPWs are filled with injunctions
against offering any opinions on the optimum size for a family or for a nation,
lest potential clients believe that family planning was a strategy to reduce families and nations to that specific size. FPWs unanimously agreed that any mention of overpopulation from a white source provoked a political backlash.

> They [local men] were saying that this is a white man's tool to put down the
> number of Africans. . . . And then the white regime that was there would
> come out and say there are too many Africans, let's use family planning . . . It
> was also because of the negative press releases from the white regime, like
> there are too many Africans, we must cut down the number of Africans so for
> them family planning was to cut down the number of Africans which was all
> wrong . . . We had to change the image completely, that it is a health issue
> only. (interview with nurse who worked in FPAR clinic)

> I for one I actually thought the [nationalist] politicians were a bit right
> because the main reason why the whites are saying there is family planning
> is population explosion, but we do not have population explosion. Our
> country is a lot bigger than England and yet our population is just a fifth of
> England. We saw a lot of land lying idle. I also believed the politicians were
> a bit right because they were using the wrong reason for family planning,
> instead of actually telling the advantages to myself, talking about economy,
> how can I look after so many children, but instead it was population explo-
> sion. It wasn't sound reasoning. (interview with Harare-based nurse)

> The thing that was hammering us [impeding our efforts] was then there
> were some whites who could talk in Parliament, that "Oh, those Africans are
> so many." In Parliament! "These Africans are so many, they don't even
> know what family planning is." That alone was a barrier for us. Some edu-
> cated people in the rural areas, they knew [what was said in Parliament].
> They said, "You are talking of this [the benefits of family planning] but why
> are they saying that?". . . . They said, "Ah no, there is something behind it."
> We tried our level best to make them understand that of course they might
> be saying that we are too many in Parliament, but . . . it is you that is facing
> those problems [of having too many children or children too close together],
> no matter what is said in Parliament you are still going to have those prob-
> lems. (interview with male former supervisor from Midlands)

A plaque from Spilhaus Centre, commemorating the FPWs "lost in action" during the war. One other FPW, a Mrs. Rafirokumwe, was killed after this picture was taken. In interviews, FPWs named several other fellow workers who they claimed had also been killed in performance of their duties, in addition to the four officially acknowledged ones. Above the plaques is a picture of Joyce Wickstead, in whose honor the lecture theater at Spilhaus Centre was named. Source: *FPAR 1978,* a promotional brochure published by the FPAR.

## FPWS' ENCOUNTERS WITH THE COMRADES THEMSELVES

In contrast to the suspicion, harassment, and threats that the FPWs received from the nationalists' supporters, their encounters with people who were actually members of the guerrilla armies were much more diverse and ambiguous. The comrades' attitudes toward family planning varied widely throughout the operational areas, depending more on the personality and individual likes and dislikes of the local guerrilla commanders than on any kind of shared ideology.

Whatever the comrades might think in private, in all public speeches or exhortations, family planning was attacked. One FPW from Matabeleland remembered hearing nationalist politicians publicly exhort crowds to reject the new methods as early as the early 1960s, before the shooting war developed.

The leaders and the comrades told the masses that the main objective of family planning was to reduce the black population and nothing else. In the early sixties a very senior political leader addressing a rally in the White City stadium in Bulawayo said family planning being a white man's idea to reduce our population must be discouraged in all sections. He said it encouraged prostitution in married women and young girls. He was applauded when he went on to say, "No one has the right to tell me how many children I should have, that's an affair between my wife and myself in our bedroom!" Imagine a top leader saying that to a crowd of about 45,000 people! Speeches like this one made our work even harder because many people cherished the statement for many years that followed. The comrades sent the message to the *mujibas* who in turn spread it to the masses.

In later years, both at *pungwes*[21] and in public actions, the comrades attacked the purveyors of family planning, both in words and in deeds.

I actually got a lot of letters from the boys in the bush saying, "We are going to kill you because of what you are talking about," because I was doing radio [hosting the ZNFPC weekly radio show]. I had to go to the police station [to receive police protection]. It was beamed all over and they received it in Mozambique. They said it was a white man's ploy to cut the number of Africans when we need soldiers. (interview with senior female FPW)[22]

The political argument came with the war, after Mozambique had got independent, when we started having political commissars addressing meetings. [AK: Did they actually talk about family planning in the meetings?] Ah yes, I came across one such address . . . The issue here was about the land, the whole fight was about the land, any idea which could be used to recover the land would come in. "We are fighting for the land, the land is ours, but our land has been taken. And now you people are accepting ideas of limiting your children! When the country is so full of other people and not you yourselves, you should have children. We have plenty of ground for children and yet you are being told to limit the number of children. These people [whites] want us to be few and so they can fight us and take us over. If we are fewer they will take us over, after all they have already taken over the better areas, the land, the farms, and we own very little in the poor areas. And you are limiting the number of children!" (interview with female FPW)

During the war the guerrillas didn't like to see us, we were just enemies to them like the Rhodesian security forces and the police. They called us sell-outs. We were not allowed to go home to our rural areas. They knew it was Mrs. So-and-So [who was coming to visit her relative in the rural areas], they wanted to know who you are and what you are doing. The people at home would reveal that she is doing family planning. So at that time we could not go to our homes, we were not traveling freely because you know your job is not wanted by the guerrillas. (interview with female FPW who worked in urban townships)

I was stationed in Gweru, but still there were these boys, some of them were coming to camp with their friends or their relatives in the townships for hid-

A FPW landrover making a stop at a commercial farm. The original caption read, "The Chipinga [now Chipinge] mobile unit has been mine-proofed to guard the staff against terrorist attacks when they travel on farm rounds." Mrs. Winnie Pasipanodya is the nurse standing. Source: *FPAR 1978,* a promotional brochure put out by the FPAR.

ing themselves so it was a problem there. I know of a man from Chivhu who was killed, he was an educator and he was killed because of his work. They said, "These people give women pills so that they don't bear children." That one was called Makiwa. He was killed not even by a gun but by an axe and another one was killed in Chivhu, it was so bad. Makiwa was killed openly. I was so sad. We were called to the office to be told that one of our educators is dead. We were told to be very careful in our approach, how you talk, and you must also educate yourselves on the tempers of these people, once you fear that the tempers are rising, you calm down. (interview with female FPW who worked in rural area)

These attacks were not always about family planning itself. In many cases, attacks on FPWs were motivated by jealousy of the FPWs' steady jobs or by other feuds that had existed before the beginning of the war. Family planning was a convenient way for people in the community to act out their hostilities, by hitching their personal grievances to the anti–family planning rhetoric of the comrades.

The community there [in a mining area in the southeast] was a problem during the wartime. Those were then ones who were giving wrong information to the freedom fighters. They were telling wrong information. [Another FPW interjects: Especially those who were anti–family planning, they went to the freedom fighters and said, "We don't like".] They were also jealous because there were very few people in the communal lands who were employed so the others were jealous. They told the freedom fighters, "We don't like this." And the boys said, "Okay, we will look into it." The freedom fighters didn't have a problem. The problem was with people in the community. (interview with former regional supervisor for FPAR)

How did the FPWs account for the comrades' expressions of hostility toward contraception? In explaining why the comrades were anti–family planning, the FPWs used two arguments. First, they said, some of the comrades were genuinely laboring under genuine misapprehensions about family planning—the comrades genuinely thought that it was forced on people by the government, or that it was intended to sterilize women so that no more soldiers for the liberation war could be born. Such misunderstandings flourished in the politically charged atmosphere of the war, buttressed by the population-control rhetoric of the white politicians.

FPWs who met comrades who "did not understand" tried to enlighten the comrades in two ways: either by referring the comrades to their clients, who would confirm that family planning was not being forced or otherwise abused in that particular area, or by reframing family planning in such a way that it could be made to appear consistent with the guerrillas' mission, to strengthen the African nation. Both strategies created an apparent distance between the practice of family planning and the coercive and abusive Rhodesian state: in the first case, by depoliticizing it, making it appear as a politically meaningless, optional health measure; and, in the second strategy, by repoliticizing it in a new way, as part of building the new Zimbabwean nation.

FPWs, using the first strategy and attempting to depoliticize their work, pointed to their harmonious relations with the community and described their work as merely offering information, not coaxing women to take up suspect "white" technologies:

One of the [FPAR] group leaders was taken and stayed three days out waiting to be killed . . . she was at work with her bicycle, uniform, and bag, then others said, "That is the one who is forcing people to take contraceptives." She was taken, she stayed there [at the comrades' bush camp] for about three days, one [government employee] being killed each day. The day it was her turn she was asked to give a motivational talk, how she does her work. She did everything and at the end she explained, "We are not forcing people, if you want contraceptives, you come and I give them to you. If you have your own methods that you are going to continue to use, you continue using them. What we want is to space your children." They [the comrades] asked the other people who were there at the *pungwe*, "Is there anyone who was forced to take pills by this woman?" They [the people] said, "No, they teach us, and if you want you take, if you don't want, you don't. Why do you want her to be killed, then?" . . . they saved her life at the *pungwe*. She is very brave, she didn't even change the area where she worked, she stayed there. (interview with female FPW who worked in Mashonaland Central)

In contrast, FPWs who used the second strategy sought to repoliticize the contraceptives, to make them consistent with the guerrillas' own agenda. They did so by claiming that contraceptives would enhance the quality of the new Zimbabweans being born and would remove the dangers of pregnancy during wartime:[23]

You would say it is not a sickly person [one who is ill as a consequence of too may children in a family] who can be a soldier, who can go to war, who can bear weapons, it's a healthy person who can do all those things. [AK: So you were agreeing with them about the war?] Yes, we needed them [the comrades], definitely we needed them, but we needed healthy people, we didn't need sickly people. (interview with male FPW)

They might say that we [the FPWs] want to reduce the population so that we don't have soldiers, but a soldier who is not educated is no good. And then there was no free education, starting from grade one you were paying fees, books, everything; so we tried to tell them about the economy, about hardships and these burdens. (interview with male former district supervisor for FPAR)

Another female FPW used a combination of both strategies:

At one time the problem I faced was the comrades from the jungle. They came to me, they were told that that CBD [community-based distributor] is forcing people to join [to use family planning]. So I was called to the base. I was taken to the bush on my way to the field. They just stopped me on the way. I don't know where they came from. They just stopped me there and I went there with my bag and everything. They asked me, "Are you the one who is forcing people to join family planning? You know we are being killed, we are dying because of this war, what do you think of that?" So what I did, I had to educate those people. I said, "No, we don't force family planning, if you want to know the truth go to those farms and talk to the people and ask them what we are actually doing. You know there are some people who are having children who are dying. You soldiers here, you are also dying, you need replacements. But if the children keep on dying without good health, can they be good soldiers?" They said no. . . . And they said, "You are very right because no war can be fought by pregnant people." And I said, "Let's say people are pregnant and you have taken them to your base. Who is going to deliver that woman when she is in labor? It's a problem, maybe there won't be enough water or maybe the war is going to start there before she has delivered, and that means that woman is going to die." And they said, "I think you are very right, no pregnant woman can fight a war. So I think if these pills are reversible then it's okay." I gave them the example of my own children, because my firstborn was born 1964 and the second one in 1970. So they could see there is no danger. I think in wartime what is needed is your own explanation. If you show them you are very afraid with what you are doing you are going to be in trouble. So you are supposed to have confidence in what you are saying.

Many FPWs adopted a broader strategy of presenting themselves to the comrades as politicized people, who could be trusted not to betray the guerrillas' locations to the regime's forces, or as people who would actively help the guerrillas. They might have to work for the whites, they implied, but their hearts were with their fellow Africans fighting for independence:

[AK: Did you ever meet the guerrillas when you were doing your work?] On so many occasions, so many occasions! Sometime they used to come to my home, I was cooking sadza for them and all the like. They really knew that's where Mr. Katerere of family planning stays. [AK: So they knew you were from family planning?] Definitely. They met me, came to my place and talked to me and I told them, "Yes, I am working at family planning, I am an educator in this area, and they said, "Tell us your job," and I had to do a little bit of education and motivation for them. Then they said, "Ah no, if it's like that we don't mind about your job unless you are going to be a sell-out to go and tell the government soldiers that there are guerrillas here. If you are going to be that sell-out that's when there is going to be a problem with you. If you are doing your job of family planning, then go ahead." . . . There was a time in early 1978 when I was called to their base at night. I came back the next morning and my wife had tears in her eyes, she thought I was dead. They asked me, they wanted to know really actually what I do, my work. I told them that even if we get independence still family planning we will need it because of this and that, all the advantages. There was one guerrilla I still remember, he said, "No you guys, we mustn't trouble this man. This family planning doesn't interfere with our war. It's not going to stop us and interfere with us. Let him go on with his job, it has nothing to do with our war" . . . Yes, I did cook sadza for them, not once but several times, many times! Many times I fed those guerrillas. So I didn't get any problems with them. I worked cooperating with them. I could just pass through this village and see those guerrillas there, "Where are you going old man?" "I am going to my work" "Okay, you can go." (interview with a male FPW who worked in Manicaland)

The senior educators for the FPAR during most of the 1970s quietly encouraged workers to cooperate with the comrades where possible:

Some of them [the comrades] would ask me to get them cigarettes from town. So we didn't have problems. In fact one of the educators met them and he told me that they said, "No, we are not opposed to family planning, in fact when we take over the country we want this to be high on the agenda". . . . I know some of our educators were in touch with them and I would take cigarettes and parcels out to those who were saying that they were handing them over to the freedom fighters. So they weren't harassed, they weren't intimidated, there was no problem. (interview with former senior educator)

One male FPW hinted at an even deeper collaboration with the comrades, behind his cover as a cooperative ally of the regime:

I was working in a very sensitive area where there was war [in 1977]. I used to go on very well with these boys. . . . The [white commercial] farmers when the war was hot they used to organize for me, so I was not going from house to house, they used to provide security and guards, and I used to give my education talk when guarded by the guards. But then what happened one time was that soon after I gave my talk the boys came to the farm and burned the barns and tractors. The following day where I was, they did it again. They were following me. The police thought, "Who was here yesterday? It was that family planning man. Ah, don't worry about family planning, that one is a government employee." They went again to the next farm, who was here, it was the family planning man, the next one, it was the family planning man. They said, "Ah no, there is this family planning man now, he is bringing the comrades." They found some packets of Peter Stuyvesant [a brand of cigarettes] [at one of the burned sites]. I was smoking Peter Stuyvesant. And I tell you it was a very frightening day. I couldn't go to my house, I was taken and tortured as a terrorist for three weeks in the cell. Fortunately enough my director [Peter Dodds] was very good, he was also a captain in the army, he saved me and said you should not have held him for three weeks. So I was lucky, but I tell you it's in two ways [that I was lucky]. When I came out of the cell I found most of my friends were killed, either by the Rhodesian army or by the terrorists. So I was safe in my cell.

Whether other FPWs went as far as this man hints that he did, all those who managed to work out a relationship with the comrades also had to maintain smooth relations with the local agents of the government. Many local police and security officers saw the FPWs as a potential source for information on the comrades. Working in an area controlled by the comrades could thus put FPWs in double jeopardy—at risk both from the freedom fighters and from the regime's forces. Several FPWs refused offers of assistance, such as transport from government employees, toward the end of the 1970s, as more and more rural areas were partially controlled by the *vakomana,* in order that their work not be seen to be connected in any way, even the most innocuous, with the government:

When we go into the TTL the first station to report to is the DC's office, then sometimes we are given a messenger, but I said, "No no no, I prefer to go by myself, I don't want a messenger, I know the areas, I can drive there. Thank you very much, but I can go by myself" . . . If you cooperate with DCs and so forth your message will be misunderstood by the people. So I think that in that way we promoted family planning even during the liberation war. (interview with former senior educator)

FPWs were often caught between the comrades and the regimes' forces. Maintaining good relations with both sides required tact and deception. They kept their contacts with the comrades secret from their superiors and from fellow Africans in the police and army.

[AK: Did you ever report the presence of the comrades to the management?] It was difficult if you go and report. I still remember another year that was 1979, we had a workshop in Sakubva there. I wanted to explain that there are some areas that we shall not go for our programs because once we understood that there are guerrillas there, it's not easy to go and work in the area where you have been given the information that there are some guerrillas now. Then those [FPAR management] came to me and said, "Where are those guerrillas? You go to the [police] camp and report those guerrillas now." So to go and report them to the Rhodesian forces, now when they will go and attack the guerrillas, you are in trouble, you are a sell-out. So it was difficult to come and tell our officers here during the war. That time they were white people. It was difficult to tell them, " I have seen the guerrillas," because they are going to say, "All right, let's go and tell the police now, and the army will go and [destroy the guerrillas' base] . . . " so you see you are a sell-out. . . . Once you meet them or if you give them any support you can't tell the office. (interview with male FPW who worked in rural areas)

I remember when I was traveling at night . . . I was stopped by the police on my way into Harare. "Where are you coming from? This is a curfew area. What are you doing, do you cooperate with guerrillas?" I said, "No, if you understand my work that I am doing with family planning, I have no friends, we are not wanted by the guerrillas because I am their enemy". . . . We [FPWs] made it clear that we are not going to report anything [to the police] because we are working for the people. If the terrorists or the fighters see us, maybe they are going to kill us, fine, but we are not going to report them to the police. . . . [The police] said, "As you go, if you see anything unusual please report it to us." (interview with former male senior educator)

While some FPWs believed the comrades were sincerely opposed to family planning, others thought that the comrades were simply being canny and molding their opposition to contraceptives to fit pre-existing male hostility to the devices. Opposition to family planning, according to the FPWs, had more to do with opportunism and political expediency than with genuine misunderstanding about the purpose of the contraceptives. They recognized and exploited the symbolic value of the struggle over women's fertility, and the resonance that this struggle had with men's and elder's embattled sense of patriarchal norms.

> Just like the digging of contour ridges and dipping of cattle [other practices promoted by the white authorities which were opposed by the guerrillas], such talk about family planning was there and regarded as a Western way of reducing the number of blacks so that we have fewer children and they come and take over the land and eventually the land is taken . . . Like the issue of contour ridges for conservation, to dig contour ridges or to take your cattle to the dip tanks to clean ticks, these were opposed as propaganda for the war. . . . So all these things, these developmental issues that would do down the enemy would be advanced. During the war you use any available propaganda. It's a question of what ideas people will buy and you advance them. (interview with female FPW who worked in peri-urban areas)

FPWs reported that the younger and more militant comrades who joined the movement later in the 1970s were the one who most strongly opposed contraceptives on ideological grounds, as a Western perversion. Older and more seasoned comrades, especially those who had been trained in socialist countries that had their own contraceptive programs, would sometimes acknowledge in private that contraceptives could be separated from the political context of colonialism in which they were proffered, and that contraceptives could be politically acceptable in an independent Zimbabwe as part of national development.

> The politicians, they were going around mobilizing people that people knew about it [reasons why contraceptives were bad] . . . They were telling us that it's the way of decreasing the Africans. If you could find an old man who is a politician, he would tell you that this is because we are still fighting, we haven't got our independence yet, but after we win we will want these things. If you talk to them privately, they can say that. Those were the old politicians. The young men were all excited . . . They [the older politicians] would tell you be strong [i.e., don't give up on family planning] because tomorrow we will also want to have this family planning.[24] (interview with female FPW from commercial farming district)

> The comrades just said, "Carry on [with your job]. There is no government that doesn't like family planning, when we are the government we will want it." (interview with female FPW who worked in rural areas)

> [The comrades] did understand [about the value of family planning] but of course politically they were saying it, they were saying no. They would say it

publicly, they could say family planning is another way to destroy us, they would say that publicly, just the same as what they would do with that FN [rifle] of the Smith people [i.e., the regime's soldiers], they would say that it has got no bullets. They would say that, they would say this AK [rifle, used by the comrades] is the only gun which has got bullets . . . they just say it because of the situation. Not that they actually hate family planning, they were just making propaganda. (interview with male former district supervisor)

One female FPW said that the comrades in her area actually protected her from angry husbands, fathers, and local politicians who believed that the new methods were both corrupting their women and were a tool of the genocidal white government:

Pills and injections were completely disliked in [her home area]. Those who didn't like them wanted to prevent prostitution. They feared that women's wombs would be closed completely, that prostitutes would become numerous, and some said that the whites were the ones who had decreed this so that the blacks would decline. They said that I had been sent by the whites . . . In the area where I traveled they wanted to kill me, but some of the comrades spoke of the goodness of family planning. I was given a letter so that I would not be killed by the others [the comrades' supporters]. Therefore, in the areas where the people said, "down with family planning!" I showed them that letter. I also carried a letter from the Rhodesian government and a badge reading, "[Her name], FPAR." (tr. AK)

FPWs reported contradictions between the comrades' political education and their personal lives. While family planning was a useful symbol of white domination and a rhetorical rallying point against white control of African bodies, for some comrades it was also something useful for their private lives. Evidently, they did not fear that they were compromising their own political integrity by using pills and injections themselves. Many among the comrades, both "top people" who formed the elite of the guerrillas movement and the civilian support networks, and also the more pragmatic of the obstreperous adolescent men who made up most of the liberation forces' rank and file, found a use for contraceptives in their private lives. As one FPW with long-standing connections in the liberation movement (and who went on to a minor municipal political career with ZANU after the war) recounted:

I was a politician myself. During my school days I was one of the youth for Dr. Nkomo [one of the founders of the parties which developed into the liberation movement] in [his township] . . . So most of the politicians were my friends and I could understand them. One funny thing was that during the Rhodesian time some of the things they wanted they didn't want other people to accept. The reason being that when you meet them they could resist in the presence of many but if you meet them privately they say, "Yes, I do this [use family planning] but I don't want the others to know." You get to some prominent people, very top people, and they say, "I am using but I don't want others to know, this is my secret" so you could just leave them. (interview with male former FPW who worked in urban townships)

Rejection of family planning on political grounds was symbolically necessary, as part of the comrades' self-construction as the opponents of genocidal white practices. However, in a different and more private context, such as the comrades' own marriages and families, the meaning of family planning shifted again so that the new contraceptive could be acceptable.

## CONTRACEPTION AMONG THE COMRADES?

It is difficult to gauge the extent to which the comrades themselves took advantage of family planning methods. Only two FPWs reported that they had regular contact with (female) comrades seeking pills or Depo injections, although two others claimed that they saw the comrades' medical officers carrying pills. Many FPWs reported that they supplied condoms to the comrades.[25] When FPWs met the comrades in the course of their work, the guerrillas were more likely to request money or minor medical supplies or to destroy the stocks of pills and injections that they found than to make any requests for contraceptive assistance. The one former comrade whom I spoke with asserted that all of her colleagues were opposed to the new contraceptives.

However, many of the people of Wedza remember that the comrades covertly used contraceptives to facilitate their sexual encounters with local girls. Like private acceptance by married women, these activities were viewed with great disapproval, as elders believed that the comrades had used these pills, which they kept secret from elders, to seduce girls away from their parents and their virginity.[26]

To us, the comrades said nothing, but we heard our sons and daughters talking about pills. (interview with Mrs. Twiza, tr. NS)

[NS: Did the comrades talk about family planning] Not the first groups, and not often. The last groups of comrades were given some pills, and they gave them to their girlfriends privately when we elders had gone home from the meetings. (interview with Mr. Nyamudzura, tr. NS)

We had no family planning lectures, but we heard our sons and daughters saying that the last group of comrades from Mozambique gave their lovers injections and pills. To us elders, they encouraged us to have children. (interview with Mr. Mbira, tr. NS)

They said nothing about family planning, but to their assistants and the girls
they gave pills privately. They did this privately, we only heard it from the
girls. (interview with Mrs. Mbira)

Evidence from the comrades themselves suggests that the use of pills did
occur, but was contested both in the base camps in Zambia and Tanzania and
while on maneuvers within Zimbabwe. In the course of their revolutionary
work, living far from the watch of their parents, young female guerrillas had
to covertly negotiate the issue of family planning. In the liberation movement,
the combination of the socialist rhetoric of women's emancipation and protra-
ditionalist sentiments espoused by the cultural nationalists was bound to pose
conflicts for the running of the camps and the missions in Zimbabwe, where
young men and women would live in close proximity to each other without
chaperones. Officially, these were often resolved in favor of tradition, with
young married couples being required to promise that they would return to the
parents' homes and carry out traditional rites involving *lobola* when the war
ended (Kriger 1992:193). Julia Zvobgo, a ZANU official involved in admin-
istering the training camps over the border in Zambia, had to supervise many
young people in the emotionally charged wartime situation. Fraternization
might happen in the camps, but "We didn't go in for family planning. . . . We
felt that family planning was something that should be decided by the parents
[of the female guerrillas]"(quoted in Weiss 1986:95).

A young guerrilla in the camps, Tainie Mundondo, reported that "[n]atu-
rally men and women fell in love. If they wanted to stay together, they
reported this and were registered. Family planning was not possible"(Weiss
1986:90). The war situation added to the cultural and moral objections to contraception. "It would have been wrong to have birth control when so many
people were dying" (ibid.). By 1978, more than 15,000 people, overwhelmingly rural Africans, had been killed in the war, and the liberal Catholic Commission for Justice and Peace estimated that one hundred were dying every
day (Gilmurray, Riddell, and Sanders 1979:31). Zvobgo also claimed that the
high death rate among civilians meant that contraception was politically as
well as morally wrong for politically sensitized women (Nhongo-Simbanegavi
1998:170). Teurai Ropa, another senior woman in ZANU, said that when
ZANU women tried to make traditional herbal contraceptives, they had to
keep their activities secret from their male colleagues, "as they were continu-
ally being bombed in the camps, the men were anxious to have children to
carry their name on, in case they died during the war" (ibid.).

Nonetheless, women guerrillas had their own strong reasons to want birth
control. Even Mundondo acknowledged that "pregnant women had a tough
time" in the liberation armies (Weiss 1986:90). Guerrillas who were pregnant
were sent to the rear in Mozambique, usually to the maternity camp at Ossibissa, for three-and-a-half months as a kind of maternity leave. Ossibissa was

regarded as a place of punishment, a scrap-heap to which unlucky women were consigned, and the desire to stay out of Ossibissa was strong (Nhongo-Simbanegavi 1998:177). After the baby was born, he or she was placed in a communal nursery and the mother was usually reassigned to support work. It was very difficult to get back to the front after becoming a mother (Davies 1983:104–5).

Although Zvobgo was opposed to the use of nontraditional contraceptives, she acknowledges "Of course I talked to the girls privately and told them to look after themselves and how best to do it [possibly a reference to traditional methods of contraception, such as rhythm or coitus interrupts?[27]]. But there was no policy about family planning" (Weiss 1986:94). Zvobgo evidently did not see anything wrong in avoiding birth by "looking after oneself," so it appears to be the use of pills and injections per se that was objectionable.

While contraceptives were officially forbidden, women guerrillas found ways to get them. Like civilian women back in the villages, they were willing to contravene officially sanctioned norms in order to enhance their own lives:

We had access to contraceptives in the bush. People brought them back from overseas and I'm glad, really I wouldn't have liked to have had a baby in the bush. We have adopted what we want from Western culture into our revolution, and we are aware of the fact that people have sexual feelings in spite of the dangers of the struggle. . . . Our attitude to contraception and abortion changed during the years of the struggle. The girls have really adopted a new way of living. . . . They are quite different from the people who have stayed in Zimbabwe. ("Nyasha," quoted in Davies 1983:105)

For these same women, their own interests prevailed over the norms that opposed contraception, which led to conflict with men: "Some of the male comrades did not like contraceptives because they thought they were murder, but really it was our duty and we female comrades were ready to defend it" (a female guerrilla, quoted in Kriger 1992:139). If these male comrades did find their female colleagues with contraceptives, the sanctions could be severe. For instance, Nhongo-Simbanegavi reports that some women in base camps in Chimoio, Mozambique, went to the capital of Mozambique to have intrauterine devices inserted. This transgression was somehow discovered, and the women were punished by being forced to have the loops removed (Nhongo-Simbanegavi 1998:171).

## CONCLUSION

Because family planning is directly implicated in the creation (or noncreation) of new lives, it was constructed as a white initiative aimed at "cutting down the nation" both physically and spiritually. The potential for the new methods to cut down the nation physically is obvious in their power to prevent births, which was expressed through denunciations of family planning for its potential to "kill the soldiers" of the next generation. The spiritual and cultural threat posed by this alien invasion into Zimbabwean bodies is apparent from the rumors that surrounded the new methods. An intrusion into a Zimbabwean woman's body was not just a medical procedure, it was also an intrusion into the heart of Shona identity. Because the bodies in question here were female, this cultural threat acquired a gendered dimension, so that the maleficent powers of the new methods of family planning were conflated with the emasculation of African men as their land, cattle, and status as adults were also stripped away. Thus, the attacks on the new methods had a gendered appeal to men as men, just as the comrades' crackdowns on divorce and male profligacy appealed to married women as women. The gendered nature of the political objections to family planning is also evident in the gender division among those who voiced their objections. Women, while they might fear or distrust the new methods for their own reasons, were relatively silent about the political danger of these methods.

The comrades' objection to family planning was not monolithic, however. While the issue clearly had great symbolic appeal to the masses, especially men, the comrades themselves held positions with respect to family planning that were much more complex than simple rejection. Some of the comrades maintained a distinction between the methods themselves, which could be useful in a future Zimbabwe, and the historic context within which they were distributed, which was at that time a context of war, colonialism, and racial oppression. Other comrades made a split between the contraceptives that they denounced in public meetings and the contraceptives that they used in their own lives. In other cases, there are hints that the issue of contraceptives was a bone of contention between male and female comrades.

The nation-builders of Zimbabwe—the early nationalist organizers of the 1950s, the members of the liberation armies, and civilian supporters—defined their nation partially in reaction to the colonial imposition of alien practices, including practices that undermined the traditional authority of men and elders. The struggles over family planning were not only struggles over actual practices, but also struggles over the symbolic significance of which men were to control African women's bodies.

## NOTES

1. When appropriate, nationalist forces and their supporters also appealed to women on the basis of their interests as women. These types of gendered appeals are harder to find in the literature, but persist in Zimbabweans' memories. Kaler (1997), Kriger (1992), and Staunton (1991) all found that women in the rural areas remember with approval how some of the comrades in the liberated zones held their husbands to a high standard of responsibility for their wives and children, thus reinforcing women's normative claims on men. In

particular, women (and some men) in Wedza recalled that the freedom fighters strongly discouraged men from divorcing or abandoning their wives on frivolous pretexts, holding men responsible for fulfilling their side of the patriarchal bargain. The predominant promise of the comrades—that ancestral lands would be returned to Zimbabweans—also had a strong appeal to women as women. Although they did not have formal title to the land, women did the bulk of the agricultural labor in the arid and overcrowded Tribal Trust Lands reserved for Africans, especially in areas with high male labor out-migration, such as the communities from which many of the women in Wedza came. Thus, the promise that prime agricultural land would be taken back from the white usurpers and returned to Africans had great appeal to women in Wedza who believed their gender-specific subsistence chores would be much easier if they had good land to till.

2. See Thompson 2000a for a comprehensive account of peasant resistance to the NLHA.

3. See Department of Health (Southern Rhodesia) *Report on the Public Health* 1949:9, 1950:14, and 1951:10. See also Gordon 1980:70.

4. Mr. Morris went on to add that he had had personal requests from the chief in Sipolilo reserve asking for the provision of clinics, without fear that they would be used to sterilize women. Sipolilo reserve was one of the strongholds of African nationalist politics in the 1950s.

5. One of the few pre-1965 statements by the organized nationalist movement came from Michael Mawema, a prominent member of the National Democratic Party, which was the leading African nationalist political party allowed to operate in Southern Rhodesia. He insisted that family planning was a tool of genocide by the white regime, an attempt to undermine the growth of the African population as a means of thwarting their political aspirations. He was taken to task in the pages of *The Rhodesia Herald* by a woman, a fellow nationalist, who signed herself "NDP Mother Number One." Although Mawema framed family planning as a threat to the African nation because it would reduce the population, "NDP Mother Number One" framed Mawema's opposition to family planning as a gender issue, claiming that he opposed it because he, like a "typical native husband," believed that his wife was only "there to suffer and produce children":

> You never gave birth, Mr. Mawema, and others like you and that is why you speak so lightly on the subject. Only your wife and other women know what it means to have unplanned families . . . You are a married man and I respect you, but please stop misleading the women, you will never share the pain of labour as your wife does. Neither will you be called upon to look after two children who look almost like twins [i.e., who are born too close together]. Or are you reasoning like a typical native husband that the wife is only there to suffer and produce children? Preach to your fellow men about the sorry condition of the African women and then cry for freedom in general as you have wonderfully been doing. Stop punishing the women to a string of unplanned *piccanins* [slang for small children]. ("Mawema Taken to Task on Family Planning," letter to the editor, *The Rhodesia Herald,* September 14, 1960)

6. There were two main liberation movements—the Zimbabwe African National Union (ZANU) and the Zimbabwe African Patriotic Union (ZAPU)—as well as some smaller splinters, which merged in 1976 to form the Patriotic Front. However, in terms of the treatment of family planning within the pages of their official organs, I found no significant difference between ZANU and ZAPU.

7. I deduce that the readership was largely male because of the very low rates of female literacy in the vernacular, and especially in English, which prevailed at the time.

8. The poor quality of medical treatment given to blacks was used as an index of white hatred of blacks. For example, the Political Commissariat Lecture Series, intended as a self-study course for Zimbabweans at home and in exile, had this to say about Rhodesian medical facilities for Africans:

> The health services for Africans in Zimbabwe are poor, insufficient and highly segregated. The hospitals and clinics are concentrated in industrial areas and white business centers to ensure the workers are fit enough to sell their labor power to their imperialist bosses. In the reserves the medical facilities are far scarcer, ill-equipped, and short-stocked. A pregnant woman will die at the doorstep of a European hospital because she is an African and cannot be admitted into a European hospital for medical attention during delivery . . . many Africans are being used as guinea pigs for testing new medications and for test operations by trainee doctors. ("Political Commissariat Lecture Series Part 2: Colonialism," *Zimbabwe News,* March/April 1978)

9. The management of this cholera outbreak became a political football bounced back and forth between the guerrillas and the Rhodesian government. While the guerrillas accused the government of dragging their feet in providing medical assistance, the *Annual Reports of the Secretary for Health* in the early 1970s accused the guerrillas of intimidating people from coming for treatment and of preventing medical relief teams from getting into the area.

10. Although rumors of such a policy circulated widely among Africans in Rhodesia during the war (and although some voices in the white community called for such measures, along with punitive taxation and disqualification from social welfare benefits for large African families), to the best of my knowledge such a policy never became official in Rhodesia. On the large white-owned commercial farms, however, subtle and not-so-subtle coercion by farm owners amounted to a de facto policy of this nature.

11. These proscriptions, along with much more extensive lists that varied regionally, are common in accounts of the period. However, more recent histories of the period (such as Staunton 1991) suggest that, under the influence of youth, hormones, and battle adrenaline, the first proscription was often disregarded.

12. It is important to note, however, that the liberation movements were somewhat ambivalent to the threats posed by all white institutions and practices, as illustrated by the guerrilla ambivalence over closing schools in the district Kriger studied (Kriger 1992:158–59). Similar concerns were voiced by many of the women in Staunton (1991) who feared that their children's and, by extension, their families' futures were being sacrificed to political zealotry.

13. Despite the emphasis on harmonious and correct marital relations, however, the guerrillas were not primarily interested in changing gender relations. While the people of Wedza by and large appreciated the guerrillas' efforts to stabilize chaotic marriages and families, these efforts clearly took place within the framework that valorized "tradition" and not women's emancipation. As Kriger says, with respect to the course of the war as a whole, "demands for changing African social relations were ultimately abandoned by the guerrillas, whose central platform was against racial discrimination" (Kriger 1992:194).

14. FPWs who worked as township nurses during those years told of rumors that any Africans who sought medical help from white-run clinics were at risk of being used as an involuntary subject for experimentation (often for veterinary purposes) or organ transplantation.

15. By the end of the 1970s, a writer forecasting Zimbabwe's medical future expressed relief at the end of political rumors, which had hampered preventive medicine in Rhodesia, and expressed confidence that

> [t]he political bogey attached to the vaccination campaigns of the early 1950s and persisting since then must be overcome. The population must be assured that this is not yet another white man's trick to get rid of them . . . (Gordon 1980:70)

16. As mentioned in the introduction, in this chapter I have not used proper names in quotes from respondents because of the politically sensitive nature of some of their stories.

17. One female FPW's husband changed his favorite beer-drinking place to avoid the political criticism of his drinking mates, who attacked his wife's work during the 1970s:

> The husbands would scold my husband: "You sir, your wife is doing bad, she is giving our wives pills, but don't you have children yourself?" He would say, "You are just opposing because it is pills [from white sources], if it was one of our Africans doctors coming with a method you would not oppose, if it was African medicine you would not complain."

Eventually, however, the threats of being beaten drove him away from this beerhall.

18. One of the first five nurses to begin working for family planning in the township of Salisbury said that the leading women in nationalist politics "would not go for that [family planning] and they were older and not having many children"—that is, that their status in life, as much as their political allegiances, made it likely that they would not be interested in family planning.

19. See Lyons 2000, Staunton 1991, Weiss 1986.

20. The guerrilla armies throughout the war had the problem of too many would-be soldiers, so that many youths who crossed the border to fight were eventually sent back to their homes because the armies could not absorb them.

21. A *pungwe* was a secret mass meeting, usually lasting all night, called by the comrades to inform local people about the progress of the war and to proselytize. Attendance at the *pungwes* was usually mandatory for all adults.

22. Her account continues, corroborating the FPWs contention that the comrades opposed family planning was on symbolic rather than substantive grounds:

> Then just after independence when the comrades were in the assembly [demobilization] points the ZANU-PF [Patriotic Front] and ZAPU asked if we could run a workshop for two weeks. They chose some cadres who were what they called political commissars, they came here [to Spilhaus Centre]. . . . As I got in [entered the room] they said, "Oh, you are Sister So-and-So, we used to plan to kill you in Mozambique." But in the end they were very motivated, they said there was nothing wrong with family planning, it was just the political situation.

23. This line of reasoning—that family planning enhanced the quality of the human stock of Zimbabwe—was later echoed in the developmentalist arguments of the ZANU-PF proponents of family planning after independence in 1980.

24. Looking back from the 1990s to the 1960s and 1970s, former freedom fighters concurred it was the political context of family planning that made it objectionable during the 1970s. Speaking at the launch of the Zimbabwe National Family Planning Council's Male Motivation Campaign in October 1993, Swithin Mombeshora, the Minister of Local Government and Urban and Rural Development, said

We as politicians took a position [in the 1970s] which was appropriate under the circumstances, that modern family planning was a colonial ploy to reduce the black African population at a time when the colonial government was vigorously encouraging large scale white immigration. (press release, October 16, 1993)

Of course, Mombeshora's retrospective assessment of the situation in the 1970s may have been colored by his government's postindependence embrace of family planning.

25. However, condoms did not carry the same political loading as the pill and the Depo injection, and are also male-controlled methods that did not have the same connotation of gender subversion as the female-controlled pills and injections.

26. Elders' dislike of the comrades' violation of norms in the matter of giving contraceptives to girls was linked to their objections to other ways in which the comrades transgressed the norms of control over fertility. The most frequent complaint against the comrades was that they impregnated local girls and left them with illegitimate babies who had no fathers. This "theft" of girls' reproductive capacities (and virginity, in some cases) was especially significant as in Shona society a child belongs to the lineage of the father, and the patrilineal spirits are important in healing childhood diseases and bringing luck in later life. Without any known patrilineal relatives, a child would not be able to participate in proper rituals for his or her success in life, and is doomed to be a "person with no name." In addition, the single mothers the comrades left behind experienced difficulty in finding anyone to marry them, as men did not want to expose their own lineage to the potential witchcraft dangers represented by the presence of another child. The women interviewed by Staunton (1991) report similar concerns.

27. This statement by Zvobgo may also be read as tacit permission for "the girls" to use family planning as long as they were discreet and "private" about their use. This reading supports the contention earlier in this chapter that for the freedom fighters the construction of meaning for family planning depended on the context in which it was being practiced or discussed. In public discourse, family planning could not be separated from the comrades' task of building a spiritually and physically strong Zimbabwean nation and so it was condemned; but in private it could be understood more benignly, as a means of "look[ing] after themselves."

# 7

# CONCLUSION: POSTINDEPENDENCE FAMILY PLANNING AND SOME THOUGHTS ABOUT THEORY

Zimbabwe achieved independence in 1980. With this came a sharp break with the white-ruled past, and, for family planning, a radical new beginning. At the end of the twentieth century, Zimbabwe had one of the highest rates of contraceptive use and one of the lowest fertility rates in Africa. Zimbabwe's postindependence fertility transition lies outside the scope of this book, so I will not go into the details except to say that it took place in a society experiencing rising incomes (at least until the structural adjustment programs of the 1990s) and expectations, and was accompanied by many of the socioeconomic features associated with trends toward lower birthrates, such as increased literacy among women, better health care, lower infant mortality, greater access to education for all children, and improved economic opportunities[1] (see Sibanda 1998 for a comprehensive up-to-date précis of Zimbabwe's contraceptive and demographic history since independence).

The family planning workers (FPWs) whom I interviewed leaned heavily toward the economic-rationality-of-small-families argument to explain why more and more people, especially men, came to use contraceptives in the 1980s and 1990s. They claimed that increases in the cost of raising a child properly, as a result of both rising prices and rising expectations for one's children, had tipped men's minds toward pills and injections. While in the early days of family planning, women wanted pills and injections to protect their health, now men wanted them to protect their purses. In other words, financial constraints have changed notions of correct manhood, expanding the parameters of masculinity to encompass a small family and a wife who goes to the family planning clinic regularly.

In addition, the political profile of family planning was radically transformed as Zimbabwe African National Union (ZANU), on achieving power in 1980, performed a remarkable about-face on its previous stance against contraception and the programs begun by the Family Planning Association of Rhodesia (FPAR).[2] After independence, when the new African government took over and family planning was no longer in the hands of a white minority state, the pill was redefined as an aid to development and a welfare program for healthier African families, rather than as an instrument of genocide.

White control of the FPAR (known as the Family Planning Association of Zimbabwe after 1979) came to an end in 1981, when Peter Dodds resigned and all his white staff followed him. Dodds quit in protest after having been accused by the new Minister of Health Herbert Ushewokunze of disregard for black women's health because of his support for Depo-Provera despite medical studies from the United States that linked it with cancer (for a detailed account of the political dimensions of the Dodds-Depo affair, see Kaler 1998). The FPAR was taken over by the government as a department of the Ministry of Health and reorganized under the name of the Child Spacing and Fertility Association of Zimbabwe (CSFAZ). This name change (the first of several before "Zimbabwe National Family Planning Council" was settled on in 1985) reflects the effort to recuperate the politically tainted image of the new methods as devices for "cutting down the nation." While ZANU-PF [Patriotic Front], as a government might have reversed its opposition to the new methods, it still had to tread carefully to avoid the old fears about the genocidal implications of family planning:

> The Child Spacing and Fertility Association's network remains unchanged from that established by its predecessor, the Family Planning Association, but it is no longer aimed at reducing the country's population growth . . . "The question of policy is a political one," explained Dr. Tom Chimbira, the 38-year-old gynecologist who heads the organization. "At the moment the government says we should not talk in terms of family limitation . . . so we talk more in terms of maternal and child health. We emphasize spacing as opposed to family limitation." ("The Accent is on Child Spacing—Not Limitation," *The Zimbabwe Herald*, October 26, 1982)

As a sign of ZANU's new approval for family planning, "by far the most important and exciting event of the year was the visit of the ZANU Women's League" to Spilhaus Centre in 1982 (*Quarterly Report of the CSFAZ*, September 1982:17). The highest-ranking ZANU women were invited to tour the center and discuss family planning technologies with the staff, and, as a result, "it was agreed that child spacing should be a subject for discussion at all levels of the party's Women's League, thus providing family planning with much needed political backing" (ibid.). While a visit from the heads of the Women's League was not as prestigious as a visit from the president himself (although that would come), this event did signal that ZANU was willing to adopt and adapt the institutional structures of family planning and to embrace the idea of providing new technologies.

The issue of population growth was also rapidly redefined by the new government, from being a source of political power for the burgeoning African nation to being an obstacle to postwar development:

> The Government's social and economic policies should cut Zimbabwe's annual population growth rate within the next five to ten years, Mr. Joseph Mapondera [of the Central Statistical Office] said yesterday ... Colonial policies were the cause of the high population growth rate. The rural people had been neglected and poor health and education facilities had been provided [resulting in high infant mortality and the desire to have many children so that some would live]. "A rapid population growth rate in any country hampers the implementation of the development programmes" [he said]. ("New Order Will Cut Birth Rate," *The Zimbabwe Herald,* April 22, 1982)

Within five years, population growth was consistently described in the national (and government-controlled) press as a development problem to be curbed by family planning. In September 1985 columnist Idi Muvake wrote that the search for "effective solutions to the problem of Zimbabwe's dangerously high 3.5% per year population growth rate" should be a national priority:

> Sound approaches to the question of population planning can be worked out ... only if we as a society progress beyond the hang-ups [lingering suspicions of family planning from the war years] which continue to grip most of us concerning this subject ... Unless population increase is carefully matched to the growth in our capacity to create wealth and provide service, we create political room for an acute maldistribution of wealth and income ... and a progressive reduction in standards of well-being. ... We need an explicit national policy that supports the position that smaller families are better—for their members and for society as a whole. ("Development Frontiers," *The Zimbabwe Herald,* September 19, 1985)

By the 1990s, family planning had become synonymous with development in official discourse. The acceptance of family planning was even used as a barometer for measuring the incorporation of minority ethnic groups into the modern nation of Zimbabwe, and, in an unconscious echo of the words of the Rhodesian social engineers, symbolized their acceptance of economic rationality. This tendency is evident from the headlines of newspaper articles about the Zimbabwe National Planning Council's [ZNFPC's] work to bring the modern benefits of family planning to "backwards" people: "Even Shangaani See Family Planning Light" (*The Zimbabwe Herald,* March 24, 1995) and "Tongas, At Last, Now Accept Family Planning" (*The Bulawayo Chronicle,* August [date unknown] 1994).

However, pills and injections still have not been entirely purified of their taint of racism and imperialism. On several recent occasions in the House of Parliament, MPs have risen to protest that the Minster of Health and the government in general have been duped into doing the work of genocidal foreigners bent on depopulating Africa. For example, in the debate on the President's state-of-the-nation address in December 1994, one member of parliament insisted that developed countries were trying to wipe out blacks by promoting family planning:

> The use of contraceptives was [described as] a move by developed countries to reduce if not eliminate the black population so that they can "take over Africa . . . I smell a rat, those people want Africans to perish through AIDS. Every action by the developed countries since the days of slavery was for their own economic gain. We should view foreign prescriptions with suspicion . . . African countries rushed to the Cairo conference [on population] like cats and rats to destroy their own people." ("Efforts to Wipe Out Blacks," ZIANA [Zimbabwe's News Agency] press release, December 15, 1994)

Only three months earlier, during the annual budget debate, the Minister of Health (who was also the only remaining white minister in the Zimbabwean cabinet) was accused of "trying to kill and exterminate the population" by asking for more funding for family planning ("Emotions Run High over Funds Allocation for Family Planning," *The Zimbabwe Herald,* September 22, 1994). One MP stated that "family planning programmes were designed by multinationals 'with an exploitative endeavour to reduce our populations'" (ibid.).

However, if the political stigma of family planning has been partially neutralized by independence, gender-based resistance to family planning still exists. FPWs who were still working for family planning said that overall they found that men had become much more receptive to the idea of their wife using the new methods because of the economic pressure on them as heads of families, and the ZNFPC has also launched major male motivation campaigns intended to remove men's concerns that FPWs were making an end run around them to get access to their wives. However, fears of prostitution and fears of losing their status as the arbiters of the outside world remain strong, in some cases winning out over the economic rationale for adopting contraception.

Chiefs, the bearers and definers of "Zimbabwean culture," have been outspoken. Chief Dotito said, at a seminar on family planning, that "most women who use the pill become promiscuous . . . he preferred the traditional family planning methods rather than to make the pill available to anyone who needed it" ("Chiefs Raise Eyebrows over Family Planning," *The Zimbabwe Herald,* May 13, 1991). Chief Mangwende, who is also a MP, said in Parliament that "Zimbabweans should not be told how many children they must have. It was up to a man and his wife . . . Women were not oppressed by men but men had 'God-given' authority over women" ("MPs Criticize Modern Birth Control Methods," *The Zimbabwe Herald,* September 1, 1994).

The lingering suspicions about contraception are still felt by women at the grassroots. In a group interview, the older members of the Zvamaoko Women's Club near Wedza concurred that

> Some of our women were divorced by their husbands in the 1970s when women started to use injections. Our African men want children, so at that time we had to hide pills, but we go for injections because they are private and easier to use than pills, because he will try to find out [find where the pills are hidden] one day . . . Some they are still hiding their pills, but they end up [get caught or found out]; their husbands get other wives. We are still fighting the war of understanding if we are talking in terms of family planning. (tr. NS)

## WHY STUDY FERTILITY? WHY THIS RESEARCH MATTERS

If the pill and Depo are on their way to being widely accepted in Zimbabwe, and if the struggles of the early family planning workers are now firmly in the past, why bother with studying contraception at all? Now that the social question of whether women "should" be using the pill and Depo seems to be on the way to being settled, why dig up the problems and concerns of decades ago? To justify excavating this history, I offer thoughts on why studying contraception matters, for social theorists as well as for those interested in the history of gender and politics in Zimbabwe.

The study of contraception offers invaluable insights on two abstract concepts that preoccupy social scientists: the nature of gender and the nature of resistance. These insights are made possible, however, only because of the intimate association between fertility control and power.

Wherever new methods of fertility control are introduced, disagreement and contention shortly follow. People disagree about many issues associated with the new methods, from the medical consequences of hormonal contraception, to the status of religious injunctions to be fruitful and multiply, to the economic viability of a large or small family. All of these questions (especially the last) have been examined by demographers, historians, economists, and sociologists. However, the most important and most often overlooked issue is the question evoked by all new technologies of fertility: In whose hands shall the power to control women's fertility rest? Their own? Their male partners? A government bureaucrat's? This question leads to the most vociferous arguments about family planning, and often underlies many other debates, including debates that may seem on the surface to be about simple technical or managerial issues.

Technologies of fertility control are fundamentally about gaining power over the body, about being able to produce changes in a female body (in the absence of any effective and popular male contraceptive). Different technologies bestow this power over women's bodies on different people or groups of people, from traditional healers to Ministry of Health bureaucrats to individual women themselves. Any shift in the locus of control of family planning has the potential to reduce the power of some people, as new technologies bring with them new gatekeepers for fertility control.

The parties to these struggles over who shall control fertility share two beliefs: first, that their own well-being and status depend on what young women do with their fertility; and, second, that they have a legitimate right to influence other people's ideas and behavior concerning reproduction. The exact identity of these stakeholders varies across time and place. In this book I have identified several stakeholding groups, including husbands, in-laws, elders, white bureaucrats, members of national liberation movements, and others, and have drawn out the details of conflicts among them, and between them and the young women who were the potential users of the new methods.

These shifts and changes in the locus of control over reproduction also affect the meanings that accreted to the pill and Depo, meanings that were created discursively in places ranging from the men's beerhall to the Ministry of Health, to the gossip circles of the extended family. In contemplating the new methods, people thought and argued in terms of whether these new technologies would reinforce, reconfigure, or undermine one's own or someone else's power. The pill and Depo were constructed variously as a means of personal emancipation, a way to enhance one's health and the health of one's family, another nail in the coffin in Zimbabwean morality, a way to ward off unwanted marriage, an invitation to prostitution, a way to displace husbandly authority, or an attack on the well-being of the lineage. The specific meanings that individuals selected and reproduced depended on where one was located in particular power relations and on the potential of these new technologies to weaken or reproduce these relations.

*[margin note: Various constructs]*

## Gender and Identity

Fertility lies at the center of struggles among many different interest groups—between men and women, between elders and juniors, and as a battleground for the nationalists and the entrenched white elite. In this book, I have stressed the wide range of social identities that created stakeholders in

*[handwritten note: Social I.Ds create stakeholders]*

the debates over Depo and the pill, but have concentrated mainly on gender as the single most salient form of identity.

However, while gender was the most prominent axis of conflict in the early days of these new technologies, gender identities were much more complex and varied than simply the question of whether one was a man or a woman. From listening to life stories in Zimbabwe, I know that the connections between gender and other forms of identity are so dense that gender cannot be reduced to a set of binary categories, but that it is a culturally constructed, constantly varying artifact.

In Zimbabwe in the 1960s and 1970s, gender was always inflected. The fact of being sexed female and gendered a woman did not predict the way that women reacted to the new methods of family planning as they emerged. The fact that conflicts over the pill and Depo were almost always expressed in terms of gender norms and violations thereof should not lead us to think that gender is merely a dichotomous variable. In this book, we meet many different kinds of women—young women, old women, mothers-in-law, and daughters-in-law. While they all possessed, and acted on, a consciousness of themselves as women and of what was in their best interests as women, these gendered consciousnesses differed according to their point in their own life-cycle and their positions in relation to other women. A woman's place in her life course—as a young bride, a mother, a sister-in-law, a mother, or a mother-in-law—determined what kind of social relations she had with the people surrounding her. Her views on the desirability of young women controlling their own fertility were apt to change depending on whether she perceived this particular locus of control as advantageous to her interests as a young woman of childbearing age, or disadvantageous to her as an older woman whose power and prestige came from her large number of descendants.

Even though fertility is by definition a sex-specific trait, analyses of gender qua gender are insufficient to account for why some women welcomed and others rejected the use of the new methods of contraception. More subtle and often less visible social relations, such as those binding members of different generations to each other or those that governed access to the alternatives to modern methods of contraception, are equally as salient to understanding what people thought about the new methods as are the relations between the two genders.

Among men the differences across the lifecycle were not as striking. Although young men, like young women, acquired power as they aged, the men did not experience the same degree of subordination in their youth. Neither did they show such unequivocal interest in the new methods as a way of circumventing their subordination as young women did. Nevertheless, for men too, attitudes toward family planning were inflected by other social identities and by their relation to the prospective user of the new methods. For men with strong nationalist sympathies, for example, their political allegiances gave them a reason to issue a blanket condemnation of the new methods, as tools of a repressive regime. For less politically committed men, ideas about family planning could be more nuanced depending on who the potential user was. Men might forbid their wives to use it, but encourage "outside women" and extramarital girlfriends to use family planning. For men as well as women, in many cases, it was not the methods per se but the relationship between the man or woman and the potential user of the methods that produced support or dislike for family planning. Even for very politically committed men, such as the comrades, family planning could be split into two conceptually distinct categories: symbolic meanings of these technologies, as signs of genocide, and the practical uses for the pill and Depo, as means of preventing undesirable pregnancies, as shown by the accounts of comrades who rejected the pill rhetorically but saw some practical use for it, either in their own lives or in a hypothesized future, in chapter 6.

Changes in political economy also inflected the construction of gender identity, as colonial structures entrenched themselves. I speculate that the effects of colonialism on masculine gender identity were particularly salient in shaping the culture of contraception in the 19670s and 1970s. The relationship between colonialism and gender is easier to see with respect to men, who were disempowered, symbolically humiliated, and deprived of the bases of masculine pride and power, including their cattle and their land. In the context of these forms of gender-specific oppression, the efforts by the white government to destock not only cattle but also children were constructed as another attack on the rights of African men qua men, a construction that would have been different in a different historic context without the same legacy of emasculation of African men. Men, inside and outside formal nationalist movements, came to perceive the new methods as part and parcel of the colonial projects that degraded not only the Shona as a people but also Shona men as men and produced a backlash against the new methods, which in turn provoked the dramas of resistance and evasion in many households. Gender identity and the perception of how family planning affects one's gender-specific interest thus changes according to both historic as well as lifecycle time.

Even if one were to hold the stage of the lifecycle and the historic moment constant—if, for example, one were to talk to one particular woman at one particular point in time—her ideas about the goodness of the new methods of family planning might still fluctuate depending on whose fertility was at stake: hers? her daughter's? her sister-in-law's? Chapter 5 provides evidence of women who would support their daughter's interest in the new methods while being opposed to their daughter-in-law visiting the same clinic, or women who would help their friends hide their use of the pill from disapproving husbands while not wanting their sister-in-law to use it, or women who would tell me about their knowledge of traditional methods but would not allow this knowledge to be shared freely with local young women. These apparently contradictory attitudes toward family planning can be explained by the fact that, in all cases, women were acting out of gendered self-interest. For some women, their status and power as a mother, mother-in-law, or grandmother meant ensuring that certain specific younger women had many children. At the same time, their status as grandmothers or mothers-in-law was not as dependent on the fecundity of certain other young women, such as their own daughters. This variation in gendered self-interests has implications for gender-specific solidarity and mutual support, as women's gendered identities might lead them to act in solidarity with some woman, while acting against others.

The strength of generational identity in Shona communities means that the reproduction of patriarchal ideas and systems of control was not simply an issue of men oppressing women and women resisting that oppression, but also a relation between the old and the young, both between the two genders and within genders. Of all the social identities that inflected gender, and thereby affected what women perceived as their best interests, the most powerful was age. As women aged, the bases from which they drew their prestige and power became more and more dependent on the compliance of a younger generation In this particular case, it depended on the younger generation being fruitful and multiplying so that the older women would be a grandmother of many and have many people in her sphere of influence. Thus, her interests in the fecundity of her daughters-in-law and other young women converged with the interests of those young women's husbands, her sons. Older women tried to enforce ideas and patterns of practice on young women, which were clearly in the interests of men as a gender, because these same practices were also in the interests of older women as an age-group.

Older women could attain status not only by acting as gatekeepers for methods of fertility control but also through their relationship to their son's reproductive life. It was thus in their interests to ensure that their sons' wives remained faithful and had many children. These qualities were implicitly promised by the payment of *lobola*, but were thought to be threatened by placing pills and injections in young women's hands. Thus, the prevailing "patriarchal bargain" provided a strong disincentive for older women to support younger women in their ventures to the clinic and the FPAR distributor. In the often-contentious relationships between mothers-in-law and *varoora,* we see the maintenance of patriarchy in the absence of men.

## Family Planning as Repression and/or Emancipation

Depo and the pill, proffered by an oppressive and racist state, yet used by many women for personal autonomy and emancipation, call into question the concepts of repression and emancipation. Viewed from one perspective—that of national politics and national liberation—these were oppressive technologies whose intent was to "cut down the nation," to hold back the natural growth of the African body politic and to corrupt and seduce young people away from cultural standards of rectitude. Seen from another perspective—that of personal autonomy and gender emancipation—these were liberating technologies, which enabled young women to gain a measure of control over their own bodies. These technologies were perceived as either oppressive or empowering, depending on the observer.

The arrival of the new methods created contradictions for women's autonomy. Her independence from her husband's and her elders' agendas for her fertility could be increased, but the means of that increase—use of the pill and the injection—locked her into greater dependence on the white state. The social relations that surrounded the arrival of the pill and the injection—the demographic and political projects of the white regime—meant that, when a woman made use of them, she was fulfilling at least two agendas—her own and that of the Rhodesian regime that wanted, albeit with some internal dissent, to have as many African women as possible bearing as few children as possible.

With Depo and the pill, private acceptors found for themselves a way of evading their husbands' or in-laws' watchful eyes and, thereby, gaining control and autonomy. Yet by participating in the projects of the FPAR, they were simultaneously involving themselves in a repressive state enterprise, motivated at least partially by a racist fear of Africans and designed to give white institutions more control over African bodies. The family planning methods thus possess a polyvalence that makes it impossible to categorize them as either emancipatory or repressive. Because these technologies were crucial to individual women's efforts to gain reproductive autonomy and the white state's ongoing efforts to manage and control the African population, they have a dual, contradictory character. The answer to the question of whether they were liberatory or constraining depends on the perspective of the one asking the question—no final judgment about the moral value of these technologies is possible.

Gender made an enormous difference as to whether the pill and Depo were regarded as oppressive or empowering. Both men and women expressed opposition to the new methods, but women's opposition was more likely to be based on health worries and concerns about possible ruptures in "proper" marital and family relations than on political grounds. The construction of family planning as a malevolent white intrusion into the bodies of African women, bodies which should properly belong to African men, did not resonate with Zimbabwean women who evidently did not think of their bodies as breach-points for racist genocide. We know that more men than women expressed their objections to the new methods on political grounds and that women were relatively silent on the dangers that these methods posed to the physical and spiritual well-being of the African nation. We also know that young Zimbabwean women were actively involved in the liberation war and the political agitation that led up to it. This gender difference in political attitudes toward the pill and Depo suggests that these women's political consciousness and their ideas of what was or was not good for the nascent nation were inflected by their interests as young women in controlling their fertility, leading them to perceive the new methods as more benign than did their male counterparts. Men's political objections to the new methods were born out of their identity not only as Africans, but as African *men*. Women's less hostile attitudes reflect a very different notion of what was good for Zimbabwe and Zimbabweans.

*[handwritten margin note: obvious?]*

## Rethinking Resistance

This book is essentially a series of stories about struggles for control over women's fertility, encompassing attempts to exercise power, to resist the exercise of power, and to grapple with the implications of losing or gaining power. In chapter 1, I defined power as something inherently productive, as the ability to produce effects rather than as inherently coercive (Cooper 1995:3). I have concentrated on the exercise of power in a very small and restricted space—the female body. Although, to paraphrase graphic artist Barbara Kriger, the (female) body is clearly a battleground for many different parties, I have shown that it quite possible for the battleground itself to act—for women to exercise power even in situations in which other people asserted their rights to control women, and even when the women themselves claimed that they were powerless. Women's claims during interviews about the strength of Shona patriarchy and their insistence that they had were subject to the wishes of their men and elders was at odds with their strategies to carve out autonomy for themselves. Implicit in these strategies was the unspoken assumption that they had a right to control their own reproduction: their problem lay in how to secure this control. The same women who described themselves as "slaves to *lobola*" were the ones who became private acceptors and, in practice, claimed control over their own bodies.

*[handwritten margin note: Power as productive]*

*[handwritten margin note: sense of injustice v sense of right]*

These women were perceptive and creative in their appropriation of resources that could give them power. They lived in a social world filled with resources for their appropriation, whether these resources were material, metaphysical, ideological, or technological. They include the invocation of our Shona culture, ideas about gender relations, access to land, children, jobs in towns, Christianity, the creation of liberated zones by the nationalist forces, and many other social and material facts. The pill, Depo injection, and structures of the FPAR were the latest in a long series of resources that could be brought into the work of enhancing power and autonomy for men, women, old, and young. The history of fertility builds on many other histories about social life in Zimbabwe, in which different elements of this universe of material and symbolic resources were involved in conflicts over different forms of control and command.

The experience of Zimbabwean women with these new technologies is different from the way that power and resistance is often imagined in sociology. In feminist and Foucauldian literature, power for women is often defined as the ability to resist or to refuse "incursion into the body," of denying would-be invaders access to the body and of refusing the disciplining of knowledge/power systems, such as biomedicine. Faith (1994), for example, states that

> Resistance . . . feminist resistance in particular, begins with the body's refusal to be subordinated, and instinctual withdrawal from the patriarchal forces to which it is often violently subjected. The act of resisting incursions into the body may be conscious, thoughtful, deliberate, ideologically situated, or it may be a primitive act of survival. Resistance is . . . the compelling "No!" (39)

However, for Zimbabwean women, gaining power over their fertility meant a compelling "Yes"—actively seeking out incursions into their bodies in the form of pills and injections, and actively inscribing themselves in the discipline of biomedicine through the work of the clinics and the FPWs.

Their use of clinical biomedicine problematizes the question of resistance to disciplinary systems. Biomedicine and other means of disciplining the body are not exclusively means of repression or control; they can also be resources that enhance individual power to resist control of the body. Even in colonial Zimbabwe, where biomedicine was firmly interwoven into the disciplining and regulating projects of colonialism, some people sought and found in it a means of liberating themselves. The structures and dictates of one system of regulating bodies—the biomedicine of the clinics and the FPAR—became a way to evade another system of regulating bodies—that of village- and family-based patriarchy.

However, for young Zimbabwean women, the choice to use the new methods was not simply a matter of enhancing their own power by playing the FPAR off against their husbands and elders. The FPAR's resources were not simply out there like mangoes to be picked and eaten for the benefit of the picker. Inscribing oneself in the colonial social engineering project of family planning also meant involvement in colonial projects of domesticating and controlling Africans. At the same time as taking power over their bodies, they were simultaneously inscribing themselves in a project of racial domination, born out of the white regime's anxiety about the political and demographic threat posed by the African population.

Just as the relationship between repression and emancipation in the case of Zimbabwean women's use of the new family planning methods is neither straightforward nor self-evident, neither is the relationship between oppression and resistance in Zimbabwean homes. The ongoing low-level struggles in homes documented in this book appear to be a straightforward case of resistance to men's and elders' desires to control the fertility of young women. Yet the domestic setting of these conflicts means that they differ from the sorts of cases of repression and resistance that dominate sociological and political science. Most scholars who study resistance focus on settings where power relations were relatively uncomplicated, even if intense or brutal. The landlord exploited the peasants, the boss exploited the workers, and very few bonds of affection or respect existed between the parties to the conflict, which might complicate or mitigate the power relation. However, in Zimbabwean marriages and families, the relations between young and old and between men and women did not consist solely of control and resistance. Within families— as distinct from states, commercial plantations, and other sites of oppression—bonds of affection and respect connected members, as did relations of exploitation. This complex tangle of relations produces complicated explanations for and definitions of the oppressive situation in which young women found themselves, in an effort to reconcile affection and respect with resistance to power.[3]

Women who used the new methods over their husbands' or elders' objections were clearly weakening male and elder power in the household and the community. Yet was this the sort of conscious, willed resistance that dominates the literature on other forms of resistance to power among peasants or workers? The exact nature of private acceptance is hard to theorize. Private acceptance may have threatened patriarchal structures of domination, but did the resistors perceive it as such? Men and elders clearly saw an attack on patriarchal norms, but it is less clear what the women thought about the relationship between their private acceptance and the implied values of patriarchy that made it necessary. I found that it was impossible to make any meaningful claims about the private acceptors' subjectivity of resistance and their consciousness of their acts as flouting of power.

The private acceptors show by their actions that they clearly believed, on some level, that they had a right to control their own bodies. They were not in thrall to patriarchal norms about respecting men's and elders' dictates as to what to do with their bodies, but neither do they appear to be consciously constructing an alternate social order or to be deliberately inverting symbolic forms of patriarchy. Women talked much more about the "how" of private acceptance rather than the "why." Their memories of being private acceptors were of actions that were pragmatic and utilitarian, rather than ideological, in character. Instruction about how to do private acceptance successfully were passed from woman to woman, as the ubiquity of the mealie-meal bin and banana leaf stories attest, but these communications were instructive and pragmatic rather than ideological.

The pragmatic nature of this form of resistance to patriarchy is shown by the absence of a performative component to private acceptance. Unlike, for example, peasants and workers who remembered and celebrated their rejec-

*[handwritten in margin: private acceptance vs. performativity]*

tion of the landlord's or the boss' or the colonialist's authority, private accep-tors did not produce folk songs, dances, stories, or anything that could amount to a cultural celebration of their resistance.[4] Peasants' and workers' forms of resistance have a quality of performativity, which private acceptance does not have.

However, private acceptance should be thought of as different from, rather than inferior to, more obvious and visible forms of resistance to power. Covert use of Depo-Provera and the pill had the power to transform women's lives and to have material impact on women's (and men's) conditions of living and to alter their relationships with their bodies, with each other, and with future generations. Indeed, Watkins, Rutenberg, and Green (1995) speculate that the transformative power of the new methods of family planning may be even greater than the power of cash income to alter women's lives, precisely because it can be invisible, known only to the woman who uses it. Women's secret use of family planning may be "quiet," as compared with "louder" forms of resistance and rejection of control, but it is no less powerful.

## FINALLY . . .

The strongest impression to be left by this project, I hope, is of the creativ-ity and agency of the people who were actively making decisions about the new methods. Far from being passive vectors through which innovations like the pill and the injection diffused smoothly through populations, these were men and women who made informed choices about what meanings they would ascribe to the new methods and how they would act on the meanings they perceived. This agency means that conflicts and resistance were not just historic accidents but are integral to any changes in fertility control.

## NOTES

1. Unfortunately, all of these improvements in the quality of life have been rolled back since Zimbabwe implemented its first Economic Structural Adjustment Program in 1992. The fertility transition in Zimbabwe appears unstoppable, however, as birthrates have continued to fall.

2. The role of donors in prodding the government to rethink family planning is an intriguing issue. The turnaround in attitudes toward family planning began at the same time as negotiations for Zimcord, a reconstruction and development plan for Zimbabwe, were going on with European countries. I could not find any evidence explicitly linking postindependence donor aid to a promotion of family planning, but international aid has always made up the largest part of the funds spent on family planning in Zimbabwe.

3. One consequence of these complex relations was the ubiquitous trope of "understanding" or "not understanding," used by both family planning workers (FPWs) and non-FPWs to explain the resistance of husbands and elders to the new methods. By describing a husband, or, less commonly, a mother-in-law, as "not understanding" rather than as cruel,

harsh, or repressive, one can avoid denouncing a person one loves and respects despite their opposition to the new methods. This rhetorical strategy provides a way to cope with the dissonance of both loving and evading the same person.

4. For examples of resistance accompanied by celebratory cultural production, see Comaroff 1985, Isaacman 1976, and Scott 1990.

# REFERENCES

Abu-Lughod, Lila. 1988. "Fieldwork of a 'Dutiful' Daughter." In *Arab Women in the Field,* edited by S. Altorki and C. F. El-Solh. New York: Syracuse University Press.

Batezat, Elinor and Margaret Mwalo. 1989. *Women in Zimbabwe*. Harare: SAPES Trust.

Benefo, Kofi. 1997. "Cultural Hybridization and West African Fertility." Unpublished paper, Population Research Laboratory, University of Southern California.

Berninghausen, Jutta and Birgit Kerstand. 1992. Forging New Paths: Feminist Social Science Methodology and Rural Women in Java New York: Zed Press.

Bledsoe, Caroline. 1990. "Transformations in Sub-Saharan African Marriage and Fertility." *Annals of the American Academy of Political and Social Science* 510:115–125.

———. 1998. "Legitimate Recuperation or Illegitimate Stalling? Time, Contraceptive Use and the Divided Man in Rural Gambia." Paper presented at the annual meeting of the Population Association of America, Chicago, March.

Bledsoe, Caroline and Allan Hill. 1993. "Social Norms, Natural Fertility, and the Resumption of Postpartum 'Contact' in The Gambia." Paper presented at the New Approaches to Anthropological Demography conference, Barcelona.

Bledsoe, Caroline, Allan Hill, Umberto D'Allessandro, and Patricia Langerock. 1994. "Constructing Natural Fertility: The Use of Western Contraceptive Technologies in Rural Gambia." *Population and Development Review* 20(1):81–113.

Bourdillon, M.F.C. 1982. *The Shona Peoples, 2nd edition* Gweru (Zimbabwe): Mambo Press.

Burke, Timothy. 1996. Lifebuoy Men, Luxe Women: Commodification, Consumption and Cleanliness in Modern Zimbabwe. Durham: Duke University Press.

Callahan, Bryan. 1997. "Veni, VD, Vici? Reassessing the Ila Syphilis Epidemic." *Journal of Southern African Studies* 23(3):421–40.

Castle, W. M and K. E. Sapire. 1976. "The Pattern of African Acceptance of Family Planning Facilities in Relation to Social Class" *South African Medical Journal* 50:965–68.

Catholic Commission for Justice and Peace [Rhodesia] (CCJP). 1976. *Civil War in Rhodesia.* Salisbury: CCJP.

Caute, David. 1983. Under the Skin: The Death of White Rhodesia London: Allan Lane.

Chavunduka, Gordon. 1978. *Traditional Healers and the Shona Patient*. Gweru: Mambo Press.

Chinemana, Frances. 1989. "Liberated Health in Zimbabwe? The Experience of Women 1981–1983." In Women's Health and Apartheid: the Health of Women and Children and the Future of Progressive Primary Health Care in Southern Africa, edited by Marcia Wright, Zena Stein and Jean Scandlyn, 90–113. Frankfurt: Medico International.

Chizengeni, S. 1979. *Customary Law and Family Predicaments.* University of Rhodesia (Centre for Applied Social Sciences) (mimeo).

Clarke, D. G. 1971. "Population and Family Planning in the Economic Development of Rhodesia." *Zambesia* 2:11–22.

————. 1972. "Problems of Family Planning Amongst Africans in Rhodesia." *Rhodesian Journal of Economics* 6:36–48

Comaroff, Jean. 1985. Body of Power, Spirit of Resistance: The Culture and History of a South African People. Chicago: University of Chicago Press.

Comaroff, John and Jean Comaroff. 1992. "Home-made hegemony: Modernity, Domesticity and Colonialism in South Africa." In *African Encounters with Domesticity*, edited by Karen Tranberg Hanson, 38–74. New Brunswick: Rutgers University Press.

Cooper, Davina. 1995. *Power in Struggle: Feminism, Sexuality and the State.* New York: New York University Press.

Cooper, Frederick and Ann Stoler. 1989. "Tensions of Empire: Colonial Control and Visions of Rule." *American Ethnologist* 16:609–21.

Cornwall, Andrea. 1990. Indigenous Methods of Reproduction, Implications for Family Planning Education: A Case Study from Southern Zimbabwe. London: Simon Population Trust.

Courville, Cindy. 1993. "Re-examining Patriarchy as a Mode of Production: The Case of Zimbabwe." In *Theorizing Black Feminism*, edited by Stanlie James and Abena Busia, 31–43. New York: Routledge.

Crawford, J. R. 1967. *Witchcraft and Sorcery in Southern Rhodesia* Oxford: Oxford University Press.

Daneel, M. L. 1971. Old and New in Southern Shona Independent Churches. The Hague: Mouton.

Davies, Miranda. 1983. Third World Second Sex: Women's Struggles and National Liberation. London: Zed Press.

Davin, Anna. 1978. "Imperialism and Motherhood." *History Workshop* 5:9–64

De Braganca, Aquino and Immanuel Wallerstein, eds. 1982. The African Liberation Reader: Documents of the National Liberation Movements. Vol.1: The Anatomy of Colonialism. London: Zed Press.

Dodds, Peter. 1977. "The Community and Family Planning." *Rhodesia Science News* 11: 314–16.

————. 1978. "Family Planning in Africa." *Rhodesia Science News* 12:160–63.

Draper, William. 1966. Untitled press release from the International Planned Parenthood Federation.

Dunlop, H. 1975. "The Publications of the Tribal Areas of Rhodesia Research Foundation." *Zambezia* 4:2.

Dwyer, Daisy and Judith Bruce, eds. 1988. *A Home Divided: Women and Income in the Third W-World.* Stanford: Stanford University Press.

Faith, Karlene. 1994. "Resistance: Lessons from Foucault and Feminism." In *Power/Gender: Social Relations in Theory and Practice*, edited by Lorraine Radtke and Hendrikus Stam, 36–66. London: Sage.

Family Planning Association of Rhodesia (FPAR). Date unknown. *Field Educator's Handbook.* Salisbury (Harare): FPAR.

————. 1978. *FPAR 1978.* Salisbury (Harare): FPAR.

Fapuhunda, Eleanor. 1978. "The Characteristics of Women Workers in Lagos: Data for Reconsideration by Labor Market Theorists." *Labor and Society* 3(2):158–71.

————. 1988. "The Nonpooling Household: A Challenge to Theory." In *A Home Divided: Women and Income in the Third World*, edited by Daisy Dwyer and Judith Bruce, 143–54. Stanford: Stanford University Press.

Feldman-Savelsberg, Pamela. 1994. "Plundered Kitchens and Empty Wombs: Fear of Infertility in the Cameroonian Grassfields." *Social Science and Medicine* 39(4):463–74.

Frederikse, Julie. 1984. None But Ourselves: Masses vs. Media in the Making of Zimbabwe. Harmondsworth, UK: Penguin.

Gaidzanwa, Rudo. 1992. "Bourgeois Theories of Gender and Feminism and Their Shortcomings with Reference to Southern African Countries." In *Gender in Southern Africa—Conceptual and Theoretical Issues*, edited by Ruth Meena, 95–125. Harare: SAPES Books.

Gelfand Michael. 1973. *The Genuine Shona.* Gweru (Zimbabwe): Mambo Press.

———. 1980. "African Customs in Relation to Preventive Medicine." *Central African Journal of Medicine* 27(1):1–8.

Geiger, Susan. 1997. TANU Women: Gender and Culture in the Making of Tanganyikan Nationalism 1955–1965. Portsmouth, NH: Heinemann.

Geisler, Gisela. 1993. "Silences Speak Louder than Claims: Gender, Household, and Agricultural Development in Southern Africa." *World Development* 21(12):1965–80.

Geraty, A. 1973. Evaluation of Family Planning Programmes in Rhodesia. MA thesis, University of Rhodesia.

———. 1974. "A Population Policy in a Multicultural Community." *Rhodesia Science News* 8:8–17.

———. 1975. "Birth Control." *Rhodesia Science News.* 9:175–78.

Gibney, Laura Margaret. 1993. Contraceptive Practices in Zimbabwe: The Influence of Educational Attainment and Personal Relationships. PhD thesis, Stanford University.

Gilmurray, John, Roger Riddell and David Sanders. 1979. *The Struggle for Health: From Rhodesia to Zimbabwe Vol. 7.* Salisbury (Harare): Mambo Press.

Ginsburg, Faye and Rayna Rapp. 1991. "The Politics of Reproduction." *Annual Review of Anthropology* 20:311–43.

Goebel, Allison. 1998. No Spirits Control the Trees: History, Culture and Gender in the Social Forest in a Zimbabwean Resettlement Area. PhD thesis, University of Alberta.

Gordon, John A. 1980. "Remoulding the Health Services of Zimbabwe." *Central African Journal of Medicine* 26(3): 67–71.

Government of Zimbabwe. 1996. *1994 Zimbabwe Demographic and Health Survey.* Harare: Central Statistical Office.

Greenhalgh, Susan. 1990. "Toward a Political Economy of Fertility: Anthropological Contributions." *Population and Development* 16(1):85–106.

Guyer, Jane. 1988. "Dynamic Approaches to Domestic Budgeting: Cases and Methods from Africa." In *A Home Divided: Women and Income in the Third World*, edited by Daisy Dwyer and Judith Bruce, 155–72. Stanford: Stanford University Press.

Haddad, L., and John Hoddinott. 1991. *Gender Aspects of Household Expenditures and Resource Allocation in the Cote d'Ivoire*. Applied Economics Discussion Paper 112. Oxford, UK: Institute of Economic Studies.

Hanks, J. 1973. "The Population Problem in Zimbabwe and The Consequences of Unlimited Growth." *Rhodesia Science News* 7:249–56.

———. 1975. "Population Problems in Rhodesia." *Rhodesia Science News* 9:pagination unknown.

Hansen, Karen Tranberg, ed. 1992. *African Encounters with Domesticity.* New Brunswick: Rutgers University Press.

Hobsbawm, Eric and Terence Ranger, eds. 1983. *The Invention of Tradition.* Cambridge: Cambridge University Press.

Holleman, J. F. 1952. *Shona Customary Law.* Cape Town: Oxford University Press.

Hooker, J. R. 1971. "Population planning in Rhodesia 1971." *American Universities Field Staff Reports: Central and Southern Africa* 15(6):1–9.

Hughes, A.J.B. 1974. *Development in Rhodesian Tribal Areas: An Overview.* Salisbury (Harare): Tribal Areas of Rhodesia Research Council.

Hunt, Nancy Rose. 1988. "'Le bebe en brousse': European Women, African Birth Spacing and Colonial Intervention in Breast Feeding in the Belgian Congo" *The International Journal of African Historical Studies* 21(3):401–32.

———. 1990. "Domesticity and Colonialism in Belgian Africa: Usumbura's Foyer Social 1946–1960." *Signs* 15(3):447–74.

International Defense and Aid Fund for Southern Africa (IDAFSA). 1977. *Zimbabwe: the Truth About Rhodesia.* London: IDAFSA.

Isaacman, Allen. 1976. The Tradition of Resistance in Mozambique: Anticolonial Activity in the Zambezi Valley, 1850–1921. London: Heinemann.

Jeater, Diana. 1993. Marriage, Perversion and Power: The Construction of Moral Discourse in Southern Rhodesia 1894–1930. Oxford: Clarendon Press.

Johnson, Thomas. 1995. "A Vanishing People?: Population, Fertility and Venereal Disease among the Ila of Northern Rhodesia, 1900–1960." Paper presented at The University of Kent, Canterbury, United Kingdom, October.

Kaler, Amy. 1997. "Maternal Identity and War in Mothers of the Revolution." Journal of the National Women's Studies Association 9:1–21.

———. 1998. "A Threat to the Nation and a Threat to the Men: The Banning of Depo-Provera in Zimbabwe 1981." *Journal of Southern African Studies* 24(2):347–76.

———. 1999. "Visions of Domesticity in the African Women's Homecraft Movement in Colonial Rhodesia." *Social Science History* 23 (3):269–309.

———. "Many Divorces and Many Spinsters: Marriage as an invented Tradition in Southern Malawi." *Journal of Family History* 26(4):529–56.

Kaler, Amy and Susan Watkins. 2001. "Street-level Bureaucrats and Would-be Patrons in Community-Based Family Planning Programs in Rural Kenya." *Studies in Family Planning* 32(3):254–69.

Kandiyoti, Deniz. 1991. "Bargaining with Patriarchy." In *The Social Construction of* Gender, edited by Judith Lorber and Susan Farrell, 98–110. Newbury Park, CA: Sage.

Kennedy, E. and P. Peters. 1992. "Household Food Security and Child Nutrition: The Interaction of Income and Gender of the Household Head." *World Development* 20(8):1077–85.

Kirkwood, Deborah. 1984. "Settler Wives in Southern Rhodesia: A Case Study." In *The Incorporated Wife,* edited by Shirley Ardner and Hillary Callan, 143–64. Sydney: Croom Helm.

Kongstedt, P., and M. Monsted. 1980. *Family, Labour and Trade in Western Kenya.* Uppsala: Scandinavian Institute for African Studies.

Kriger, Norma. 1988. "The Zimbabwean War of Liberation: Struggles Within the Struggle." *Journal of Southern African Studies* 14(2):304–322.

———.1991. *Zimbabwe's Guerrilla War: Peasant Voices.* New York: Cambridge University Press.

Kuuya, Tsitsi, and Cecelia Manyame [for Zimbabwe Women's Resource Centre and Network]. 1994. *Impact of the Interaction between Men and Women on Women and Development in Zimbabwe: Culture Survey.* Harare: ZWRCN.

Lan, David. 1985. *Guns and Rain: Guerrillas and Spirit Mediums in Zimbabwe*. Berkeley: University of California Press.

Lyons, Tanya. 2000. Guns and Guerrilla Girls: Women in the Zimbabwean National Liberation Struggle. Lawrenceville, NJ: Africa World Press.

MacCormack, Carol P. 1988. "Health and the Social Power of Women." *Social Science and Medicine* 26 (7):677–63.

Martin, David and Phyllis Johnson. 1981. *The Struggle for Zimbabwe: The Chimurenga War.* Harare: Zimbabwe Publishing House.

Maxwell, David. 1993. "Local Politics and the War of Liberation in North-east Zimbabwe. *Journal of Southern African Studies* 19(3):361–86.

McCarthy, Elizabeth. 1971. "Communications and Family Planning." Address to the Rhodesia Science Congress.

McClintock, Anne. 1995. Imperial Leather: Race, Gender and Sexuality in the Colonial Contest. London: Routledge.

McNicoll, Geoffrey. 1981. "Institutional Determinants of Fertility Change." *Population and Development Review* 6(3):441–62.

Meekers, Dominique. 1993. "The Noble Custom of Roora: The Marriage Customs and Practices of the Shona of Zimbabwe." *Ethnology* 32:35–54.

Merton, R. K. 1972. "Insiders and Outsiders: A Chapter in the Sociology of Knowledge." *The American Journal of Sociology* 78 1:9–47.

Mhloyi, Marvellous. 1991. "Fertility Transition in Zimbabwe." Paper presented at the Course of Fertility in Sub-Saharan Africa conference in Harare, Zimbabwe, November.

Ministry of Information (Rhodesia). 1975. *The Man and His Ways.* Salisbury (Harare): Ministry of Information.

Moore, Henrietta and Meghan Vaughan. 1995. Cutting down Trees: Gender, Nutrition and Agricultural Change in the Northern Province of Zambia 1890–1990. London: James Currey.

Munachonga, Monica. "Income Allocation and Marriage Options in Urban Zambia." In *A Home Divided: Women and Income in the Third World*, edited by Daisy Dwyer and Judith Bruce, 173–94. Stanford: Stanford University Press.

Murphree, M. W. 1977. "What Happens to Africa's 'White Tribes'?" *The Rhodesia Herald*, 19 May.

Mutambirwa, Jane. 1979. "Traditional Shona Concepts on Family Life and How Systems Planned on The Basis of These Concepts Effectively Contained the Population Growth of Shona Communities." *Zimbabwe Journal of Economics* 1(2):96–103.

Nhongo-Simbanegavi, Josephine. 1998. *Zimbabwean Women and the Liberation Struggle: ZANLA and Its Legacy 1972–1985*. D.Phil. thesis, St Antony's College, Oxford.

Obbo, Christine. 1993. "HIV Transmission: Men are the Solution." In *Theorizing Black Feminisms: The Visionary Pragmatism of Black Women*, edited by Stanlie James and Abena Busia, 160–81. New York: Routledge.

Pankhurst, Deborah and Susie Jacobs. 1988. "Land Tenure, Gender Relations and Agricultural Production: the Case of Zimbabwe's Peasantry." In *Agriculture, Women and Land; the African Experience*, edited by J. Davison, 202–27. Boulder, CO: Westview.

Parpart, Jane L. 1986. *Sexuality and Power on the Zambian Copperbelt 1926–1964*. Boston University: Working Papers in African Studies #120.

Paxson, Heather. 1997. "Rationalizing Sex: Conception, Contraception and Abortion in Urban Greece." Unpublished paper, Department of Anthropology, Stanford University.

Peel, J.D.Y. and T. O. Ranger, eds. 1982. *Past and Present in Zimbabwe*. Manchester: Manchester University Press.

Percival, Linda. 1989. "Family Planning Practices Among Urban and Rural Women in Zimbabwe." Paper presented at the annual meeting of the American Educational Research Association, San Francisco, March.

Philpott, R. H. 1969. Motive and Methods in Population Control: An Inaugural Lecture Given in the University College of Rhodesia. Salisbury (Harare): University College of Rhodesia.

Ranchod-Nilssen, Sita. 1992. "Educating Eve: The Women's Club Movement and Political Consciousness Among Rural African Women in Southern Rhodesia 1950–1980." In *African Encounters with Domesticity*, edited by Karen Tranberg Hansen, 195–217. New Brunswick: Rutgers University Press.

Ranger, Terence. 1985. Peasant Consciousness and Guerrilla War in Zimbabwe: A Comparative Study. Berkeley: University of California Press.

Ray, Sunanda, Mary Bassett, Caroline Maposhere, Portia Manangazira, J. O. Dean Nicolette, Roderick Machekano, and Josephine Moyo. 1995. "Acceptability of the Female Condom in Zimbabwe—Positive but Male-Centered Responses." *Reproductive Health Matters* 5:68–79.

Sapire, K. E. 1971. "Family Planning." *Rhodesia Science News* 5:104–110.

Schmidt, Elizabeth. 1992. Peasants, Traders and Wives: Shona Women in the History of Zimbabwe 1870–1939. Hanover, NH: Heinemann.

Scott, James C. 1990. *Domination and the Arts of Resistance: Hidden Transcripts*. New Haven: Yale University Press.

Seidman, Gay. 1984. "Women in Zimbabwe: Postindependence Struggles." *Feminist Studies* 10(3):419–40.

Sibanda, Amson. 1998. "The Course and Structure of Fertility Decline in Sub-Saharan Africa: Evidence From Kenya and Zimbabwe." Paper presented at the annual meeting of the Population Assocaition of America, Chicago, March.

Sibanda, Misheck J. 1989. "Early Foundations of African Nationalism." In *Turmoil and Tenacity: Zimbabwe 1890–1990*, edited by Canaan S. Banana, 25–49. Harare: College Press.

Silberschmidt, Margarethe. 1992. "Have Men Become the Weaker Sex? Changing Life Situations in Kisii District, Kenya." *Journal of Modern African Studies* 30(2):237–53.

Snow, David and Robert A. Benford. 1992. "Master Frames and Cycles of Protest." In *Frontiers in Social Movement Theory*, edited by Aldon Morris and Carol McClung Mueller, 133–55. New Haven: Yale University Press.

Spilhaus, Paddy. 1961. "Family Planning." Address to the Anglo American Corporation medical and welfare officers, Ndanga, Northern Rhodesia (Zambia), October.

———. 1981. *Pioneering Family Planning in Rhodesia 1957–1970*. Salisbury (Harare): Self-published.

Stack, Carol. 1997. All Our Kin: Strategies for Survival in a Black Community. New York: Basic Books.

Staunton, Irene, ed. 1991. Mothers of the Revolution: The Wartime Experiences of Thirty Zimbabwean Women. Harare: Baobab Press.

Still, Elizabeth. 1973. "Problems of Family Planning in Rhodesia." *Family Planning* 21(4):91–95.

Stott, Leda.1989. *Women and the Armed Struggle for Independence in Zimbabwe*. M.Sc. thesis, University of Edinburgh.

Szreter, Simon. 1993. "The Idea of Demographic Transition and the Study of Fertility Change: A Critical Intellectual History." *Population and Development Review* 19(4):659–94.

Thiesen, R. J. 1977. "Variables of Population Growth." *Zambezia* 5(2):161–68.

Thompson, Guy. 2000a. Cultivating Conflict: Modernization and "Improved" Agriculture in Colonial Zimbabwe, 1920–1965. PhD dissertation, University of Minnesota.

———. 2000b. "Peasants, Production and the NLHA, 1945–1965." In *The Zimbabwe Economy, 1945–1990*, edited by Alois Mlambo and Evelyn Pangeti. Harare: University of Zimbabwe Press.

Vambe, Lawrence. 1972. An Ill-Fated People: Zimbabwe Before and After Rhodes. London: Heinemann.

Van Rensburg, N. J. 1972. *Population Explosion in Southern Africa.* Pretoria: Self-published.

Vaughan, Megan. 1989. "Measuring a Crisis in Maternal and Child Health: A Historical Perspective." In *Women's Health and Apartheid*, edited by Marcia Wright, Jean Scandlyn, and Zena Stein, 130–42. Frankfurt: Medico International.

———. 1991. *Curing Their Ills: Colonial Power and African Illness* Stanford: Stanford University Press.

Watkins, Susan Cotts. 1993. "If All We Knew About Women Was What We Read in *Demography*, What Would We Know?" *Demography* 30(4):551–77.

Watkins, Susan Cotts, Naomi Rutenberg and Steven Green. 1995. "Diffusion and Debate: Controversy About Reproductive Change in Nyanza Province, Kenya." Paper presented at the annual meeting of the Population Association of America.

Watkins, Susan Cotts, Naomi Rutenberg and David Wilkinson. 1997. "Orderly Theories, Disorderly Women." In *The Continuing Demographic Transition*, edited by G. W. Jones, R. M. Douglas, J. C. Caldwell and R. M. D'Souza, 213–45. Oxford: Clarendon Press.

Watkins, Susan Cotts, Nancy Luke and Ina Warriner. Forthcoming. "This *Rariew*, It Doesn't Rhyme with Western Medicine: Recognition and Treatment of a Reproductive Illness in Rural Kenya." In *Cultural Perspectives on Reproductive Health*, edited by C. Makhlouf Obermeyer. Oxford: Oxford University Press.

Weinrich, A.K.H. 1979. Women and Racial Discrimination in Rhodesia. Paris: Unesco.

———. 1982. African Marriage in Zimbabwe and the Impact of Christianity. Geneva: Unesco.

Weiss, Ruth. 1986. *The Women of Zimbabwe*. New Jersey: Red Sea Press.

West, Michael O. 1994. "Nationalism Race and Gender: The Politics of Family Planning in Zimbabwe 1957–1990." *Social History of Medicine* 7:447–71.

Wilmoth, John and Patrick R. Ball. 1992. "The Population Debate in American Popular Magazines, 1946–1990." *Population and Development Review* 18:631–38.

Wolf, Diane. 1996. "Introduction." In *Feminist Dilemmas*, edited by Diane Wolf, 3–55. Boulder: Westview.

Yuval-Davis, Nira and Floya Anthias, eds. 1989. *Women, Nation, State.* London:Macmillan.

Zimbabwe Women's Bureau. 1981. *We Carry a Heavy Load: Rural Women in Zimbabwe Speak Out.* Harare: Zimbabwe Women's Bureau.

## FILES OF THE NATIONAL ARCHIVES OF ZIMBABWE (NAZ)

B/137/3
B/137/4
B/137/5
B/137/8 [FPAR Minutes of Meetings]
F/118/3 [Mashonaland Reports Vol.1]

## PERIODICALS CITED

*Annual Reports of the Child Spacing and Fertility Association of Zimbabwe*
*Annual Reports of the Family Planning Association of Rhodesia*
*Annual Reports of the International Planned Parenthood Federation Regional Secretary*
   *for Europe, the Near East and Africa*
*Annual Reports of the Secretary for Health [Rhodesia]*
*Annual Reports of the Secretary for Internal Affairs [Rhodesia]*
*Annual Reports of the Zimbabwe National Family Planning Council*
*African Times*
*Bantu Mirror*
*Bulawayo Chronicle*
*The [Rhodesia] Herald*
*The [Zimbabwe] Herald*
*Mhuri Inofara [The Happy Family]*
*Northern News*
*Parliamentary Debates*
*Rhodesia Science News*
*Southern Rhodesia Cabinet Conclusions*
*Zimbabwe News Agency*
*Zimbabwe News*
*Zimbabwe People's Voice*
*Zimbabwe Review*

# INDEX

**About the Author**

AMY KALER is Assistant Professor in the Department of Sociology at University of Alberta.